GLOBAL
WARNING

TIM LaHAYE
ED HINDSON

HARVEST HOUSE PUBLISHERS

EUGENE, OREGON

Cover by Dugan Design Group, Bloomington, Minnesota

Cover photos © Digital Vision / Getty Images; Visible Earth / NASA

Published in association with Joel Gotter at Intellectual Property Group, 9200 Sunset Blvd., Ste. 820, Los
Angeles, CA 90069.

ACKNOWLEDGMENTS

We want to express our gratitude to Dillon Burroughs and
Thomas Lee for their research and editorial assistance, and to
Amanda Stanley, who graciously typed the original manuscript.

GLOBAL WARNING
Copyright © 2007 by Tim LaHaye Ministries, LaHaye Publishing Group, LLC and Ed Hindson
Published by Harvest House Publishers
Eugene, Oregon 97402

ISBN-13: 978-0-7369-2145-9

CONTENTS

INTRODUCTION:

THE FINAL WARNING

But mark this: There will be terrible times in the last days.
2 TIMOTHY 3:1

THE WORLD IS IN SERIOUS TROUBLE, and everyone knows it. Something ominous is about to happen. Even the most powerful people on earth sense that we are running out of time. Never before in all of human history has the world seemed so vulnerable to disaster and at a loss for a workable solution to the world's problems. Despite today's amazing technological advances, increasing prosperity, and growing number of opportunities for a better life, many people readily admit to a growing sense of unease about the future. In fact, most would agree we are living in one of the most precarious, chaotic, and even dangerous times in history. Consider the following:

The Economy: Bubbling underneath the current booming world economy is a multitrillion dollar international debt that continues to increase exponentially. Many governments have given up trying to repay their debts and now struggle just to keep up with the interest payments on their debts. To make these payments, these governments must take out loans totaling more than a billion dollars a day, which in turn further increases the global debt. Like a gambler who continues to max out all his credit cards, the world's day of reckoning will eventually come—and when it does, a depression dwarfing that of the 1930s is certain to follow.

Crime: According to the U.S. Department of Justice, American residents last year experienced approximately 23 million crimes involving homicide, rape, assault, robbery, burglary, and theft. Those in the 12-to-24-year-old age range were by far the largest group to be involved in violent crimes. A major contributing factor is drug use, which continues to grow at an alarming rate. Nearly 2 million people, many of them juvenile, were arrested for drug abuse violations last year. Currently, there are more than 7 million people over the age of 18 in correctional facilities across the country.

Natural Disasters: Earthquakes, floods, tornados, hurricanes, and other natural disasters have been steadily increasing in both number and intensity for more than 100 years now. A staggering 960,000 people have died worldwide as a result of various natural disasters just within the last 15 years alone. Scientists expect the trend to continue, with the majority of deaths taking place in low- to mid-developed countries. While many are concerned about the challenges of global warming, very few take seriously the global warnings predicted in the Bible.

Terrorism: The constant threat of international terrorism has the world continually on edge. As the situation in the Middle East continues to worsen, many Americans and Europeans fear that further attacks against the Western world are imminent. Increased vigilance and technological surveillance have prevented some potentially horrendous incidents from occurring, but it is reasonable to assume that it is only a matter of time before terrorists strike a crippling blow of similar proportions to 9/11 or even greater.

Technology: Despite its many wonderful benefits, modern technology is also responsible for the development of weapons of mass destruction, which threaten the very existence of life on planet Earth. Nuclear bombs no longer have to be launched by intercontinental missiles. They can be packed in suitcases or dropped from pilotless drones.

Coupled with these worrisome trends are a number of additional significant global indicators that seem to point to the fact that we are racing headlong toward the last days. Just what do these "signs of the times" mean? Are we indeed moving toward some kind of cataclysmic disaster? Is there any way to know for certain what's going to happen in the future? And what about the Bible's predictions about the end of time? Do those predictions fit with the warning signs we see around us today?

In the pages that follow, we have researched the Scriptures as well as the international indicators of our times to answer these questions. We have given preference to Dr. LaHaye's position on certain matters but in all things essential we are in agreement that the world is running out of time and Jesus is coming soon.

Throughout the ages, man has attempted to discern the future through a number of occultic means such as divination, fortune-telling, astrology, spiritism, and witchcraft. Even today, communication with demonic entities is often sought by the practitioner in order to aid in his or her attempt to achieve a certain amount of prophetic success. Over the years, some of these so-called prophets have attained a certain degree of notoriety as a result of their predictions. Such seers include Mother Shipton, Madam Helena Blavatsky, science fiction writer H.G. Wells, Edgar Cayce, and Jeane Dixon. Perhaps the most famous of these "prophets" was a sixteenth-century Frenchman named Michel de Nostradame, better known as Nostradamus, who has attained a significant following that persists to this very day. Skeptics of Nostradamus are quick to point out that his reputation as a prophet has been largely manufactured by modern-day supporters who match his vague and often cryptic writings to events *after* they have already occurred. In fact, his writings are so tenuous that they remain essentially useless in trying to predict any event in advance with even the smallest degree of certainty.

A RELIABLE PROPHETIC SOURCE

Anyone can make predictions based on their own experience, judgment, and available data, and these "prophecies" may or may not come true. Stock market analysts and weathermen do this all the time. However, the only reliable source of prophecy that is truly 100 percent accurate is the Bible. Nearly one-fourth of the Bible's content was prophetic at the time that it was written, and to this day, more than 500 of these prophecies have been fulfilled down to minute detail. Since these fulfilled prophecies have come to fruition in a literal manner, we have an intellectual basis for believing that those which are yet future will likewise be fulfilled literally. Once we understand this, we can take comfort in the knowledge that God has a plan and purpose for this world, and has lovingly revealed it to us in advance through His Word. In fact, God said this about Himself and the future:

Remember the former things of old, for I am God, and there is no other; I am God, and there is none like Me, *declaring the end from the beginning, and from ancient times things that are not yet done,* saying, "My counsel shall stand, and I will do all My pleasure" (Isaiah 46:9-10 NKJV).

It is ironic and unfortunate that a number of skeptics over the years have failed to recognize the undeniable importance of prophecy, especially when one realizes that *fulfilled prophecy credentials the Bible itself.* It also stands to reason that the Bible's content is not man-made but instead has its origins outside of our own space-time continuum because *it records history before it happens.* Prophecy is just that—history written in advance.

There is another important reason why one should make a determined effort to study prophecy. It was precisely because the religious leaders of Christ's day were not proficient in their study of prophetic Scriptures that they failed to recognize Jesus as the Messiah when He appeared on earth the first time. Now today, as we stand on the threshold of the end times, those who have rejected the study of prophecy may likewise be unprepared for Christ's second coming.

THE GREATEST OF ALL PROPHETS

Jesus not only fulfilled prophecies during His first appearance on earth; He Himself was the greatest of all prophets. His words, recorded in the New Testament, give insights into the future as no other prophet before Him. His detailed prophecies give us a clear understanding of the future. No book written before or since has provided such a prophetic chart of human destiny like the Bible.

Besides the hundreds of prophecies that have already been fulfilled in times past, there are large numbers of yet-to-be fulfilled prophecies that focus specifically on the conclusion of this present age, or the *last days* or *end times.*

One extremely significant end-time prophecy that was fulfilled quite recently was the regathering of the Jews to their homeland and the re-establishment of the nation of Israel in 1948. Since then, there has been a constant stream of fulfilled prophecies leading us ever closer to the return of the Lord. In fact, the return of Christ looms as an imminent event that could occur before any more of these predictions come to pass.

We believe that we are living in the last days. The ominous signs of the *Global Warning* are all around us. The crisis of war in the Middle East, the tensions and breakdowns of international diplomacy, and the threat of nuclear destruction all loom as ominous storm clouds over the Earth. It seems it is only a matter of time until an extremist dictator of a rogue nation or terrorist faction will acquire a nuclear bomb, the system to deliver it, and be willing to push the button.

As we watch the warning signs of the times flashing on the horizon of the global community, we recognize that the human race may well be running out of time. We may have dodged the proverbial apocalyptic bullet in the past but there is no guarantee that we can do it again in the future. The truth is that we may well be on our way to the next world war sooner than we think.

1

AT THE BRINK
OF DISASTER

*"The main aim of any American president is
to prevent World War III."*
—SEYMOUR M. HERSH, *THE SAMSON OPTION*[1]

THE PAST CENTURY HAS CERTAINLY experienced its share of disasters. Over 83 million lives have been lost in the first two world wars alone. Approximately two million people died in the Korean War, over one million in the Vietnam conflict, as many as 200,000 in the first Gulf War, and countless others in the numerous conflicts continuing to rage around our world today.

Most notably in recent history, the disaster of 9/11 revealed the vulnerability of the United States to outside attack. Three thousand Americans lost their lives that day as terrorists targeted the Twin Towers, the Pentagon, and even unsuccessfully aimed at the White House in what could only be considered an act of war. However, unlike past wars, today's acts of terror no longer involve land or governmental expansion. According to conservative radio host Rush Limbaugh, "This is a religious war.... There is no room for compromise in a religious war...no room for 'settlement.'"[2]

Today, terrorist groups continue to infiltrate, irritate, and make their influence known in Western nations. According to *Newsweek*'s article "Terror in

Our Time," there has instead been an increase in terrorist attacks and major threats since the world's turning point at 9/11. A few examples include:

- April 11, 2002: Truck bomb explodes outside a synagogue in Tunisia.
- June 14, 2002: Car-bomber attacks American Consulate building in Karachi, Pakistan, killing 11 people.
- March 11, 2004: In a sophisticated attack, terrorists set off bombs in four crowded Madrid commuter trains…191 people are killed and more than 1,700 are injured.
- August 11, 2006: British authorities uncover an alleged plot to explode bombs on ten airliners traveling from Britain to the United States. The alleged bombers would smuggle liquid explosives onboard disguised as beverages and other common objects. Twenty-four people are detained for questioning.[3]

Where will terrorists strike next? The growing numbers of attacks worldwide says we can expect more to come. Research that we share below reveals our world could very well be on the brink of disaster.

Potential Disasters

According to the Center for Defense Information in Washington, D.C., there are several threat scenarios available for hostile regimes or terrorist cells to attack on American soil. These scenarios are very real possibilities in other locations around the globe. The most likely options include the following:[4]

A Dirty Bomb

The most accessible nuclear device for terrorists today would be a radiological dispersion bomb. This so-called "dirty bomb" would consist of waste by-products from nuclear reactors wrapped in conventional explosives, which, upon detonation, would spew deadly radioactive particles into the environment. What's disconcerting is that radioactive waste material is relatively easy to obtain. According to reports by BBC, over the last decade there have been over 175 instances of terrorists or criminals trying to obtain or smuggle radioactive substances.[5]

Radioactive waste is widely found throughout the world, and in general is not as well guarded as nuclear weapons. For example, in the United States radioactive waste is located at more than 70 commercial nuclear power sites in 31 states. Enormous quantities also exist overseas—particularly in Europe and Japan. Tons of wastes are frequently transported over long distances, including between continents.

In Russia, the security precautions for guarding such nuclear waste is especially poor, and the potential for diversion and actual use by Islamic radicals has been shown to be very real indeed. In 1996, Islamic rebels from the breakaway province of Chechnya planted—but did not detonate—such a device in Moscow's Izmailovo Park to demonstrate Russia's vulnerability. This dirty bomb consisted of a deadly brew of dynamite and one of the highly radioactive by-products of nuclear fission—Cesium 137.

While such concoctions would not likely kill as many people as died on 9/11, worst-case calculations for an explosion in downtown Manhattan during noontime give an estimate of more than 2,000 deaths and many thousands more suffering from radiation poisoning.

At a March 28, 2006 hearing before the Senate committees on Homeland Security and Governmental Affairs, the Government Accountability Office announced that its undercover agents had smuggled enough material for two dirty bombs across the U.S. border.[6]

If such a bomb were to explode and harm people, the treatment of those exposed to it would be greatly hampered by inadequate medical facilities and training. For example, the United States has only *one* hospital emergency room dedicated to treating patients exposed to radiation hazards—located at Oak Ridge, Tennessee.[7]

Dr. Henry Kelly, president of the Federation of American Scientists, said in a testimony before the U.S. Congress, "With urban areas especially difficult to decontaminate after a radiological attack, any abandonment could be permanent, potentially costing trillions of dollars."[8] A credible threat to explode such a bomb in a U.S. city could have a powerful impact on the conduct of U.S. foreign and military policy, and could possibly have a paralyzing effect on international relations. Not only would the potential loss of life be considerable, but the serious consequences of having to mass-evacuate highly populated urban centers would loom large in the minds of policy-makers.

Attacks on Nuclear Power Plants

A terrorist attack on a commercial nuclear power plant using a commercial jet or heavy munitions could have a similar effect as the explosion of a radiological bomb and cause far greater casualties. If such an attack were to cause either a meltdown of the reactor core (similar to what happened in the Chernobyl disaster) or a dispersal of the spent fuel waste on the site, extensive casualties could be expected.

According to a survey by the Project on Government Oversight, however, security guards at *only one of four* nuclear power plants are confident their plant could defeat a terrorist attack.[9] As a result, much attention has been given by counterterrorism teams to this potential problem since 9/11.[10] In studies by the Nuclear Energy Institute, computer models have shown that American nuclear plants *could* withstand direct airplane crashes even if the crash were to cause a radiation leak, yet the security threat remains.[11]

Direct Obtainment of Nuclear Material or Weapons

All nuclear-related threats pale in comparison to the possibility that terrorists could build or obtain an atomic bomb itself. An explosion of even low yield could kill hundreds of thousands of people. A relatively small bomb of 15 kilotons, if it were detonated in Manhattan, could immediately kill upwards of 100,000 inhabitants, followed by a comparable number of deaths in the lingering aftermath. Experts say the blast from a single ten-kiloton nuclear bomb in Washington, D.C. would destroy everything within a half mile radius, contaminate 3,000 to 5,000 square miles with toxic levels of radiation, and kill 300,000 people within a matter of minutes.[12]

"Lack of knowledge has never been an obstacle to any nation in developing nuclear weapons. The problem is in obtaining the necessary tools and materials."[13] That raises an important question: Have terrorist groups ever tried to build a nuclear bomb?

According to the Council on Foreign Relations, the answer is yes. In the mid-1990s, al-Qaeda agents repeatedly attempted to purchase highly enriched uranium in Africa, Europe, and Russia. In November 2001, Osama bin Laden announced that he had obtained a nuclear weapon, although U.S. intelligence officials dismissed his claims.

State-sponsored terrorists have also attempted to obtain nuclear weapons. Iraq sought nuclear weapons as early as 1981, when Israeli jets destroyed Saddam Hussein's Osiraq nuclear reactor outside Baghdad. When U.N. inspectors arrived in 1991, they found that Saddam was probably within three years of having enough highly enriched uranium to build a bomb.[14]

Fortunately, bomb-grade nuclear fissile material is heavily guarded in most, if not all, nuclear weapon states. Of greatest concern today are potentially hostile governments, such as recent efforts by both Iran and North Korea, to obtain and test nuclear weapons or to achieve the capability to develop nuclear weapons. Other nations, including Egypt,[15] have expressed intent to create such weapons in the near future. According to the Dubai-based *Middle East Economic Digest,* at least *six additional nations* are developing nuclear programs. These include Egypt, Saudi Arabia, Morocco, and Algeria, with plans in the infant stages for both Tunisia and the United Arab Emirates.[16]

Iran has been of particular concern in recent news. With high-level remarks directed toward the United States and especially Israel, combined with the continued development of nuclear capabilities, this worry has not been without reason. "Iran is today the leading example of a country that is simultaneously exploiting the current nonproliferation regime and sneaking around it."[17]

In January 2006, Israeli acting prime minister Ehud Olmert firmly stated that "under no circumstances, and at no point, can Israel allow anyone with these kinds of malicious designs against us [to] have control of weapons of mass destruction that can threaten our existence."[18] Why the great concern? According to Akbar Hashemi Rafsanjani, chairman of Iran's Expediency Council, "The use of even one nuclear bomb inside Israel will destroy everything.... It is not irrational to contemplate such an eventuality."[19] As a result, tensions will continue to increase as Iran, North Korea, and other such nations seek to arm themselves with nuclear capabilities.

In his 1995 book *Fighting Terrorism,* former Israeli prime minister Benjamin Netanyahu wrote, "It can only be a matter of time before this terror is turned inward against the United States, the leader of the hated West, and the country responsible in the eyes of militant Muslims for having created Israel and for maintaining the supposedly heretical Arab regimes."[20] His insight, mentioned over a decade ago, continues to serve as a major concern for Americans today.

UNCONVENTIONAL WEAPONS

Following the attacks of 9/11, packages with small amounts of anthrax began to appear in the mailboxes of key U.S. individuals and corporations, creating a massive scare. This type of unconventional warfare reminds us of the ongoing concern such weapons could bring in future attacks. Four major unconventional weapons currently include anthrax, nerve gas, attacks on water supplies, and the destruction of major oil markets.

Anthrax Mailings

> *"The United States is ripe for a terrorist attack using biological weapons and is nowhere near ready for it."*
> —DR. MICHAEL OSTERHOLM, CHIEF OF DISEASE EPIDEMIOLOGY, MINNESOTA DEPARTMENT OF HEALTH [21]

Within the one-year period following 9/11, five Americans died as a result of anthrax mailings.[22] The 2001 anthrax attacks (also known as Amerithrax, the name the FBI assigned to the case) occurred over the course of several weeks beginning on September 18, 2001. Letters containing anthrax were mailed to several news media offices and two U.S. senators. In addition to the five individuals who died, 17 others were treated. The crimes remain unsolved.

Five letters were mailed during the first of the two waves. These were directed to ABC News, CBS News, NBC News, and the *New York Post* (all in New York City), and the *National Enquirer* in Boca Raton, Florida. Two additional anthrax letters, bearing the same Trenton, New Jersey postmark, were dated October 9 and were addressed to Senators Tom Daschle of South Dakota and Patrick Leahy of Vermont. The Daschle letter even caused a temporary shutdown of government mail service.

What did these mysterious notes say? The note that was addressed to Senators Daschle and Leahy read:

09-11-01
YOU CAN NOT STOP US.
WE HAVE THIS ANTHRAX.
YOU DIE NOW.
ARE YOU AFRAID?

DEATH TO AMERICA.
DEATH TO ISRAEL.
ALLAH IS GREAT.

Notice the final three sentences: "Death to America. Death to Israel. Allah is great." The goal by these radicals is the destruction of Israel as well as America due to its connection with Israel. This confirms that today's terrorist warfare is rooted in religious belief.

Nerve Gas

It is known that al-Qaeda terrorists staged a crippling VX nerve gas attack on Jordan's intelligence headquarters in April 2004. According to one Jordanian official, "We found primary materials to make a chemical bomb which, if it had exploded, would have made nearly 20,000 deaths."[23] In the same article, Jordan's King Abdullah confirmed that the vehicles containing these materials had entered the country from Syria.

According to Grant Jeffrey's *The Next World War,* "Jordanian officials claim that the arrested suspects confessed to plan to detonate a chemical (VX nerve gas) bomb on the Amman headquarters of the intelligence services. The terrorists admitted as well that the planner was Abu Musab Al-Zarqawi, the leader of al-Qaeda in Iraq."[24] Despite Al-Zarqawi's death in June 2006, such plans continue to cause concern over the possibility of terrorist attacks through means of VX nerve gas or similar substances.

Water Supplies

In the spring of 1993, Milwaukee was devastated by the largest outbreak of waterborne disease ever in America. Cryptosporidium, a protozoan, passed undetected through two water treatment plants and caused more than 400,000 illnesses (mostly diarrhea) and between 50 and 100 deaths out of some 800,000 customers who drank the water. Cryptosporidium is often present in animal waste, but authorities never figured out what had happened. The principle established was that this was a possible means of carrying out terrorist attacks.

When it comes to water system sabotage, two types, vandalism and terrorism, must be considered. *Vandalism* would interrupt the supply of water and reduce its quantity. *Terrorism* would contaminate the water and reduces its quality. Because drinking water is essential to human life, making it inaccessible for any period of time would cause widespread panic. Supply interruptions could be caused by the destruction of or interference with reservoir dams, water towers, or pumping stations. In some areas, a simple backflow by a vacuum cleaner or bicycle pump with poisonous waste could cause problems for residents in that region. Another possibility of danger would include a truck bomb or other explosive device set off beneath a water pumping station.

According to Tom Curtis, an executive of the American Water Works Association, "For instance, one city has six giant pumps, and they're all in one building. If you crashed an airplane into that building or blew it up, it would cause half a million people to lose their water supply almost instantly. Pumps of this size must be custom-built and can take as long as 18 months to replace."[25]

While some of the scenarios being discussed in popular media today are founded on urban legend rather than facts, the danger is still very real. In fact, according to the Homeland Security Web site, water is one of five core areas of protection, including several strategic initiatives intended to help protect our nation from water supply disasters.[26]

Oil Market Attacks

Yet another unconventional weapon is a terrorist attack designed to hurt a major oil market. An intentional destruction of a major pipeline or oil transportation route would wreak devastating effects on world oil market prices. "Oil is just very much in the crosshairs around the world," said John Kilduff, senior vice president for energy risk management at Fimat USA in New York. "There's no country, there's no production that can come to the rescue of any kind of terrorist attack."[27]

Interestingly, during the 2006 United Nations sessions in New York City, Venezuelan leader Hugo Chavez verbally assaulted the American govern- ment and even called the president "a devil." In another context he recently claimed that "if the United States attacks, we won't have any other alternative [but to] blow up our own oil fields. They aren't going to take that oil." Such comments, along with Chavez's growing alliance with Iran's Ahmadinejad, continue to increase already-heightened oil price tensions.[28]

According to Shibley Telhami, the matter of protecting today's oil is critical. He notes:

> ...there is no escaping that the region that has grabbed the greatest global attention during the past half century in matters of oil, the Middle East, remains critical for future energy supplies. In a way, all the scrambling to develop resources around the world today is intended to delay the day of reckoning. Although the Middle East produces a quarter of world oil supplies, it holds between two-thirds and three-quarters of all known oil reserves.[29]

In 2004, the world's top oil exporters included sensitive nations such as Iran, Iraq, Kuwait, and Saudi Arabia in the top 15.[30] Four of the top five nations with the greatest known oil reserves are Arab nations, and those reserves total *613 billion barrels.* Because Arab nations control such an enormous amount of the world's oil, any decisions made regarding the War on Terror are extremely significant.[31]

NEW TECHNOLOGIES FOR WAR

Today's emerging technologies also offer terrorists and hostile nations new opportunities for attack. Growing concerns exist today regarding electromagnetic pulse attacks (EMPs), pilotless drone planes, and Internet communications among today's enemies. Our nation's top leaders agree. In launching his preemption doctrine, President George W. Bush announced, "The gravest danger our nation faces lies at the crossroads of radicalism and technology."[32]

EMPs

One of the scariest signs of our perilous times, especially for people who live in a technologically advanced country, is the potential threat of an electromagnetic pulse or EMP attack from a rogue nation. For those who may not know, an electromagnetic pulse is a phenomenon that occurs when a nuclear warhead is detonated anywhere from 25 to 300 miles above the Earth's surface. Radiation from the explosion interacts with the atmosphere and ionosphere to produce high energy electrons that speed across the Earth's magnetic field to produce an instantaneous and invisible electromagnetic pulse.

Although people themselves are not usually harmed, an EMP has the ability to disrupt and destroy electrical systems that are within the detonation's line of sight. The higher the altitude of the explosion, the greater the affected area. A single ballistic missile equipped with a nuclear warhead launched over the United States and detonated 100 miles above the earth could affect roughly one-fourth of the country. A more powerful missile launched from a place such as North Korea and exploded at an altitude of 300 miles could impact electrical systems across the entire continental United States.

In March 2005, the Senate Judiciary Subcommittee on Terrorism, Technology and Homeland Security held a hearing on the EMP threat. The following observation was made:

> An electromagnetic pulse (EMP) attack on the American homeland, said one of the distinguished scientists who testified at the hearing, is one of only a few ways that the United States could be defeated by its enemies—terrorist or otherwise.... And it is probably the easiest. A single Scud missile, carrying a single nuclear weapon, detonated at the appropriate altitude, would interact with the Earth's atmosphere, producing an electromagnetic pulse radiating down to the surface at the speed of light. Depending on the location and size of the blast, the effect would be to knock out already stressed power grids and other electrical systems *across much or even all of the continental United States, for months if not years.*[33]

While EMPs are commonly referenced in popular culture, such as in the film *Ocean's Eleven* or television shows such as *Lost* and *24,* the real-life impact of such a weapon could cripple large areas dependent upon electrical power systems. According to the Federation of American Scientists, "The pulse can easily span continent-sized areas, and this radiation can affect systems on land, sea, and air. The first recorded EMP incident accompanied a high-altitude nuclear test over the South Pacific and resulted in power system failures as far away as Hawaii."[34] This article later noted that a strategically placed EMP released over Kansas could potentially extend over all of the continental United States.

In a worst-case scenario, there would be no lights, no running water, cars would stop running, planes would crash, and television, radio, Internet, and cell phone communications would end. In one shot the affected portion of the nation would fall into chaos. Due to this horrific potential, U.S. military and government plans against this type of disaster have been under discussion at least since 1988. But very little specific action has been recommended for preventing such an attack.[35]

So far, little has been done to safeguard electrical systems from an EMP attack. In fact, U.S. military and civilian systems have become increasingly dependent on advanced electronics that are more vulnerable to an EMP than older electronic devices—a trend that is likely to continue. Since nuclear weapons were originally designed to decimate a particular target area, and since the electrical systems in that area would simultaneously be destroyed, there seemed little reason to protect those electrical systems from the effects of the resulting electromagnetic pulse. However, in the years following the end of the Cold War, the situation has changed dramatically. The proliferation of nuclear technology and ballistic missiles among other nations has altered the nature of the EMP threat. In addition, the rise of terrorist groups that have no state identity who are motivated to attack the United States without regard for their own safety are a relatively new phenomenon and are difficult to deter, as evidenced by the response to the 9/11 attacks.

As our world's dependence upon electronic technology continues to grow, its vulnerability to an EMP attack likewise increases. And there are several potentially hostile adversaries who currently have the ability to launch an EMP attack. Certain types of unsophisticated low-yield nuclear weapons can be employed to generate a successful attack by a rogue nation or terrorist cell intent on destruction. Designs for these low-scale weapons have been illegally trafficked for nearly three decades. Furthermore, an EMP attack using a few nuclear weapons could damage an area the size of the entire continental United States, far exceeding the impact the same number of weapons would have if used in a conventional method on specific cities or military sites. It is increasingly obvious that "protective shields" of missiles need to be developed to defend against such attacks.

Pilotless Drones

According to the technology website PhysOrg.com,

> The technology for remote-controlled light aircraft is now highly
> advanced, widely available—and, experts say, virtually unstoppable. Models with a wingspan of five metres (16 feet), capable of
> carrying up to 50 kilograms (110 pounds), remain undetectable
> by radar. And thanks to satellite positioning systems, they can
> now be programmed to hit targets some distance away with just
> a few metres (yards) short of pinpoint accuracy.[36]

At the international level, "we are observing an increasing threat from
such things as remote-controlled aircraft used as small flying bombs against
soft targets," said the head of the Canadian secret services, Michel Gauthier,
at a conference in Calgary recently.[37] In May of 2006, U.S. Web site Defense
Tech published an article by military technology specialist David Hambling,
entitled "Terrorists' Unmanned Air Force." According to his research, "Little
attention has been given to the more imminent threat posed by unmanned
air vehicles in the hands of terrorists or rogue states."[38]

According to a number of studies, armed militant groups have already
attempted to use unmanned aircraft. For example, on April 11, 2005, Lebanese Hezbollah flew a pilotless drone over Israeli territory on what was
called a surveillance mission. The Israeli military confirmed this event and
responded by flying warplanes over southern Lebanon.[39]

The United States has not allowed the potential for pilotless drones to
go unnoticed, In November 2002, *CBS News* reported the United States's
use of a pilotless drone spy plane named *The Predator* in the deaths of six
al-Qaeda suspects in Yemen. According to the report, "The Predator has
become a deadly tool and powerful psychological weapon that seemingly
comes from nowhere to deliver a fiery strike."[40]

Internet Communications

> *"The U.S. is dangerously behind the curve*
> *in countering terrorist use of the Internet."*
> —BRUCE HOFFMAN [41]

Internet technology has increasingly been used as a weapon in recent years. *The 9/11 Commission Report* cites four specific instances in which hijackers accessed information from the Internet to plan or facilitate the 9/11 attacks.[42] According to Professor Gabriel Weimann of Haifa University, there are some 4,800 terrorist or terrorist-related Web sites currently on the Internet.[43]

A few excerpts from a recent report to the House Permanent Select Committee on Intelligence reveals the growing number of ways terrorists or rogue nations are using Internet communications and other technologies to plan attacks:[44]

- Three British al-Qaeda operatives were indicted in March 2005 on charges of having carried out detailed reconnaissance of financial targets in Lower Manhattan, Newark, New Jersey, and Washington, D.C. The men were alleged to have amassed more than 500 photographs of the sites—many of which had simply been downloaded from the Internet.

- A British government report on the July 2005 suicide bomb attacks that targeted three London subway trains and a bus concluded that this was a "modest, simple affair by four seemingly normal men using the Internet."

- Before the attacks on 9/11, al-Qaeda had only one Web site. "Today, the movement is present on more than 50 different sites," which he said provide a "virtual sanctuary—an effective, expeditious and anonymous means through which the movement can continue to communicate with its fighters, followers, sympathizers and supporters worldwide."

Al-Qaeda, in particular, has long facilitated online communications for three critical functions, according to this report. First, terrorists use the Internet for recruitment and fundraising and to shape public opinion in the Muslim world. Second, they use it for terrorist training and instruction. As the *Washington Post* has reported, "Training materials, targeting guidance, weapons know-how, and fund-raising will become virtual (i.e., online)."[45] Third, terrorists are using the Internet for operational planning for attacks through both e-mail communication and the access it provides to an array of useful information.

A *USA Today* article, for instance, cited U.S. and foreign officials who reported that bin Laden and others were using sports chat rooms, pornographic bulletin boards, and other Web sites to hide "maps and photographs of terrorist targets" and to post "instructions for terrorist activities."[46] According to Grant Jeffrey's research:

> Today, terrorists use steganography [hidden messages] that relies on software such as S-Tools, White Noise Storm, MP3 Stego, and Steghide. These computer programs allow users to embed secret messages within computerized digital information—including audio, video, or photographic image files that are transmitted across the Internet.
>
> ...The FBI is concerned that al Qaeda and other terrorist groups may be sending messages to cells in America and Europe by embedding instructions within the video transmissions used by bin Laden. This explains why the White House requests Western television networks to refrain from re-broadcasting bin Laden's messages, in case they might contain hidden steganographic information.[47]

One additional online tool that has intelligence officials concerned is Google Earth.[48] An online satellite mapping tool, Google Earth allows users to zoom in on specific locations from any Internet connection. According to a British report, "Terrorists attacking British bases in Basra are using aerial footage displayed by the Google Earth Internet tool to pinpoint their attacks.... Documents seized during raids on the homes of insurgents last week uncovered print-outs from photographs taken from Google. The satellite photographs show in detail the buildings inside the bases and vulnerable areas such as tented accommodations, lavatory blocks and where lightly armoured Land Rovers are parked."[49]

THE FIVE MOST ATTRACTIVE TARGETS

Al-Qaeda and other terrorist organizations have made it clear that their plans to destroy their enemies include the destruction of economic structures.

According to The Strategy Page, an intelligence group that tracks terrorism trends, the top five most attractive targets to terrorists today include locations with the potential to cause horrific damage to Western economies.[50] These include, in no particular order:

- *Abqaiq Oil Processing Complex:* This Saudi Arabian facility processes up to *6.8 million barrels* of Saudi oil a day. It then pumps it out to shiploading facilities. Abqaiq is one of the best-guarded sites in the world. An unsuccessful al-Qaeda assault in February 2005 resulted in security being improved even further. If Abqaiq were put out of action, the Saudi economy would be in great danger.

- *The Strait of Malacca:* This strait is the narrow seaway providing the quickest passage between the Pacific and Indian oceans. Approximately 20 percent of all world trade moves through this strait, traveling on an average of 130 ships per day. Such a small section of sea opens opportunities for pirate-like activity, in addition to vulnerability to naval mines that could sink large ships in shallow channels. This would disrupt traffic and cause economic disruption. A total or near-total shutdown of the straits would cause economic panic, particularly in East Asia, and serious shipping delays. Shipping costs would also spike upward. The potential economic impact of such a shutdown is estimated to run into the hundreds of billion dollars.

- *The Druzhba Pipeline:* This Russian oil pipeline is over 4,000 kilometers long, making it the longest in the world. It travels through southern Russia, close to the volatile Caucasus. The pipeline, which distributes 1.2 million barrels a day, supplies oil to the Ukraine and then points west, supplying even Germany. A service disruption due to terrorism or war would cripple the economies the pipeline supplies, ultimately driving up oil prices worldwide.

- *The Strait of Hormuz:* Dr. Mark Hitchcock observes a key example in the Strait of Hormuz.[51] Located between Iran and the United Arab Emirates, it is a narrow passageway with only two one-mile wide channels for sea traffic at its narrowest point. The

best estimates are that 15-17 million barrels of oil pass through
this point each day, representing approximately 20 percent of
the world's oil supply. The strait is vulnerable to Iranian antiship
missiles (bought from China) and naval mines, which are available on the black market. A terrorist attack here would pose a
detrimental impact on the world oil market, sending gas prices
soaring for an indefinite amount of time.

• *The Suez Canal:* This canal, located beside Egypt, is more vulnerable than the Strait of Malacca. At its narrowest point, it's only
1,000 feet wide. Sink one or more ships, and 1.3 million barrels
of oil have to find a different route each day, as well as millions
of tons of other cargo. Worse, the canal is a major portion of the
Egyptian economy. A canal shutdown could cause widespread
political unrest in Egypt.

ARE WE THERE YET?

Is our world really at the brink of disaster? An analysis of today's available weaponry and those who use those weapons indicate that our world is
extremely vulnerable. And the next major terrorist attack somewhere on our
globe or even a third world war could be right around the corner.

When the religious leaders of Jesus' time confronted Him and asked
Him for a sign, He replied, "When evening comes, you say, 'It will be fair
weather, for the sky is red,' and in the morning, 'Today it will be stormy,
for the sky is red and overcast.' You know how to interpret the appearance
of the sky, but you cannot interpret the signs of the times."[52] Today's signs
indicate that our world may very well stand on the brink of disaster. As we
examine some of what is happening in our world today, we cannot help but
discover that the end may be closer than we think.

2

IT'S LATER THAN YOU THINK

*"One would be very hard-pressed to find another time in
history when there was more at stake—or when the major
prophetic signposts were lined up pointing to the end."*
—Dr. Mark Hitchcock[1]

*"We're now at the dawn of an era in which an extreme fanatical
religious ideology, undeterred by the usual calculations
of prudence and self-preservation, is wielding state power and will
soon be wielding nuclear power."*
—Charles Krauthammer[2]

According to a 2005 study by the U.S. Senate Committee on Foreign
Relations, the reported risk of attack by weapons of mass destruction is
as high as 70 percent within the next ten years. In addition, the report
highlights that:

- It is highly likely that one or two new countries will obtain nuclear
  weapons in the next five years, with a total of two to five new
  countries joining the realm of nuclear capabilities over the next
  decade.
- The most likely weapon of mass destruction to be used will be a
  "dirty bomb" in which radioactive material is included within a
  conventional explosive device.
- The risk of a nuclear attack over the next five years is 16.4
  percent.[3]

The Senate's first estimate will likely be proven true. In 2006, North
Korea proclaimed to have tested an underground nuclear device. A second
nation, Iran, continues to develop nuclear capabilities, and many suggest
Iran is very close to being able to develop a nuclear missile.

Potential dirty bomb attempts have surfaced recently as well. According to a July 2006 report, border guards seized a British boat on its way to making a delivery to the Iranian military after discovering it was packed with radioactive material that could be used to build a dirty bomb. The most alarming part of this account is that the ship was not stopped until reaching a checkpoint at the Bulgarian-Romanian border![4]

The third statistic cited above notes that the chance of a nuclear attack in the next five years is over 16 percent. If you were told the flight you were about to board had a 16 percent chance of crashing, would you still take it? Of course not! When it comes to life-and-death situations, a 16 percent chance is far too high. Unfortunately, these are the very real percentages we face today of nuclear attack.

Based on these and other events, *Bulletin of the Atomic Scientists* has recently moved its Doomsday Clock ahead, marking the time as five minutes until midnight. What is the Doomsday Clock? Quite simply, it is a figurative measurement that conveys how close humanity may be to catastrophic destruction—the figurative midnight—and monitors the means humankind could use to obliterate itself. "First and foremost, these include nuclear weapons, but they also encompass climate-changing technologies and new developments in the life sciences and nanotechnology that could inflict irrevocable harm."[5] They have measured changing signs in the following three areas.

THE SIGNS OF DOOMSDAY
Nuclear Proliferation

For four decades, the United States and the Soviet Union defined the extent of the world's nuclear concerns. This simple scenario allowed for a fairly easy way to measure the possibility of a nuclear threat.

Today, while both countries continue to host more than 1,000 warheads on high alert, ready to launch within tens of minutes, a deliberate attack by Russia or the United States on the other is unlikely. Unfortunately, however, new countries have joined the ranks of those with nuclear weapons, and the possibility of a nuclear exchange between these countries remains much more likely. In 1999 and again in 2001, India and Pakistan threatened each other with nuclear arms.

Despite past successes in limiting the spread of nuclear weapons to countries around the world, nuclear proliferation seems to present a growing danger today, with countries such as North Korea and Iran actively pursuing the capability to produce nuclear weapons. Nuclear terrorism also poses a risk given the fissile materials that remain unsecured in many parts of the world, making them more available to groups that seek to use them for destructive purposes.

Environmental Problems

Although nothing of any real significance occurred anywhere in the world on January 30, 2007, the day proved to be an interesting one for news. Broadcasters across the country on this cold Tuesday morning warned that millions would die from the effects of global warming by the end of the century. The sobering information stemmed from an about-to-be-released report from the Intergovernmental Panel on Climate Change (IPCC), a conglomerate of scientists from around the world who had assembled in Paris under the auspices of the United Nations. Among their more alarming findings:

1. There's a 90 percent chance that human-caused emissions are responsible for global warming.
2. Mediterranean shores will eventually become uninhabitable during the summer months.
3. Droughts are likely to further ravage semiarid regions of Africa and southern Asia.
4. Sea levels will rise from 11 to 16.9 inches by the year 2100 and will continue to rise for the next 1,000 years.
5. Temperatures will increase by 2.5 to 10.4 degrees Fahrenheit worldwide.

The United Nation's IPCC chairman Rajendra Pachauri said he hoped the report would shock world governments into action. "I hope this report will shock people, governments into taking more serious action, as you really can't get a more authentic and a more credible piece of scientific work." Achim Steiner, the executive director of the United Nations Environment Program, said the findings presented should cause government decision-makers to accelerate efforts to slash carbon emissions.[6]

Unfortunately, the announcement came on a day when the eastern United States was experiencing one of the coldest winters on record. Alaska had just received record amounts of snowfall. And it was even snowing in the seaside town of Malibu, California, home to the movie stars, for the first time in 30 years.

According to the latest non-United Nations endorsed, nonpoliticized data, global mean temperatures have increased only one degree Fahrenheit over the past century, having risen slightly during the period from 1919 to 1940, decreased between 1940 and the early 1970s, increased again in the 1990s, and then remained essentially flat since 1998. Satellite data shows that atmospheric temperatures have remained stable since 1979.

Within one hour of the release of the grim data, another television program featuring lighter fare was about to begin—ABC's popular *Live with Regis and Kelly* show. For this particular episode, Pat Sajak was subbing for the vacationing Regis Philbin. Mr. Sajak had been a weatherman in Los Angeles prior to his rise to stardom as the host of the wildly successful *Wheel of Fortune* game show. Mr. Sajak had saved a copy of a June 24, 1974 edition of *Time* magazine and began reading, live on the air, from an article titled "Another Ice Age." Had Al Gore been watching his television at that moment, he probably would have seethed with anger over what Mr. Sajak stated. Among other things, the article said:

1. The atmosphere has been growing gradually cooler for the past three decades and the trend shows no indication of reversing.

2. Since the 1940s, the mean global temperature has dropped about 2.7° F.

3. Man is responsible for the cooling trend. The University of Wisconsin's Reid A. Bryson and other climatologists suggest that dust and other particles released into the atmosphere as a result of fuel burning may be blocking more and more sunlight from reaching and heating the surface of the earth.

4. The effects of the cooling trend could be extremely serious, if not catastrophic. Scientists figure that only a one percent decrease in the amount of sunlight hitting the earth's surface could tip the climatic balance and cool the planet enough to send it sliding

down the road to another ice age within only a few hundred years.

5. University of Toronto climatologist Kenneth Hare warns, "I don't believe that the world's present population is sustainable if there are more than three years like 1972 in a row."

Mr. Sajak then joked that the government regulations that had been implemented to stop the impending ice age had apparently worked a little too well over the course of the last 30 years, resulting in global warming.

For his role in the documentary film about global warming, *An Inconvenient Truth,* Al Gore received an Academy Award nomination and a Nobel Peace Prize nomination. It apparently didn't seem to matter to either of the nominating committees that Gore's claims have serious problems. Early in 2006, Al Gore announced to George Stephanopoulos on ABC that "the debate in the scientific community is over." Global warming is a confirmed fact, end of discussion. His movie depicts a series of dire consequences—melting ice sheets, rising sea levels, hurricanes, diseases—that will destroy us unless we allow the government to force us to change our wicked carbon dioxide-emitting ways...now!

Clearly disturbed by Mr. Gore's scare tactics and fact bending, Richard Lindzen, a professor of atmospheric science at MIT, wrote in the *Wall Street Journal* that "Al Gore is wrong. There is no 'consensus' [among scientists] on global warming...their research is forced, whether the evidence supports it or not, into Mr. Gore's preferred global warming template—namely, shrill alarmism."

In his conclusion, Lindzen states that "nonscientists generally do not want to bother with understanding the science. Claims of consensus relieve environmental advocates and politicians of any need to do so. Such claims also serve to intimidate the public." And because the human cause of the so-called "crisis" can never be established, Mr. Lindzen continues, "its use in promoting visions of disaster constitutes nothing so much as a bait-and-switch scam. That is an inauspicious beginning to what Mr. Gore claims is not a political issue but a 'moral' crusade."[7] Any thinking person is certainly concerned about the possibility of global warming, but we insist that such concerns be based on real facts, not political hype.

Emerging Technologies

According to the Doomsday Clock measurements,

> advances in genetics and biology over the last five decades have
> inspired a host of new possibilities—both positive and troubling.
> With greater understanding of genetic material and of how physi-
> ological systems interact, biologists can fight disease better and
> improve overall human health.... [Negatively] the emergence
> of nanotechnology—manufacturing at the molecular or atomic
> level—presents similar concerns, especially if coupled with chemical
> and biological weapons, explosives, or missiles. Such combinations
> could result in highly destructive missiles the size of an insect and
> microscopic delivery systems for dangerous pathogens.[8]

BIBLICAL PROPHECIES

Our world's experts have discovered numerous reasons why the end of
the world may be closer than we think. What's remarkable is that the Bible
has a lot to say on this issue.

Shortly before His crucifixion, Jesus shared what is known as the Olivet
Discourse with His followers, which is recorded in Matthew 24–25. We not
only consider this discourse to be an important prophecy of future events, we
also believe it provides an outline of the future to which all other prophetic
sections of the Bible should be related.

While every part of the Olivet Discourse proves a remarkable preview of
the future, the first few verses give us a unique historical context that enables
us to sense when the great events it describes are about to unfold:

> Jesus left the temple and was walking away when his disciples
> came up to him to call his attention to its buildings. "Do you see
> all these things?" he asked. "I tell you the truth, not one stone
> here will be left on another; every one will be thrown down."
>
> As Jesus was sitting on the Mount of Olives, the disciples came
> to him privately. "Tell us," they said, "when will this happen, and
> what will be the sign of your coming and of the end of the age?"
>
> Jesus answered: "Watch out that no one deceives you. For
> many will come in my name, claiming, 'I am the Christ,' and

will deceive many. You will hear of wars and rumors of wars, but see to it that you are not alarmed. Such things must happen, but the end is still to come. Nation will rise against nation, and kingdom against kingdom. There will be famines and earthquakes in various places. All these are the beginning of birth pains."[9]

SHOULD WE TAKE IT LITERALLY?

Sometimes when individuals seek to understand prophetic texts from the Bible, they are unsure whether they should read the passages literally or in a more symbolic way. We can be grateful that history provides us with an example of a very literal fulfillment in the first two verses of this prophecy, for that indicates to us how we should understand the rest of the Olivet Discourse. In these verses, Jesus prophesied not only that the temple would be destroyed, but also that its ruin would be so complete that not even one stone would be left standing upon another.

History records that Christ's words were fulfilled to the letter in A.D. 70. In that year, the Roman army, under the command of Titus, destroyed the city of Jerusalem. Fires raged throughout the city and in the temple area itself. After the flames burned themselves out, the soldiers saw that large amounts of gold had melted and flowed into the crevices between the building blocks of the temple. In order to recover the precious metal, the Romans had to take the buildings apart, stone by stone. And so Jesus' prophecy was fulfilled literally—not one stone was left upon another.

Some of those stones were later excavated by Israeli archeologists and may be seen today lying on the street below the Temple Mount. Every time we see pictures of these stones in Jerusalem, we see the pinpoint accuracy of Jesus' prediction.[10] And we get a clear indication about how the rest of the Olivet Discourse should be interpreted.

WHAT WILL BE THE SIGN?

Even at the time Jesus spoke, His disciples asked, "What will be the sign of your coming and of the end of the age?" They were looking beyond what would happen in A.D. 70 and focusing on the dramatic events that would precede the second coming of Christ. Jesus responded by revealing several significant signs that will be evident on the earth before His return. And before Jesus explained those signs, He offered two warnings regarding the end times.

The Sign of Deception

First, Jesus stated, "Watch out that no one *deceives* you. For many will come in my name, claiming, 'I am the Christ,' and will *deceive* many."[11] In the discourse, Jesus specifically notes six concerns regarding deceptive teachers and leaders:

1. "Watch out that no one *deceives* you" (24:4).

2. "For many will come in my name, claiming, 'I am the Christ,' and will *deceive* many" (24:5).

3. "Many false prophets will appear and *deceive* many people" (24:11).

4. "If anyone says to you, 'Look, here is the Christ!' or, 'There he is!' *do not believe it*" (24:23).

5. "False Christs and false prophets will appear and perform great signs and miracles to *deceive* even the elect—if that were possible" (24:24).

6. "If anyone tells you, 'There he is, out in the desert,' do not go out; or, 'Here he is, in the inner rooms,' *do not believe it*" (24:26).

While there have always been false teachers, today's world offers a larger number of "options" than any other time in history. In 1970 there were 26,350 *Christian* denominations alone. By 1995, over 33,820 Christian denominations had been defined, an explosion of over 7,000 new denominational groups in only 25 years.[12] That amounts to more than one new denomination every day during this time period!

In terms of world religions, there are at least 4,200 identifiable religions honoring millions of so-called gods.[13] As a result, our world is now flooded with an abundance of competing spiritual information regarding who God is, who Jesus is, and what truth is. In addition, many have abandoned the concept of absolute truth altogether, thus helping to plunge our world into further deception as it approaches the end times.

The Sign of Wars and Rumors of Wars

There have been approximately 15,000 wars in recorded human history.

Humanity has often been eager to settle disputes or expand borders through violent conflict. But the twentieth century alone experienced wars resulting in more deaths than all of the centuries before it combined.[14]

In addition to the many wars and threats of war around the world today, our society is approaching what Newt Gingrich has called the beginning of World War III. In an interview on NBC's *Meet the Press*, Gingrich based his statement on the following evidence:

- The British home secretary saying that there are 20 terrorist groups numbering 1,200 terrorists in Britain.
- Seven people in Miami being videotaped pledging allegiance to al-Qaeda.
- Eighteen people in Canada being picked up with twice the quantity explosives that were used in the Oklahoma City bombing, with an explicit threat to bomb the Canadian parliament and saying they'd like to behead the Canadian prime minister.
- In New York City, reports that people in three different countries were plotting to destroy the tunnels of New York.

Gingrich went on to explain, "We are in the early stages of what I would describe as *the third world war,* and frankly, our bureaucracies aren't responding fast enough."[15]

But how did Jesus respond to such reports? He said, "See to it that you are not alarmed." Why not? Jesus provided two reasons in Matthew 24:

1. "Such things must happen…"
2. "…but the end is still to come" (verse 6).

Clearly, wars are not the sign of the end. Yet Jesus did use war as part of His answer to the disciples' question about signs. This can only mean that this sign had to include a special kind of war.

A Special Kind of War

Matthew's Gospel uses two Hebrew expressions here that his Jewish friends would have easily recognized. The first is, "Nation will rise against nation, and kingdom against kingdom" (24:7).[16] Here Jesus was speaking of a war started by two nations, each side soon joined by the surrounding nations until all the nations involved in the prophet's vision in Isaiah 19:1-2 are included. So in Matthew 24, the entire world is in view. In other words, "When you see a war started by two single nations that is soon joined by the kingdoms of the world—followed by unprecedented famines, pestilence, and multiple earthquakes at the same time—you have *the sign*."[17]

This was similar to what occurred in June 1914 when the archduke of Austria, Prince Francis Ferdinand, was shot by a Serbian zealot in the very area of the world where U.N. forces remain stationed today to keep peace. One month later, Austria declared war on Serbia, then other nations joined—until all but seven "neutral" nations joined the conflict. According to some researchers, this was the start of the "big four" (World War I, World War II, Communist Russia, and Communist China) that accounted for three-fourths of all deaths by atrocities during the twentieth century.[18]

Widespread Famine

More than 70 million people died of famines in the twentieth century. While statistics from earlier centuries are scarce, estimates state that at least two million people died during famines in the seventeenth century, 10 million during the eighteenth century, and 25 million in the nineteenth century. So the twentieth century was marked by more deaths by famine than the previous three centuries combined![19]

The organization World Vision continues the fight against famine today, noting that in the most dire regions of the world—such as Darfur, Sudan—as many as 10,000 people have died *per month* recently due to a combination of famine and civil strife.[20] In 2002, the BBC aired a special report that highlighted ten nations in which millions of individuals, often the vast majority of the nation's population, faced traumatic famine and resulting epidemic deaths.[21] Though famine has been eliminated from many parts of the world, numerous individuals around the world, particularly in African nations, continue to struggle against this plight.

Worldwide Plagues

Historians called World War I the Great War, and rightly so, as it was to that point the greatest war in human history. It lasted four years, from 1914–1918, and ended in the same year a flu epidemic spread throughout Europe.

By far the most destructive influenza pandemic in history, it killed nearly 100 million people worldwide in just 18 months—far more than the number of human lives lost in World War I.[22] Furthermore, many of the victims of the Spanish flu were healthy young adults, in contrast to most influenza outbreaks which predominantly affect juvenile, elderly, or otherwise weakened patients. Three parts of this first sign Jesus gave—a special kind of war, famines, and plagues—began their fulfillment in the first part of the twentieth century, setting the stage for their ultimate fulfillment in the future.

Polio epidemics have swept across the United States several times over the past century. The first major outbreak was in 1916, when 27,000 people suffered paralysis and 6,000 died. The largest outbreak was in 1952, when 58,000 cases were reported and more than 3,000 people died.[23]

However, by far the greatest epidemic of our current era is the HIV/AIDS crisis. Greater than perhaps any epidemic in human history, the statistics are overwhelming. According to the Global Health Council:

- By the end of 2005, 40.3 million people were living with HIV/AIDS, including 17.5 million women and 2.3 million children under the age of 15.

- 4.9 million people became newly infected with HIV in 2005, including 700,000 children. Of these, 3.2 million new infections occurred in Sub-Saharan Africa.

- In 2005 alone, a total of 3.1 million people died of HIV/AIDS-related causes.

- Worldwide, only one in ten persons infected with HIV has been tested and knows his or her HIV status.[24]

A major shift of focus in Christian missionary service has begun to occur in the twenty-first century, with more attention toward medical, practical, and spiritual support of those infected with the HIV/AIDS virus.[25] While methods of assistance and legislation have caused much controversy, the fact remains that the global proportions of this epidemic makes it one more indicator that the end may be closer than we think.

Multiple Earthquakes

The fourth part of the sign Jesus mentioned in Matthew 24:7, multiple earthquakes, is more difficult to track. The largest earthquake of the past century was a magnitude 9.5 quake that struck Chile on May 22, 1960. More than 2,000 people were killed in Chile, Hawaii, Japan, and the Philippines as a result of this earthquake and the deadly tsunami that followed. The most powerful earthquake in the United States, and the second largest in the world over the past century, was a magnitude 9.2 quake in Alaska, which struck on Good Friday in 1964. This great earthquake and ensuing tsunami ended 125 lives and caused about $310 million in property loss.[26]

The deadliest earthquake of the twentieth century, by far, was a magnitude 8.0 that struck Tianjin, China, on July 27, 1976. The official casualty figure was 255,000, but unofficial estimates of the death tolls go as high as 655,000. Counted together, the top ten deadliest earthquakes of the twentieth century have caused over one million casualties.[27]

The twenty-first century has already experienced an enormous number of natural disasters as well. For example, the underwater earthquake that created the 2004 tsunami in East Asia resulted in over 212,000 deaths in several nations. And the United Nations' head of emergency relief has warned that a natural disaster in any of the world's largest cities could set off a catastrophe that could be 100 times worse than the 2004 tsunami.[28] More recent disasters such as Hurricane Katrina have shown that even the United States is not immune from horrific catastrophes.

While there have been many earthquakes all through history, the frequency of these quakes and the amount of destruction they cause have increased tremendously since the early part of the twentieth century, which supports this fourth part of the sign given by Jesus in Matthew 24:7.

The Rest of the Story

The second notable Hebrew expression in Matthew's Gospel is this: "all these [the four parts of the one sign] are the beginning of birth pains" (24:8). That is, when a woman enters labor, the first birth pains are not the only ones, but rather, they are the first in a series. In most cases, a pattern begins, with each following labor pain coming slightly sooner to the one before and with greater intensity than the one before. When contractions are within three minutes of one another, the mother knows the time to give birth is near.

While World War I did not mark the "end of the age," it did signal the beginning of birth pains—pains that continue to occur in our time.

A NEW KIND OF WAR

One of the most violent and extreme words in our world today is *caliphate.* A startling interview in the *Christian Science Monitor* with a spokesman for the Muslim organization Hizb ut-Tahrir defined it this way: "Muslims should abolish national boundaries within the Islamic world and return to a single Islamic state, known as 'the caliphate,' that would stretch from Indonesia to Morocco and contain more than 1.5 billion people."[29]

In September 2006, Islamic Movement leader Sheikh Raed Salah told a rally of 50,000 that Jerusalem would become "the capital of the new Muslim caliphate sooner than is thought." Salah also noted that history tells of many occasions in which the al-Aqsa mosque in Jerusalem was occupied by foreign conquerors, but the occupiers left after a short time, and thus will also be the fate of the Israeli occupation." According to Salah, "The Israeli occupation will leave Jerusalem soon."[30]

The concept of an Islamic caliphate continues to drive the U.S. military battles within Iraq as well. In a January 2007 CNN report, it was announced that most insurgents who are battling U.S.-led forces in Iraq's Anbar province are local Iraqis loyal to al-Qaeda and not foreign fighters, according to the U.S. commander in the region. During a video news conference from the provincial town of Falluja, Major General Richard Zilmer said the insurgents intended to create a strict Islamic state similar to Afghanistan's Taliban regime before the U.S.-led invasion toppled it in 2001. They want "a caliphate state out here," he said. "They want to turn back the hands of time. It is antithetical to progress and, again, any positive future."[31]

U.S. vice president Dick Cheney, in September 2004, referred to Osama bin Laden and his followers as "wanting to re-establish what you could refer to as the seventh-century Caliphate to be governed by sharia law, the most rigid interpretation of the Qur'an."[32] General Abizaid, the top American commander in the Middle East, warned that the caliphate's goals would also include the destruction of Israel.[33]

These goals are ultimately promoted by teachings in the Quran and Hadith. It's why since 9/11 the first name of bin Laden, *Osama,* has been the number-one favored name for newborn male infants in a dozen or more Muslim countries. In some nations, seven out of ten baby boys are the namesakes of the terrorist.[34]

One of the great concerns in our world is the current rise in Islamic extremism. While certainly the vast majority of those who practice Islam do not practice acts of terror, the radicals who do are often motivated by their religious beliefs.

On a state level, Iran is controlled by a Shiite government committed to the destruction of Israel and its allies. What many do not understand, however, is that the beliefs behind this political stance derives from an end-times story of their own.

THE "OTHER" END-TIMES STORY

Like Judaism and Christianity, Islam has its own end-times story. The Shiite version, summarized by *Washington Post* writer Charles Krauthammer, explains:

> Like Judaism and Christianity, Shiite Islam has its own version of the messianic return—the reappearance of the Twelfth Imam. The more devout believers in Iran pray at the Jamkaran mosque, which houses a well from which, some believe, he will emerge.
>
> When Ahmadinejad unexpectedly won the presidential elections, he immediately gave $17 million of government funds to the shrine. Last month Ahmadinejad said publicly that the main mission of the Islamic Revolution is to pave the way for the reappearance of the Twelfth Imam.
>
> And as in some versions of fundamentalist Christianity, the second coming will be accompanied by the usual trials and tribulations, death and destruction. Iranian journalist Hossein Bastani reported Ahmadinejad saying in official meetings that the hidden imam will reappear *in two years*.[35]

Other reporters have noted that "Ahmadinejad's 'vision' at the United Nations could be dismissed as pure political posturing if it weren't for a string of similar statements and actions that clearly suggest he believes he is destined to bring about the return of the Shiite messiah."[36]

The Twelfth Imam

The mystical Twelfth Imam, venerated by many in Iran, allegedly disappeared as a child in the year A.D. 941. Shiite Muslims believe he will return and rule for seven years in perfect justice. In a November 16, 2005 speech in Tehran, Ahmadinejad said that the main mission of his government is to "pave the path for the glorious reappearance of Imam Mahdi (may God hasten his reappearance)."

The Mahdi ("director") is believed to be a direct descendant of Muhammad the prophet (Muhammad Abu'lkasem). He is believed to be the one who is guided by Allah and will rule the coming global Islamic government (caliphate). The Quran teaches that there will be a period of judgment of the Islamic caliphate that will last at least 1,000 years following the great crisis that ends this age—somewhat similar to the Bible's prophecy regarding the millennium, which is mentioned in the book of Revelation.

Muhammad declared that Allah had inspired and sent six major prophets. They were Adam, Noah, Abraham, Moses, Jesus, and Muhammad. Then at the end of the age Allah would send a seventh and final prophet called Al-Mahdi. All of these prophets are regarded by Islam as Muslims, or those who are in submission to Allah as the one true God.[37]

According to political science professor John von Heyking at the University of Lethbridge in Canada, a group in Iran called the Hojjatieh believe that humans can stir up chaos to encourage the Mahdi to return. Ayatollah Khomeini banned the group in the early 1980s because they rejected one of the primary commitments of the Iranian revolution: the concept of *vilayat-i faqih* (Guardianship of the Islamic Jurists). In other words, they opposed the notion of an Islamic republic because it would hinder the Twelfth Imam's return on account of it being too just and peaceful.

Today, in addition to the possibility of Ahmadinejad himself being a member (or a former member), the group has connections to Qom ultra-conservative cleric Mesbah Yazdi whom Iranians frequently refer to as the "crazed one." Alarmingly, four of the 21 new Iranian cabinet ministers are Hojjatieh members. Some reports state that cabinet ministers must sign a formal pledge of support for the Twelfth Imam.

Professor Heyking observes,

> The possibility of Ahmadinejad belonging to this group does not make a lot of sense, at least if one wishes to regard him as a pragmatic politician. Why would the president of the Islamic republic object to the existence of that Islamic republic? Moreover,

his recent references to the Twelfth Imam have been to promote Iran as a "powerful, developed and model Islamic society." Today, we should define our economic, cultural and political policies based on the policy of Imam Mahdi's return. "We should avoid copying the West's policies and systems." Most Iranians would have interpreted this statement as typical Iranian nationalist and Islamist rhetoric aimed against the West and as a reference to his policy of using oil money to improve the plight of the poor. However, helping the poor is central to Islamic social teaching and he need not have referred to the "Imam Mahdi's return" to say this.[38]

Western observers need to be able to understand the ideological and religious overtones of the current situation in Iran. Ahmadinejad's peculiar references to the Twelfth Imam are not a mere eccentricity to be taken lightly.[39]

Recently the Web site of the governmental Islamic Republic of Iran Broadcasting network posted a transcript from a nationally televised program that outlined the official government position regarding the Imam Mahdi. The transcript states:

> With the reappearance of Imam Mahdi...conflicts, differences and discriminations that stem from lack of faith and atheism in the society will be eliminated. The shortcomings of religions and schools of thought will be clarified and Islam will prevail as the perfect pinnacle of faith. In other words, methods will become one and oneness will appear in people's beliefs.[40]

Joel Rosenberg, bestselling author of *Epicenter*, notes in his research that "he [Ahmadinejad] believes he was chosen by Allah to bring about the downfall of Judeo-Christian civilization, and to usher in the End of Days, and he is getting more brazen and more dangerous with each passing month."[41]

The Imam's Return

Kenneth Timmerman also notes that reports in government media outlets from Tehran have quoted Ahmadinejad stating that the Twelfth

Imam will reappear in two years. At the same time, Ahmadinejad has repeatedly vowed to pursue Iran's nuclear programs—in open defiance of the International Atomic Energy Agency and European Union negotiators. "While many Shiite Muslims worship the 12th *imam,* a previously secret society of powerful clerics, now openly advising the new president, are transforming these messianic beliefs into government policies."[42]

According to the Hadith, a sacred Islamic text, "The Mahdi will be of my family, of the descendants of Fatimah.... he will have a broad forehead, a prominent nose. He will fill the earth with equity and justice as it was filled with oppression and tyranny, and he will rule for seven years."[43]

Princeton University Professor Bernard Lewis, one of America's leading authorities on the Muslim world, recently gave a lecture at Hebrew University in Jerusalem in which he warned that the political and religious leadership in Iran are actively preparing for the end of the world.

> Ahmadinejad and his group clearly believe, and I don't doubt the sincerity of their belief, that we are now entering an apocalyptic age, which will result in the triumph of their messianic figure," Lewis said, referring to the Twelfth Imam, or the Mahdi. "Muslims, like Jews, believe that there are things you can do to hasten the messiah. M.A.D. (the Cold War strategic doctrine of Mutually Assured Destruction) doesn't work with these people."[44]

Lewis also noted that "Iran is a mortal threat and one also has to take account of the apocalyptic mood of Ahmadinejad and his circle. Islam, like Judaism and Christianity, has an end of time scenario."[45]

WHAT DOES THIS MEAN FOR ME?

One of the past century's great prophecy teachers and scholars, Dr. John Walvoord, made this observation in response to his study of Scripture and the world's changing events:

> I have been studying prophecy for many years, and while I do not believe it is possible to set dates for the Lord's return, I do sense in the world today an unprecedented time of world crises that can be interpreted as being preparatory for the coming of the Lord.

If there ever was a time when Christians should live every day as though Christ could come at any time, it is today.[46]

Should we be concerned regarding these signs and current events that indicate how close the end may be? Yes, but our concern should not cause us to panic. Our understanding should lead us, as Dr. Walvoord eloquently stated, to "live every day as though Christ could come at any time."

In the next chapter, we'll discover more events that are setting the stage for the last days. And we'll see that these events have global ramifications that will affect every person on this planet.

3

SETTING THE STAGE FOR THE LAST DAYS

"When these things begin to take place, stand up and lift up your heads, because your redemption is drawing near."
—LUKE 21:28

IT WAS THE HANDSHAKE SEEN AROUND THE WORLD: The Israeli prime minister and the chairman of the Palestine Liberation Organization shaking hands on the White House lawn in September 1993. And all the world was watching by television, wondering if this new treaty would really work. The handshake was the symbolic culmination of several months of secret negotiations between the Israelis and the Palestinian Arabs.

Two simple letters signed by the late Israeli prime minister Yitzhak Rabin and PLO chairman Yasser Arafat marked the beginning of a new hope for peace in the Middle East back in those euphoric days. Both agreed to recognize the other's right to exist in peace and security. And before it was all over, they were celebrating in an elaborate ceremony on the outskirts of ancient Jericho.

"Enough of blood and tears," Rabin announced. "Today we are giving peace a chance."[1] Within a few months, the entire effort began to unravel. From the beginning, there were detractors. Hard-liners in Gaza protested with strikes and street riots. Iran denounced the peace effort, and Syria remained cautious, still insisting on its right to the Golan Heights. Other Arab nations took a wait-and-see position.

In the meantime, Arab-Israeli relations completely fell apart. Rabin was assassinated by an Israeli extremist. Ariel Sharon eventually replaced Rabin, and tensions between his and Arafat's governments finally led to the intafada ("uprising") in the fall of 2000, which lasted for nearly four years. On September 11, 2001, 19 Islamic extremists highjacked four American commercial passenger planes and flew them into the World Trade Center in New York City and the Pentagon in Washington, D.C., causing the deaths of some 3,000 innocent people.

9/11, as it has come to be known, sparked an international war against terrorism that has seen American troops invade both Afghanistan and Iraq. But the results of the U.S. military occupation in Iraq has led to 3,000 American military deaths and over 30,000 Iraqi civilian deaths in what has degenerated into what John Ankerberg, in a book published in 2007, calls a "middle east meltdown."[2]

Many people believe the only permanent solution to the ongoing conflict will be a peace treaty backed up and enforced by a powerful military leader who will bring the world back from the brink of disaster.[3] A Middle East peace settlement is clearly predicted in the Bible in Daniel 9:25-27, and other prophecies from this same passage have already been fulfilled. Daniel predicted the rebuilding of Jerusalem "in times of trouble" (verse 25), which was done in the days of Nehemiah. Daniel then looked down the corridor of time and saw the Anointed One, the Messiah, "cut off" (verse 26), which speaks of Christ's death. Looking beyond the death of Christ, Daniel predicted, "War will continue until the end" (verse 26). And so it has.

THE PROSPECT OF PEACE

The Arab-Israeli conflict goes deeper than just the Palestinian question over the issue of control in Israel's occupied territories. Certainly this is an important issue in the current debate, but the continuous attacks on Israel by Hamas and Hezbollah guerrillas shows a deeply embedded hatred that will not easily be resolved. This points to the need for a peaceful settlement of gigantic proportions.

The prophet Daniel predicted the rise of a future world leader who will sign a peace treaty ("covenant," Daniel 9:27) with Israel, but he will break that agreement in three-and-a-half years and attack Israel. While Bible scholars have debated the interpretation and application of this passage for centuries, it seems to speak of an era not unlike our own. Daniel tells us of a future age when knowledge and travel will increase (Daniel 12:4); he seems to have a global picture in mind.

Daniel also predicted an alliance of ten nations growing out of the old Roman Empire (Daniel 7:7-14), symbolized by the ten horns of the creature that represents the last world system. Bible scholar John Walvoord suggests, "The final confederacy of ten nations will constitute the revived Roman Empire, which will have the economic and political power necessary to control the Mediterranean."[4]

The unification of the European Economic Community (now the European Union) in 1992 signaled a serious step in the direction of a global economy like the one described in the Bible. This European Union (EU), which calls for the eventual economic and political union of the United States and Europe, has been a long time coming since it was first proposed after World War II and formalized by the Rome Treaty in 1957.[5] Since Bible prophecy points to a final economic, military, and political giant that sits on seven hills (i.e., Rome), we have to wonder if we are not now witnessing the coming together of the final alignment of the nations at the end of the age.

IRRECONCILABLE DIFFERENCES

The great tragedy of the ongoing crisis in the Middle East is that without Christ, there is no hope of lasting peace. Men may talk of peace, plan for peace, and work for peace, but there will be no lasting peace. The irreconcilable differences between the Arabs and the Jews go back 4,000 years. These old hatreds and prejudices will not go away as a result of mere human efforts. No amount of education, psychology, social welfare, or government planning can eradicate that unresolvable hatred. It can be corrected only by the love of Christ.

During the church age, all people, including Jews and Arabs, are called to faith in Jesus Christ, the Prince of Peace. Only in Him can there be lasting peace between mortal enemies. In Christ, all men are equal brothers. There is neither Jew nor Arab nor Gentile. We are one in Christ.

This great truth bonds the hearts of all Christians, no matter what their national or ethnic origin. In Christ, no one group is better than another. No one person takes precedence over another. All are equal in Christ. It was this truth—that a slave and a master were equal brothers in Christ—that broke the bond of slavery in the Roman world. When we kneel before Christ and submit to His lordship, we find that the ground is level at the cross.

This leaves the Christian in a unique position, however. On the one hand, he is to preach the gospel to all people, including Arabs and Jews. He is to love them both with the love of Christ. On the other hand, most Christians believe that God is not finished with His people Israel. He still has a plan for their future after the times of the Gentiles have been fulfilled. Therefore, most Christians sympathize with Israel's right to exist as a people and a nation.

The tension calls Christians to love two peoples who do not love each other and demonstrate the power of the gospel to both groups. It is not easy to affirm Israel's right to her land without offending Arabs. And it is not easy to express concern for the Palestinians without offending the Israelis. But it must be done—for Christ's sake and the gospel.

Christians must also guard against the temptation to hate Arabs, or any Muslims, because of the conflict in the Middle East. It is possible to rightly affirm the just cause of war as a response to injustice without hating our enemies. This is not easy to do, especially when we have lost loved ones to that enemy. Despite the crisis in the Middle East and the problems that stem from it, we must pray that God will give us grace not to hate the Arabs but to demonstrate the love of Christ to them.

AN INEVITABLE DESTINY?

One of the tragedies of the war in Iraq is the widening division between many of the Arabs and some people in the West. Though cooperation is possible and Western and Saudi flags have flown side by side in the past, there is still a deep resentment toward the United States within the hearts of many Arab peoples.

Some people have speculated that the current crisis has set the prophetic stage for the future.[6] The Western world is calling for a peaceful resolution of the conflict. This will require greater cooperation between Arabs and the West. Yet the old hatreds remain deeper than ever. The barbaric cries of "Death!" to all who oppose the Arabs do not give much hope to a lasting, peaceful solution.

This is the great dilemma that has confronted the Jewish people for centuries. They have often tried to live at peace with their Muslim neighbors.[7] History attests to the fact that in the past, Jewish communities often flourished among the Arabs—in Egypt, Syria, Iraq, and Iran. But sooner or later, the Jews came under persecution and often were forced to flee for their lives.

Thus future Arab-Israeli relations are very much in doubt. The Jews were without a national home for nearly 2,000 years after the Romans destroyed Jerusalem in A.D. 70. For centuries they were forced to live among Christians and Arabs alike as they wandered the earth in search of a home. Finally, in 1897, an Austrian Jew named Theodor Herzl cried out to the leaders of Europe. "There is a land without a people," he said, "and there is a people without a land. Give the land without a people to the people without a land."[8] Herzl wrote the book *Judenstat,* which called for the rebirth of the State of Israel. At the same time, he convened the World Zionist Congress in Switzerland to share with others his hopes and plans for the future of the Jewish people.

Later, on December 9, 1917, British general Edmund Allenby took Jerusalem from the Turks without firing a shot. The Turks had allied with the Germans during World War I and their losses included Palestine. On May 24, 1920, the League of Nations ratified Britain's mandate over Palestine and opened the door for Jews to return to their ancient homeland.

A Significant Prophecy Fulfilled

Many Christians believe that the Jewish people's return to Israel is the most significant evidence of fulfilled prophecy in our time. John Phillips says, "It is one of the greatest signs of the end times."[9] He points to Isaiah 60:9-10 as dramatic testimony to this prophetic fulfillment: "Surely the isles shall wait for me, and the ships of Tarshish [Europe] first, to bring thy sons from far.... And the sons of strangers shall build up thy walls, and their kings shall minister unto thee" (KJV).

When the United Nations met to vote on the partitioning of Palestine on November 27, 1947, there was little hope of Israel getting the necessary two-thirds vote. At the last minute, the Soviet Union surprised everyone and voted *for* the establishment of the State of Israel and the vote passed! On May 14, 1948, the British High Commissioner for Palestine stepped down and the Zionist Council in Tel Aviv proclaimed the State of Israel established with David Ben-Gurion as prime minister and Chaim Weizmann as president.

Several Arab states, including Egypt, Jordan, and Iraq, immediately proclaimed a holy war against the newly reborn Israel and attacked on all sides. But to the world's great surprise, Israel not only defended itself but also forced the Arabs to accept a truce. In 1956 President Gamal Abdel Nasser of Egypt tried to attack Israel and was decisively turned back. In 1967, Nasser provoked the Israelis into the Six-Day War. By the time it was over, Israel had conquered the Sinai, the old city of Jerusalem, the West Bank, and the Golan Heights. Israel's military superiority shocked the secular world. But Bible scholars recalled the prophetic prediction that the Jews would "never again…be uprooted from the land I have given them" (Amos 9:15).

By 1973 Anwar Sadat was in power as Egypt's president. His independence became clear when he threw a group of Russian military advisers out of the country. That same year, the Arab world had placed an oil embargo against the United States. Then Sadat caught the world by surprise when he attacked the Sinai Peninsula while Syria attacked the Golan Heights on October 6, 1973, which was Yom Kippur, or the Jewish Day of Atonement. Again the Israelis won a decisive victory, but this time with heavy losses.

In the years that followed, Sadat made an incredibly statesmanlike move and traveled to Israel to meet with Prime Minister Menachem Begin and to address the Knesset, the Israeli congress at Jerusalem. Later, Begin and Sadat met with President Jimmy Carter of the United States in 1978 at Camp David, Maryland to discuss the Camp David Peace Accords. Their goal was to establish a lasting peace in the Middle East. In March of 1979 Israel and Egypt signed a formal peace treaty in Washington, D.C. A leading Arab nation had committed itself to peace with Israel!

THE ESCALATING DRAMA

In many ways, Israel's survival in the midst of a sea of Arabs is indeed miraculous! While we could speculate that Israel's presence in the Holy Land may be only temporary, that seems unlikely. The Jewish people seem to be there to stay. Many, including prophecy expert Dr. John Walvoord, believed "the times of the Gentiles" (Luke 21:24) may be coming to a close and the great end-times drama is about to unfold.[10]

God promised Abraham that He would bless them that blessed Him and curse those who cursed Him (Genesis 12:3). Many Christians view this promise as binding on nations and how they treat Israel. The prophet Jeremiah put it even more strikingly when he said, "All who devour you [Israel] will be devoured; all your enemies will go into exile. Those who plunder you will be plundered; all who make spoil of you I will despoil" (Jeremiah 30:16).

Given the Arab wars and hostilities against Israel, it is clear that Israel has suffered unjustly at the hands of her neighbors. And unreasonable acts such as unprovoked missile attacks against Israel certainly do not make sympathizers out of most Americans or Europeans. Nor do such acts of terrorism commend the Islamic faith to the rest of the watching world.

CRIES FOR PEACE

There is something shocking and horrifying about war that makes us all shudder. The ultimate finality of the highway to death makes it terrifying indeed. So much so that in the midst of every war, there are cries for peace. We would think that modern, educated people would avoid the destructiveness of war at all costs. But there is something basically destructive in the psyche of human depravity that makes war an inevitable reality.

All over the world, efforts are constantly being made to stop conflicts and propose settlements for opposing parties. This has been an especially difficult prospect in the Middle East, where underlying tensions go back for centuries and where religious issues provoke bitterness and hatred. That is why a proposed peace settlement in the Middle East raises such high hopes. It promises an end to many centuries of hostilities and the beginning of a new order for the future.

The immediate solution would seem to be a peace treaty "that settles disputes, disarms antagonists, and provides absolute guarantees," writes Walvoord.[11] Such a treaty would probably be backed up by military force, but if the past is any indicator, any settlement that is reached will only be temporary in nature. Conflicts are bound to resurge again and again despite Western efforts to the contrary.

THREATS OF WAR

The Bible promises both peace and war in Israel's future. The Old Testament Scriptures indicate that a great world leader will come onto the scene promising lasting peace in the Middle East. He will sign a peace treaty with Israel. Most Christians believe this leader will arise from the European Economic Community, though some think he may be from the Middle East itself.

We can only *speculate* at this point as to how that peace settlement may come about. The continued threat of war, an economic crisis, or an oil shortage could all be factors that trigger further conflict in the Middle East. Whatever the case, the call for peace will eventually outcry the call for war. The Bible predicts a treaty between Israel and a powerful world leader that will result in peace and prosperity for the nation and people of Israel (Daniel 9:27).

But this peace will be short-lived—only three-and-one-half years. At that point the world leader will break his covenant with Israel. He will then go on to violently persecute the people of Israel for the next three-and-one-half years. Jesus called this time the "great tribulation" (Matthew 24:21 KJV). Jeremiah called it "a time of trouble for Jacob" (Jeremiah 30:7). The Scriptures indicate that God will use the Great Tribulation to awaken Israel to the truth about their Messiah.

In Israel's most desperate hour, the Lord Jesus, the Prince of Peace, will return to spare Israel and bring His resurrected bride, the church, back with Him to rule in His millennial kingdom on earth. Jesus Himself warned, "If those days had not been cut short, no one would survive" (Matthew 24:22). But God, in His great wisdom and mercy, has promised to spare the world for a better future when there will be peace for 1,000 years while Christ reigns in Jerusalem upon the throne of David.

SETTING THE STAGE FOR THE END

The Old Testament prophets predicted that the Jews would eventually return to the Promised Land and that Israel would be reestablished as a nation before the end of the times of the Gentiles. Jesus predicted, "Jerusalem will be trampled on by the Gentiles until the times of the Gentiles are fulfilled" (Luke 21:24). It would seem that time is running out for the Gentiles and that the stage is now set for the end times.

It is always possible that the end is still hundreds of years into the future, but it is not very probable. The precarious nature of international events and the ever-present threat of nuclear war remind all of us how near the end could actually be. Given the depravity of human nature, it is not likely that we can continue to escape the final apocalypse much longer.

It is also possible that Israel's present return to the Holy Land will end in failure and that the Jewish people will be expelled only to return again later in fulfillment of Bible prophecy. But with circumstances being what they are, that probably won't happen. It seems unlikely that God would not choose to use the present-day setting to bring about the end that Jesus and the prophets predicted. In fact, everything in Bible prophecy points in that direction.

The exact timing of last-day events may be indefinite, but several prophetic elements are already *now* in place:

- Israel is back in the Promised Land for the first time in nearly 2,000 years.
- The Arab nations are bent on driving Israel into the Mediterranean Sea.
- The intervention of the major Western powers in the Middle East indicates the times of the Gentiles are still operable.
- Attempted peace settlements, though desirable, seem destined to failure in resolving the Arab-Israeli conflict.
- Popular resentment against Israel among the Arab peoples is deeper than ever before.
- Extremist attempts to rally the Arabs into a jihad ("holy war") against Israel shows how quickly an Arab coalition could form in an attempt to invade Israel.
- The political unification of Europe may fulfill the Bible's prophecies of a great end-times revived Roman Empire.
- The stage is now set for a prominent world leader to arise from the West and promise peace for the entire world.
- A global economy is now upon us. It is only a matter of time until the whole world is one economic unit waiting to be taken over by a sinister power.
- The potential of nuclear war remains an ever-present reality.

While we must be careful not to set dates or to speculate on the exact details of prophetic fulfillment, we can be certain that the world is rushing headlong toward an apocalyptic destiny. It is only a matter of time until the nuclear threat is beyond human control in the Middle East. Everyone realizes that we are standing on the edge of a new day in world politics. The dramatic changes we have witnessed in Europe, the Middle East, and the former Soviet Union tell us that the world is undergoing a massive transformation. The aftermath of World War II finally has been shaken from us like an old rag. Eastern Europe is awakening to a new day of hope and freedom.

At the same time, there is great concern about where all these changes are taking us. Charles Colson, the former chief counsel for President Richard Nixon, recently said, "We sense that things are winding down, that somehow freedom, justice, and order are slipping away. Our great civilization may not yet lie in smoldering ruins, but the enemy is within the gates. The times seem to smell of sunset."[12] He goes on to suggest that Western civilization is facing the greatest crisis encountered since the barbarians invaded Rome.

A major factor in this demise of Western Civilization is our neglect of God's revelation, which has pushed us to the limits of our own rationalization. We have abandoned rationality for irrationality in the attempt to hold onto belief in something—anything—beyond ourselves.

All through the twentieth century, we allowed godless secularism to replace the Judeo-Christian values of our society. God has been deliberately and systematically removed from prominence in our culture and in our intellectual lives. We have made Him irrelevant to our culture. Tragically, we have also made our culture irrelevant to God. In so doing, we have abandoned our spiritual heritage. The Christian consensus that once dominated Western culture is now shattered. The world of the twenty-first century is already mired in the quicksand of secularism, relativism, and mysticism. It is a wonder we have survived as long as we have.

We should not be surprised, therefore, that spiritual confusion is rampant. Almost daily someone launches a new religion, predicts the end of the world, or announces himself to be the Messiah. Is it any wonder that a nonbelieving world shakes its head and walks away?

In the place of biblical Christianity, people are now calling for a new world order that consists of the very elements Scripture warns will signify the empire of the Antichrist once he comes on the world scene:

1. *World Government*

Globalists are now insisting that national governments should surrender their sovereignty to a one-world government. Such a government would operate through a world headquarters, a world court, and even a world military.

2. *World Economy*

This aspect of globalism is already upon us. No developed nation of any kind can survive today without networking with the global economy. There is almost no such thing as a product that is not dependent on parts, trade, or investments from foreign countries.

3. *World Religion*

This will be the final phase of the new world order. The idea of a new world religion of peace and cooperation is already being proposed. Religious unity has been endorsed by the Catholic pope, the Dalai Lama, and leaders of the World Council of Churches.

What we are witnessing today may well usher in the fulfillment of the biblical prophecies of the end times. Revelation 13 predicts the rise of a powerful world ruler who is able to control the world politically and economically. This ruler will have at his side a false prophet who promotes a one-world religion.

"We are past the point of no return," announced Jacques Delors, the father of European unification.[13] The Europe of the future may well become a political union, the United States of Europe. If this happens, Europe, not America, will be the strongest and most powerful "nation" on earth—economically, politically, and even militarily. And as the current European Union continues to expand into the former Soviet satellites of Eastern Europe and even into Russia itself, Europe could one day stretch from the Atlantic Ocean to the Pacific Ocean for the first time in history.

Many people believe that the resurgence of the New Europe fulfills the biblical prophecies of a revived Roman Empire in the last days. Like the architects of the Tower of Babel, advocates of the new world order believe that "coming together" will consolidate what were formerly volatile or weak economies and foster global peace and cooperation. Former German chancellor Helmut Kohl said, "The United States of Europe will form the core of a peaceful order...the age prophesied of old, when all shall dwell secure and none shall make them afraid."[14]

The real tragedy in all this talk of global unity is the absence of any emphasis on the spiritual roots of democracy and freedom. The gospel has been blunted in Western Europe for so long that there is little God-consciousness left in the European people. Without Christ, the Prince of Peace, there can be no hope for manmade orders of peace and prosperity. There will be no millennium without the Messiah!

In the present configuration of nations, the Islamic world seems out of step with all the talk of a new world order. There is little or no room in Islam for pluralism on religious or political issues. Muslims believe they are right and all others, including Christians and Jews, are infidels. Yet, the Bible predicts a global religious system in the last days.

Where Are We Now?

What is now more clear than ever is that we have taken a quantum leap toward the fulfillment of the biblical prophecies of the last days. The stage is now being set for the final climatic act in the long history of the human drama. Things could not have been arranged more perfectly for the fulfillment of the prophecies of the end times:

1. The fall of communism has paved the way for a *world economy* and a *world government*. The global web is tightening around us every day.

2. Secularism is giving way to *New Age mysticism* as the do-it-yourself religion of our times. The end result will be the watering down of religious beliefs so that they are more palatable to everyone.

3. Global economic interdependence will eventually lead to a *global political system* that dominates national sovereignty.

4. *Materialism* and *selfism* will replace spiritual values. Mankind will be left in the mindless pursuit of material prosperity as the basis for meaning and value in life.

5. The *spiritual vacuum* that results will leave the world ready for

the ultimate deception: The Great Lie of the Antichrist that will deceive the whole world.

6. A *world leader* will quickly arise on the international scene promising to bring peace and economic stability to the entire globe. He will receive the support of the European community and eventually control the whole world.

7. A *crisis in the Middle East* will trigger this world leader's intervention militarily and politically. He will eventually sign a peace treaty with Israel, only to break it later.

8. A *false prophet* of international fame will suddenly emerge to gain control of the world religious system and use it to reinforce the worship of Antichrist.

9. All resistance to the world system will be crushed by a massive *worldwide persecution*. Men, women, and children will be slaughtered in the name of the world state.

10. *Israel* will have a central role in the conflict with the world state. The Antichrist will break his covenant with Israel and invade her land, setting the stage for the Battle of Armageddon.

How Close Are We to the End?

There is no doubt that we are fast approaching the final chapter of human history. The hoofbeats of the four horsemen of the Apocalypse can now be heard in the distance. The stage is set for the final act of the human drama. The clock is ticking away the last seconds of any hope for a reprieve. We are being swept down the corridor of time to an inevitable date with destiny.

How much time is left? Only God knows. We who are Christians believe we must use every means at our disposal to preach the gospel of God's saving grace everywhere we can while there is still time. This is not the time to rest on our laurels. Rather, we have a window of opportunity, by the grace of God, and we need to take advantage of it right now. It is time for us Western Christians to take seriously the responsibility to evangelize the world.

If we do not meet this challenge and fulfill our obligation, every kind of false religious cult, every kind of secular materialism, and every kind of moral perversion will rush to fill that vacuum. The Bible alone has the truth that can set men and women free from the chains of spiritual oppression. It alone can fill the void people sense in their lives.

Jesus Christ said of this crucial hour: "As long as it is day, we must do the work of him who sent me. Night is coming, when no one can work" (John 9:4). To the ancient church at Philadelphia, our Lord said, "I have placed before you an open door that no one can shut" (Revelation 3:8). God has also given today's church an open door to preach the gospel. May we who are Christians rise to the occasion, recognizing that ultimately, the struggle for world dominion is between the forces of Christ and the forces of Satan.

4

EXPANDING THE AXIS OF EVIL

"There is a new generation that is willing to fight America, and this is something that America cannot stop."
—PALESTINIAN SHEIKH KHALIL AL ALAMI, OFFICIAL OF THE AL-AQSA MOSQUE[1]

IN HIS 2002 STATE OF THE UNION ADDRESS, U.S. president George W. Bush defined the modern "axis of evil" with the following words:

> Our goal is to prevent regimes that sponsor terror from threatening America or our friends and allies with weapons of mass destruction. Some of these regimes have been pretty quiet since September the 11th. But we know their true nature. North Korea is a regime arming with missiles and weapons of mass destruction, while starving its citizens.
>
> Iran aggressively pursues these weapons and exports terror, while an unelected few repress the Iranian people's hope for freedom.
>
> Iraq continues to flaunt its hostility toward America and to support terror. The Iraqi regime has plotted to develop anthrax, and nerve gas, and nuclear weapons for over a decade. This is a regime that has already used poison gas to murder thousands of its own citizens—leaving the bodies of mothers huddled over their dead children. This is a regime that agreed to international

inspections—then kicked out the inspectors. This is a regime that has something to hide from the civilized world.

States like these, and their terrorist allies, constitute an *axis of evil,* arming to threaten the peace of the world. By seeking weapons of mass destruction, these regimes pose a grave and growing danger. They could provide these arms to terrorists, giving them the means to match their hatred. They could attack our allies or attempt to blackmail the United States. In any of these cases, the price of indifference would be catastrophic.[2]

In Bush's words, the common themes were nations seeking weapons of mass destruction (WMDs) or sponsoring terrorism. The fact that the number of nations involved with the axis of evil is expanding is one of the most alarming issues in the War on Terror today.

THE PLAYERS IN THE AXIS OF EVIL

As mentioned above, the three original players of the axis of evil included Iraq, Iran, and North Korea. Because Iraq's status has changed since this speech and the nation is addressed elsewhere in this book, we'll concentrate here on the concerns regarding Iran and North Korea.

Iran

> *"Iran can pursue her nuclear ambitions with impunity as she confidently holds the ever-important oil card."*
> —MARK HITCHCOCK, *IRAN: THE COMING CRISIS*[3]

> *"How to handle Iran and, in particular, its pursuit of nuclear weapons is a problem from Hell."*
> –KENNETH POLLACK, *THE PERSIAN PUZZLE*[4]

A September 2006 *Time* magazine article quoted a political analyst who said, "A genuine, eyeball-to-eyeball crisis between the U.S. and Iran may be looming, and sooner than many realize....*we are headed for conflict.*"[5] One of the major concerns in the news today is whether the United States will initiate military action against Iran.

Why? Iran, with the world's fourth-largest military force, continues to defy U.N. sanctions in its development of nuclear power that could launch weapons of mass destruction toward targets hundreds of miles away. In addition, Iranian supreme leader Ayatollah Ali Khamenei announced on February 8, 2007 that if the United States were to attack Iran, the country "would respond by striking U.S. interests all over the world."[6]

Regarding Israel, Iran has repeatedly declared its official hatred. Iran's president has publicly declared that "the main solution is for the elimination of the Zionist regime Israel"[7] and believes his role is to help usher in the end of the world. According to past reports, Iran not only plans to complete its quest for nuclear technology but share it with other allies (Islamic nations).[8]

Further, much evidence has been provided from intelligence sources to show that Iran has been a supplier of the Hezbollah movement that recently attacked Israel from Southern Lebanon. In addition to all this, U.N. countries holding veto rights are continuing to stand *against* strong sanctions on Iran, though limited sanctions were passed in December 2006.

Other contributing factors to Iran as a partner in the axis of evil include:

- *Supporting Terrorist Groups:* In addition to its own national plans, "Iran today is the mother of Islamic terrorism."[9] Iran supports *at least* a dozen terrorist groups in Afghanistan, Iraq, and around the globe.[10] George W. Bush specifically highlighted Iran's assistance to groups within Iraq, stating the United States "will respond firmly" if Iran escalates military action in Iraq and endangers American forces.[11]

- According to *U.S. News & World Report,* "Tehran openly provides funding, training, and weapons to the world's worst terrorists, including Hezbollah, Hamas, the Palestinian Islamic Jihad, and the Popular Front for the Liberation of Palestine, and it has a cozy relationship with al Qaeda."[12]

- *Oil Market Controls:* Within both its military and terrorist connections, Iran's economic power is based on its oil reserves. One writer notes that while "Iran only pumps about 4 million barrels of crude a day...[it] is the second largest oil producer among the eleven members of OPEC, and the world's fourth largest exporter of crude oil."[13] Furthermore, Iran's military could cut off the transport of oil from surrounding nations with significant oil reserves, including Iraq, Kuwait, and Saudi Arabia. Such a move would be devastating to world oil prices over the long term.

- *Iran's President:* Mahmoud Ahmadinejad became the sixth prime minister of Iran on August 3, 2005. Recent publicity stunts by him have included attempts to directly challenge president George W. Bush in a live debate,[14] prayers and references to the Twelfth Imam in his past two U.N. speeches, and even proposing to have developed an herbal remedy to cure AIDS.[15] With his unique combination of political power, drive for nuclear capability, and radical Islamic eschatology, his leadership will continue to ignite controversy with the Western world. As one U.K. reporter has written, "This man should give us all nightmares."[16]

- *Governmental Control of Media:* Government authorities in Iran are highly conscious of the power of the media. According to a BBC report, they use a two-pronged approach. In homes, they enforce controls on the media that stifle freedom of expression, although there are still outlets on TV, radio, in the press, and on the Internet that provide alternative points of view. Internationally, Iran utilizes satellite TV and radio to promote its views in a variety of languages in an effort to influence world opinion. "All broadcasting is run by the authorities. It reflects the views of the Supreme Leader Ayatollah Ali Khamenei and his allies in the conservative clerical establishment."[17]

North Korea

In July 2006, North Korea caused an uproar around the world by testing not one but *seven* nuclear missiles. The United Nations quickly replied with sanctions, and talks are in process, at the time of this writing, with North Korean government leaders regarding possible nuclear disarmament.

North Korea, the world's only unreconstructed Stalinist country, has not been conclusively linked to a terrorist attack since the bombing of a Korean Air flight in 1987. However, it continues to be listed as an axis of evil power both regarding its development of weapons of mass destruction and because it sells advanced missile technology to states that sponsor terrorists.

Even more worrisome has been North Korea's actual testing of nuclear missiles. In addition, it also says it has other weapons. These "more powerful" weapons, according to earlier Pentagon assessments, are stockpiles of chemical weapons with nerve and asphyxiation gases. North Korea is also thought to have an active but primitive biological weapons program that might be able to produce anthrax, cholera, and plague.[18] Having such, however, is a violation of international treaties.

What's more, North Korea cooperates with other state sponsors of terrorism. According to the Council on Foreign Relations, North Korea has reportedly sold ballistic-missile technology to countries that the U.S. State Department lists as sponsors of terrorism. These nations include Iran, Syria, Libya, Pakistan, and Yemen. Such technology could be used to deliver chemical, biological, and nuclear weapons. Their motive? As a financially depressed and isolated country, these sales are the primary source of hard currency for the nation, and the proceeds allow North Korea to fund its own missile programs.[19]

Interestingly, North Korea's sales have included deals with fellow axis of evil partner Iran. Yet the two administrations are as different as night and day. While Iran seeks such weapons as part of its radical Islamic fundamentalism, North Korea's communism espouses atheism and no offical state religion. Such a contrast has caused Alireza Jafarzadeh to write, "Although North Korea is also designated by the State Department as a state sponsor of terrorism with nuclear weapons, it does not pose even remotely the same threat as Iran does because North Korea lacks the Iranian regime's extremist ideology."[20]

Beyond the Axis of Evil

In addition to Iran and North Korea, several other nations have raised eyebrows due to their connections with one of these two groups or other terrorist organizations. Why are these groups important? On September 20, 2001, just days after 9/11, Bush announced the new American policy toward terrorist groups: "From this day forward, any nation that continues to harbor or support terrorism will be regarded by the United States as a hostile regime."[21] Among the nations often connected in these matters today are Russia, China, Syria, and Venezuela, as well as several coalitions of important note.

Russia

Russia has signed a one-billion-dollar deal to sell missiles and other weaponry to Iran. In addition, they have agreed to sell missiles to the Syrian government and the Palestinian Hamas.[22] Why?

Russia hosts the world's only company involved in building nuclear power stations in outside nations. This company is currently working on projects in China, India, and Iran. In total, the company has 31 reactors within Russia, with plans for several more by 2030.[23] Future locations for nuclear development by this Russian corporation include northern Turkey[24] and Morocco.[25]

According to reports cited by Joel Rosenberg, over 1,000 Iranian nuclear scientists have been trained in Russia or by senior Russian scientists. Russia has vowed to finish building Iran's first nuclear power plant in Bushehr, despite intense international pressure to stop helping Iran go nuclear.[26]

In a frightening statement from U.S. intelligence, it was revealed that top-secret Iraqi documents discovered during the Iraqi war in 2003 revealed that Russian intelligence helped Saddam Hussein by sharing the precise composition and locations of American fighter aircraft, helicopters, naval ships, cruise missiles, tanks, armored vehicles, artillery, and even the locations and numbers of special-forces units. Even after the war began, such information continued to flow, including movements of specific U.S. military forces.[27]

Interestingly, Russia's president Vladimir Putin has been said to be planning a way to stay in power beyond his term ending in 2008. According to one senior politician, "He will not leave...I think he will find the kind of formula in which he would step down, but stay on."[28] If that happens, it would be cause for concern.

Putin has visited Tehran, defended missile sales to Syria, and invited Hamas leadership to Moscow, and these moves have caused prophecy scholars to note the important role Russia will play in the end times, a topic we address in a later chapter.

While Russia remains mostly friendly to the United States and Western Europe at this time, Russia's economic ties to Muslim nations and growing economic partnerships with Asian and Arab nations continue to pose a problem in implementing resistance to Russia's support of nations known to help terrorist groups.

China

The most populous nation in the world, China, is home to over 1.3 billion people. And it is also a major trade partner with Iran. In October 2004 the two countries signed a preliminary accord worth $70 to $100 billion, in which China will purchase Iranian oil and gas and help develop Iran's Yadavaran oil field near the Iraqi border. Earlier in that same year, China agreed to buy $20 billion in liquefied natural gas from Iran over the next quarter-century.[29]

With such deeply connected economic ties to Iran, China has been hesitant to agree to strong U.N. sanctions. Unfortunately, the result is that over time China will increasingly side with a nation that has a clear desire to destroy both Israel and the United States, causing a difficult tension between China and Western nations.

To further complicate the situation, China also borders North Korea. The Chinese government has taken a strong stand against North Korea's nuclear development, yet at the same time it has taken a softer stance on Iran. Because of China's spiking economic growth and thirst for oil, China's future relations with the axis of evil nations could become complex.

Syria

Hezbollah's Syrian connections reach back to the 1970s, when Hafez al-Assad began serving as president of Syria. Though this connection did not hurt relations with the West at the time, that has changed. Al-Assad's son and successor, Basher as-Assads, has been subjected to U.S. sanctions because of his continued support for the Hezbollah terrorist movement.

Author Gary Kah notes the significant problem a military conflict in Syria could cause:

> Attacking Syria would be like attacking Russia, especially since Russia still has thousands of military advisors, strategists, and Special Forces in that country.... Nevertheless, in order to stamp out terrorism, America will have no choice but to deal with Syria

at some point. Why? Syria either supports or is home to more terrorist organizations than any other Islamic state.[30]

Venezuela

In his 2006 speech to the United Nations, Venezuelan president Hugo Chavez verbally assaulted America, even calling the U.S. president "a devil." Chavez has also claimed, as we mentioned in chapter 2, that "if the United States attacks, we won't have any other alternative [but to] blow up our own oil fields. They aren't going to take that oil."[31]

During a special report, Fox News noted a trip by Chavez to China, where he was "blasting Israel for committing what he calls genocide in Lebanon, comparing Israel to Adolf Hitler. On a six-day visit to China, Chavez said, 'Israel often criticizes Hitler but they have done the same thing, perhaps even worse.' He also denounced Israel's 'fascist attitudes,' saying the country must be brought in front of an international tribunal."[32]

Rising anti-Semitism from Venezuela toward Jews and Israel in particular have also added to the concerns regarding the nation. During the 2006 Israel-Hezbollah conflict, Chavez recalled the Venezuelan ambassador to Israel and has not sent him back even long after the ceasefire agreement. Venezuela has also stopped issuing tourist visas to Israelis.

The Anti-Defamation League says anti-Israel demonstrations, anti-Jewish graffiti, and other displays of anti-Semitism have become dangerously commonplace within Venezuela. One Venezuelan reporter noted 195 anti-Semitic references in official and pro-government media during a 65-day period. Such changes now have the 25,000-person Jewish population in Venezuela in a highly uncomfortable position, prompting Jewish leaders there to gather regarding responses to their predicament.[33]

Additional warning signs from Venezuela include Chavez's threats to sell F-16 fighter jets to China or Iran[34] and his proposal to create a referendum to allow himself to remain president until 2031. These actions and others have made Venezuela a nation to be watched carefully.

Other Groups

The now-expanding axis of evil includes not only nations, but also terrorist groups or political movements that often exist in multiple nations.

Each of the following has had a significant impact on our world and is an important factor in the War on Terror.

Al-Qaeda

Made popular during the 9/11 attacks, al-Qaeda has evolved as one of the most significant terrorist movements of our time. Heavily funded and typically militant, it began in 1988 under the leadership of Osama bin Laden and is responsible for numerous acts of terror in countries all over the world.

Al-Queda exists in various forms in dozens of countries. Proponents of militant jihad, the group's overriding objective is to establish a worldwide caliphate governing the entire globe via the dictates of Islamic sharia law. A task crucial to the achievement of that goal is the destruction of America by any means necessary.[35]

Hezbollah

According to *Council on Foreign Relations,*

> Hezbollah is a Lebanese umbrella organization of radical Islamic Shiite groups and organizations. It opposes the West, seeks to create a Muslim fundamentalist state modeled on Iran, and is a bitter foe of Israel. Hezbollah, whose name means "party of God," is a terrorist group believed responsible for nearly 200 attacks since 1982 that have killed more than 800 people, according to the Terrorism Knowledge Base.[36]

Experts note that Hezbollah is also a significant force in Lebanon's politics and a major provider of social services, operating schools, hospitals, and agricultural services for thousands of Lebanese Shiites. It also operates the al-Manar satellite television channel and broadcast station.[37] Connections to other terrorist organizations include Hamas, and Hezbollah has significant influence in neighboring Syria and the nation of Iran.[38]

Hamas

Hamas is the largest and most influential Palestinian militant movement. In Arabic, the word *hamas* means "zeal." However, it's also an Arabic acronym for Harakat al-Muqawama al-Islamiya, or Islamic Resistance Movement.

Hamas grew out of the Muslim Brotherhood, a religious and political organization founded in Egypt that has branches throughout the Arab world. Beginning in the late 1960s, Hamas's founder and spiritual leader, Sheikh Ahmed Yassin, preached and did charitable work in the West Bank and Gaza Strip, both of which were occupied by Israel following the 1967 Six-Day War. In 1973, Yassin established al-Mujamma' al-Islami (the Islamic Center) to coordinate the Muslim Brotherhood's political activities in Gaza. Hamas also established itself as the Muslim Brotherhood's local political arm in December 1987 following the eruption of the first intifada, a Palestinian uprising against Israeli control of the West Bank and Gaza. Hamas published its official charter in 1988.[39]

Hamas combines Palestinian nationalism with Islamic fundamentalism. Its founding charter commits the group to the destruction of Israel, the replacement of the Palestinian Authority with an Islamist state on the West Bank and Gaza, and raising "the banner of Allah over every inch of Palestine." In January 2006, the group won the Palestinian Authority's general legislative elections, setting the stage for a political power struggle. Since attaining power, Hamas has continued its refusal to recognize the state of Israel, a stance that has led to major economic sanctions.

In addition to its military wing, Hamas devotes much of its estimated $70 million annual budget to an extensive social services network. It funds schools, orphanages, mosques, healthcare clinics, soup kitchens, and sports leagues. Hamas's social efforts help to explain the broad support it summoned to defeat Fatah in the Palestinian Authority's elections.

Hamas's military wing is believed to have more than 1,000 active members and thousands of sympathizers. In 2004, more than 200,000 Palestinians marched in the funerals of Hamas leaders Yassin and Rantisi. As of January 2006, according to the Council on Foreign Relations, Hamas is believed to have killed more than 500 people in more than 350 separate terrorist attacks since 1993.

Israel Today magazine reports that in 2006, the military wing of the ruling Hamas group, Izz al-Din al-Kassam, has begun issuing a chronological report of its "resistance activities" on a daily basis. It lists rocket launchings, mortar shells fired, and roadside bombs planted in the names of fighters who have died for their cause.

"We hereby announce the blessed operations we have carried out," the first report stated. "We shall continue to hit the enemy using all means. With the help of Allah, each of their bombardments will be answered with a bombardment—blood for blood."[40]

Wahhabism

This extremist movement of Islam considers itself to be a purist reform movement. It is a fundamentalist form of Islam that was founded in Saudi Arabia in the eighteenth century by Mohammad Ibn Abdul-Wahhab and the ruling Saudi dynasty, which felt that the local practice of Islam needed to return to its original purity. An offshoot of the Sunni Hanbali legal school, it is based on a literal translation of the Quran and rejects mysticism in any form.

Saudi Arabia today remains the heartland of Wahhabi Islam. Its adherents include members of the current Saudi royal family. The Saudi religious establishment requires strict segregation of the sexes and bans women from driving.

Other followers of Wahhabism include Afghanistan's Taliban and Osama bin Laden. A *New York Times* article reported that

the faith that drives Osama bin Laden and his followers is a particularly austere and conservative brand of Islam known as Wahhabism, which was instrumental in creating the Saudi monarchy, and if sufficiently alienated, could tear it down.

Throughout its history, the Wahhabis have fiercely opposed anything they viewed as *bida,* an Arabic word, usually muttered like a curse, for any change or modernization that deviates from the fundamental teachings of the Koran....

The ferocity with which the Wahhabis fight for their cause is legend. One Arab historian described followers of the sect, founded in the 18th century, as they engaged in battle: "I have seen them hurl themselves on their enemies, utterly fearless of death, not caring how many fall, advancing rank after rank with only one desire—the defeat and annihilation of the enemy. They normally give no quarter, sparing neither boys nor old men."

Today Wahhabis extol the purist state ruled by the Taliban as one that subscribes to their vision, and they would seek to replicate it.[41]

In a 2003 U.S. Senate subcommittee report on Wahhabism, the summary stated, "There is clearly a problem of Wahhabi/Saudi extremist influence in American Islam."[42] While Wahhabism is a belief system rather than a terrorist organization, its followers have been cited repeatedly as having financial or other connections in worldwide terrorist acts. As such, Wahhabism's influence within Saudi Arabia continues to create difficulties for Saudi-U.S. relations and further complicates the playing field in the Middle East.

Al-Mahdi Army

Led by Muqtada al-Sadr, the Al-Mahdi Army is named after the Twelfth Imam and consists of several thousand militant loyalists in Iraq. This smaller yet vocal group has made the cover of *Time* magazine and gotten attention from other news sources due to their involvement in conflicts in parts of southern Iraq. Their primary spiritual motivation is to work toward speeding up the Mahdi's (the Twelfth Imam's) return through tribulation in the present world.[43]

Palestinian Islamic Jihad Movement

The stated goal of this terrorist organization is the destruction of Israel and its replacement with an Islamic state. They define jihad as acts of war against Jews. However, the Palestinian Islamic Jihad also opposes Arab governments whom they see as being too Western. Its military wing, the al-Quds Brigades, has claimed responsibility for numerous militant attacks in Israel, including suicide bombings.

Islamic Jihad is significantly smaller than Hamas and lacks the wide social network that Hamas has. It was formed in the Gaza Strip in 1979 and is connected in part with Hezbollah and has ties with al-Qaeda. In recent years it has received attention for backing Saddam Hussein in 2003 and staging a March 30, 2003 suicide bombing at a crowded pedestrian mall in the Israeli town of Netanya. In 2003 the Islamic Jihad also announced that it was sending suicide bombers to Iraq to help fight what it called the "American invasion."[44]

WHY DO THEY HATE?

In his excellent article "Why Radical Muslims Hate You,"[45] Rusty Wright shares some of the key reasons that many of the aforementioned groups despise America. While these may not apply to every group above, these basic concepts help us better understand "why the rest hates the West."

Historical Roots of Hatred

While Americans grieved over the tragedy of 9/11, news programs showed some Palestinians celebrating over what had happened. One Hamas publication stated, "Allah has answered our prayers."[46] In London, one Muslim group circulated stickers praising the Magnificent 19, the highjackers.[47]

If you are an American or a non-Muslim, you are considered an infidel. Why? An infidel is a person who is considered an unbeliever, according to Islam. In addition, Islam combines the concepts of religion and politics, causing a cultural view that despises the democracy of America and its connections with Israel. From this worldview, radical Islam moves from anger toward "infidels" to violence, encouraging physical acts of jihad toward its enemies.

Bin Ladin calls on Muslims to "obey God's command to kill the Americans and plunder their possessions...to kill Americans and their allies, both civil and military."[48] He and his sympathizers seek to eliminate Western influence and restore Islamic dominance over the world.

Cultural Roots of Hatred

Culture is also a factor in some of the radical Muslim hatred of the West. In 1948, Sayyid Qutb visited the United States for Egypt's Ministry of Education. His stay left him shocked with what he perceived as moral decadence and sexual promiscuity.[49] He wrote that even American religion was tainted by materialism and consumerism. According to Qutb's report, churches marketed their services to the public like merchants and entertainers. Qutb especially despised clergy-sanctioned dances at church recreation halls. As an Egyptian man who was dark-skinned, Qutb also experienced racism in America. He later returned to Egypt and became what Georgetown University religion and international affairs professor John Esposito calls "the architect of radical Islam."[50]

Political Roots of Hatred

Bernard Lewis notes an essential difference between Christianity and

Islam regarding government and religion. Jesus, the founder of the Christian faith, said, "Give to Caesar what belongs to him. But everything that belongs to God must be given to God."[51] For much of history, this has been understood as recognizing the existence of two distinct authorities, one spiritual and the other political.[52]

Islam knows no such distinction. Muhammad was both a religious and political leader. He led both as the Prophet and the civil ruler. Under his successors, the caliphs, Islam grew into a tremendous empire and world religion.

With this mind-set, Western nations are viewed by radical (and numerous non-radical) Muslims as imperialists. In the eyes of some, the very concept of democracy is enough to declare destruction and jihad.

Abu Muhammad al-Maqdisi, leader of the Bayat al-Imam extremist group whose operatives were arrested in Jordan in 1995, states that Jews and Christians become "combatants" and infidels because of their participation in elections and as a result of their endorsement of democracy and its values. For al-Maqdisi, democracy is a prohibited innovation that contradicts Islamic values and embodies a new heretical religion. Its followers are "infidels" and "polytheists," even if they consider themselves as Jews or Christians by religion.

In his words: "Democracy is the rule of the masses or the rule of paganism, which is conducted according to a constitution [written by humans] and not according to Allah's laws.... It [democracy] has become the mother of laws and is considered [by the masses] as a holy book." Further, he concludes that "democracy is a religion that is not Allah's religion."[53]

Religious Roots of Hatred

Another reason some radical Muslims show hatred involves religion. In the Islamic worldview, any religion other than theirs causes: 1) a Muslim attempt to convert non-Muslims, 2) a call to tax enemies and allow a peaceful though separate coexistence, or 3) a call to physically overtake or even kill others who will not convert to Islam. As one popular writer has noted, "Radical Islam does not want us to be quiet—they want us to be dead."[54]

On May 8, 2006, President Ahmadinejad of Iran sent a letter to George W. Bush, in which he called on Bush to accept Islam. He ended his letter by commenting, "Mr. President, history tells us that repressive and cruel governments do not survive."

In a Hadith (sacred Muslim text), Muhammad tells his followers to call people to Islam before waging war against them:

> Fight in the name of Allah and in the way of Allah. Fight against those who disbelieve in Allah. Make a holy war.... When you meet your enemies who are polytheists, invite them to three courses of action. If they respond to any one of these, you also accept it and withhold yourself from doing them any harm. Invite them to [accept] Islam; if they respond to you, accept it from them and desist from fighting against them.... If they refuse to accept Islam, demand from them the Jizya [the tax on non-Muslims specified in Sura 9:29]. If they agree to pay, accept it from them and hold off your hands. If they refuse to pay the tax, seek Allah's help and fight them (Sahih Muslim 4294).[55]

Muslim scholars have held debates in recent years in which they are beginning to change their views regarding a peaceful coexistence with Jews and Christians based on their interpretations of the Quran and hadith.[56] Again, while much of this attitude lies within radical Islam, these religious roots of hatred are growing in strength among those who are not radical Islamists.

WHERE WILL IT LEAD?

As the radical views toward non-Muslims grow in popularity, how will they affect our future world? If Iran, for instance, develops a nuclear weapon, the nation could then share its technology with other likeminded nations or terrorist groups who could, in turn, wreak havoc and cause massive destruction upon places and people. This frightening prospective scenario should cause us to wake up from our slumber and prepare ourselves for the right response to such a danger.

5

THE NUCLEAR NIGHTMARE

"The heavens will disappear with a roar;
the elements will be destroyed by fire,
and the earth and everything in it will be laid bare."
—2 Peter 3:10

THE WORLD IS A VERY DANGEROUS PLACE these days. With major terrorist attacks on the rise worldwide and the thwarting of additional attacks, even the most naïve among us has been forced to take the Islamic threat more seriously than ever before.

The Middle East continues to be a boiling cauldron of tension, conflict, terrorism, and war. Our television screens are constantly bombarded with images of Palestinian suicide bombers, Israeli reprisals, and Iranian threats. It is more evident than ever before that we are on the brink of a conflagration that would easily engulf the whole world. The threat of nuclear and chemical weapons in the hands of irresponsible rogue nations is greater than it has ever been.

Until recently, the exclusive nuclear weapons club included only five members: Britain, China, France, Russia, and the United States. Today, the number of nations possessing or attempting to possess nuclear weapons is escalating dangerously. In a recent article in *Atlantic* magazine, entitled "How to Get a Nuclear Bomb," William Langewiesche wrote, "The danger comes from a direction unforeseen in the past, that this technology might now pass into the hands of the new stateless guerillas, the jihadists, who offer none of the targets that have underlain our nuclear peace—no permanent infrastructure, no capital city, no country called home."[1] He goes on to point out that there is plenty of weapons-grade fissile material in the world today that a terrorist could eventually steal or buy enough of it for making a single garage-made device.

In his landmark study *Power,* Adolf Berle, professor emeritus of law at Columbia University, stated, "Power and love are the oldest known phenomena of human emotions. Neither wholly yields to rational discussion."[2] He also observed, "Power is a universal experience; practically every adult has had a measure of it, great or small, for a brief moment or for an extended time."[3] Then he warned, "Except in rarest fortune, power leaves men before their lives are over."

Berle postulated five natural laws of power:[4]

1. Power fills any vacuum in human organization.

2. Power is invariably personal.

3. Power is based on a system of ideas or philosophy.

4. Power is exercised through, and depends on, institutions which limit and control it.

5. Power acts in relation to a field of responsibility.

Berle saw power as the human effort to control chaos. He suggested that in any contest between power and chaos, power would win. But he also acknowledged that such victories are always temporary in nature until the contest between power and chaos are renewed.

John Kotter has defined power as the measure of a person's potential to get others to do what he or she wants them to do, as well as being able to avoid doing what he or she does not want to do.[5]

Charles Colson has stated, "The history of the last fifty years has validated Nietzsche's argument that man's desire to control his own destiny and to impose his will on others is the most basic human motivation."[6] Nietzsche argued that the "will of power" would eventually fill the vacuum of values in the modern world, and he was right. We are now witnessing the culmination of the deterioration of Western culture. For nearly a century, modern man has been told that he is an animal, and now he is starting to live like one. And also like an animal, he has no allegiance to the morals or values of the past. Modern man has struck out on his own and is now adrift on the sea of relativity.

Aleksandr Solzhenitsyn wrote,

> If the world has not approached its end, it has reached a major watershed in history equal in importance to the turn from the Middle Ages to the Renaissance. It will demand from us a spiritual blaze; we shall have to rise to a new height of vision, to a new level of life, where our physical nature will not be crushed, as in the Middle Ages, but even more importantly, our spiritual being will not be trampled upon, as in the Modern Era.[7]

It is this sense of destiny that compels most evangelical Christians at the present hour. It is obvious to virtually everyone that what has been viewed as the traditional Western culture is in danger of extinction. Whether this threat is real or perceived, it staggers the heart with the fear of a secularist future in which God, religion, and religious values have no place.

A godless secular state is the environment necessary to justify war for the common good of the state. As our culture continues to become more secularized, the stage will be set for the justification of war against all who oppose the will of the state. As good a system as democracy is, it can only survive with a moral foundation. Otherwise, a majority of people can legitimatize anything they choose. Just because something is politically correct doesn't make it morally right.

FROM PEACETIME TO WARTIME

Just prior to the dawn of the new millennium, the Berlin wall was dismantled, Germany was reunited, the Soviet satellites were set free, and the Soviet Union itself became the democratic Commonwealth of Independent States. Unfortunately, when everyone was beginning to believe peace was in sight, Saddam Hussein upset the plans by maliciously invading Kuwait. It wasn't long before news headlines read, "Geneva Peace Talks Fail," "War in the Middle East," "U.S. Bombs Baghdad," and "Israel Hit by Missiles." Satellite broadcasts gave us all front-row seats to the most televised war in modern history.

Prophetic speculation began running at fever pitch. Many were convinced

Armageddon was just around the corner. But the U.S.-led coalition squashed Iraq in one of the most effective wars ever fought. God intervened to give the world a reprieve. What could have been the worst war in modern history was over in a few weeks.

When Saddam Hussein ordered the invasion of Kuwait on August 2, 1990, he unleashed a bloodbath that would eventually claim 100,000 Iraqi lives. What would possess someone to do such a horrible and irrational act? We believe the only legitimate answer is Satan. He is the father of pride, arrogance, extravagance, lies, and murder. The history of our world is sadly dotted with the aftermath of his destructive work in the hearts of people.

A subsequent decade of negotiations and weapons inspections ended with the invasion of Iraq by a global coalition and the removal and eventual execution of Saddam. Today we watch with wonder as the conditions of war, stated so clearly in the Bible, appear to be coming together before our very eyes.

The actions of the late Saddam Hussein of Iraq and those of Mahmoud Ahmadinejad of Iran remind us of a very real, soon-to-come madman, the Antichrist, who will bring war and destruction to this planet while promising peace and prosperity. It may well be that the hopes and dreams of a new world order will one day smolder in the ashes of a world gone crazy.

THE NUCLEAR EPIDEMIC

A recent article in *U.S. News & World Report* announced, "The West's attempt to prevent the spread of nuclear weapons has failed, and a dangerous new era of nuclear proliferation has begun."[8] The article goes on to report that the Russian economy has unleashed a flood of uranium ore and tons of plutonium on the black market. Much of this is coming from the Muslim Central Asian republics and could well end up equipping Iran, Iraq, or Syria with nuclear warheads in the near future. In addition, it is now obvious that North Korea is also on the verge of creating a nuclear bomb, with Japan and Taiwan not far behind.

Stephen Budiansky notes that every country that has ever attempted to build a nuclear bomb has done it by building their own bomb-making complex.[9] The technology already exists and can easily be copied. The real problem for would-be nuclear powers, he says, "is obtaining plutonium or highly enriched uranium to fuel the explosive chain reaction." He further notes that North Korea has developed its own supply from graphite, which exists there in abundance.

There are also growing concerns over the mental stability of Kim Jong II, supreme ruler of North Korea. He has been considered to be erratic—perhaps even irrational. But now there are stories of dementia, paranoia, and other mental problems that may color and even compound the severity of his oppressive rule. His regime is widely believed to be the most bloody and tyrannical in the world today.

Recently, North Korea took advantage of America's preoccupation with Iraq and al-Qaeda terrorists by withdrawing from the nuclear non-proliferation treaty and reactivating a nuclear plant capable of producing weapons-grade plutonium. Is this a move that bodes ill for the security of the world—a threat of nuclear blackmail against the United States? Or is it just a ploy to extort renewed financial aid from America?

A number of years ago, America's leaders decided that the fall of the Soviet Union would produce a "peace dividend," allowing the United States to lower the state of its military preparedness and save on the cost of supporting military bases and troops. Along with downsizing the military establishment, the U.S. government downsized its military expectations, abandoning the idea that it must be prepared to fight multiple wars at the same time.

Today, the U.S. military finds itself spread dangerously thin. There are 200,000 troops in the Gulf area, with over 50,000 in Afghanistan attempting to rebuild that devastated nation while flushing out al-Qaeda terrorists. All the while, the United States is maintaining its presence with NATO on the North Korean border and on several other fronts as well.

If America were forced to engage North Korea at this time, while it is so busy elsewhere, it could be the proverbial "straw that breaks the camel's back." Whether Kim intends to press this issue only time will tell. But the bellicose dictator is unpredictable at best, and who knows what lurks in the mind of a delusional leader?

> *"The breakup of the [Soviet Union] poses the biggest
> proliferation threat facing the world today."*[10]
> —CARLA ANNE ROBBINS

U.S. government officials have already reported "shopping" expeditions to Russia and Kazakhstan by delegations from Iraq, Iran, and Libya. The instability that resulted from the transfer of power from the Soviet Union to the Commonwealth of Independent States has often resulted in temporary losses of control at various weapon sites. There is no way to avoid the fact that the continued instability of the Russian government means uncertainty for the world's future. While the United States has officially expressed confidence in Russia's ability to safeguard its nuclear weapons and technology, it is also obvious that some Russian nuclear scientists could easily be hired on the world market.

God has given Christians an open window of unparalleled opportunity to evangelize the spiritually deprived peoples of Eastern Europe and parts of Asia. We must act quickly before that window closes, for we have no guarantee that the United States and Russia will remain on friendly terms.

How Close Is Disaster?

Albert Einstein warned that the atomic age would propel the world toward unprecedented catastrophe. In his blockbuster bestseller *The End*, Ed Dobson reminds us that "Hiroshima is a microcosm of what could and might happen.... The current nuclear arsenal has the potential to wipe out civilization as we know it."[11] Scientists now estimate the staggering proportions of the holocaust that could result from a nuclear war:

Human Toll	*Environmental Toll*
750 million to 1 billion people killed	water contamination
340 million seriously injured	radiation fallout
33 percent of the survivors incapacitated	toxic rain
inability to grow food	uncontrollable fires

Nuclear war will kill at least one-third of the earth's population and render the environment unsuitable for those who survive. "Everything would change forever," Dobson writes.[12] Futurists Alvin and Heidi Toffler have said, "We appear to be plunging into a new dark age of tribal hate, planetary desolation, and wars multiplied by wars."[13] The world scene is tenuous at best. The Tofflers note that there are nearly 200 members in the United Nations, and 60 of them have waged war over the last 50 years. They state, "In fact, in the 2,340 weeks that passed between 1945 and 1990, the earth enjoyed a grand total of only three that were truly war-free."[14] Since then, the situation has only worsened.

The Tofflers observe that we have a *trisected global society* with three types of politico-economic systems: 1) agrarian, 2) industrial, and 3) informational. These move at various "clock speeds" as they intersect one another. Thus, a crisis in one sector can trigger a response in another, as in the case of Somalia (agrarian) or Iraq (industrial). The Tofflers write,

> Nothing marks today's moment of history…more strikingly than the acceleration of change…. This acceleration, partly driven by faster communications, means that hot spots can erupt into the global system almost overnight…. A "small" war in a remote place can, through a series of often unpredictable events, snowball into a giant conflagration.[15]

IRAN IN THE CROSSHAIRS

The battle of Ezekiel 38–39 has long piqued the interest of students of Bible prophecy. It involves the invasion of Israel by a great nation from the north. Most generally believe this to be Russia, or the Islamic states that made up part of the former Soviet Union, or some successor of the ancient Ottoman (Turkish) Empire. Whichever the case may be, the King James Version of the Bible says that in that fateful invasion, five-sixths of the invading army will be destroyed (Ezekiel 39:2). That is an awesome and frightening prediction. With Iraq facing imminent devastation from civil war, one cannot help but wonder how its Islamic neighbors will respond in the event of catastrophe in that ancient land of Babylon.

The prophet Jeremiah predicted, "The Lord has opened his arsenal and brought out the weapons of his wrath, for the sovereign Lord Almighty has work to do in the land of the Babylonians…. At the sound of Babylon's capture, the earth will tremble; its cry will resound among the nations" (50:25,46). It is entirely possible that Israel or the United States will be brought to the place where they must use nuclear capabilities against a rearmed Iraq in the future. Such a nuclear strike would bring the ancient land of Babylon to an ignominious end.

That possibility raises many questions. What could shake the earth, humanly speaking, other than the use of nuclear weapons? And what might force Israel to use such extreme measures? There could be many possibilities, but foremost among them could be a strike against Israel that involved nonconventional weapons.

On January 16, 2003, the world was abuzz with news that weapon inspectors had found 11 empty chemical warheads in Iraq. The Associated Press reported: "UN inspectors found 11 empty chemical warheads in 'excellent' condition at an ammunition storage area in southern Iraq on Thursday, and the components were not reported in Iraq's declaration meant to account for all banned weapons, a UN spokesman said." Iraqi officials first said that those weapons had been reported in their 12,000 page disclosure documents. Later they maintained they had forgotten that the warheads were stored in that facility, which was built some eight years after Iraq was supposed to have surrendered or destroyed her weapons of mass destruction (WMD).

That same day, inspectors interviewed Iraqi physicist Faleh Hassan, the director of Razi, a military installation specializing in laser development. After exchanging heated words with Iraqi officials, Hassan was taken to a protected U.N. location for further investigation, and copies of some provocative documents were taken with him.

The world waited and was ready for the report of the U.N. inspectors, followed by President George W. Bush's revelations about the possibility of secret Iraqi weapons of mass destruction. Though no such weapons were reported, that does not mean they never existed. Many believe they were moved to Syria.

ISRAEL ON EDGE

To say that Israel is on edge these days would be a gross understatement. Israeli citizens hold regular chemical and biological attack drills, donning awkward but hopefully lifesaving gear in a moment's notice. It is an exercise that has been refined many times over during the years since the Gulf War and especially in light of the ketusha rocket assaults on Israel by Hezbollah during the summer of 2006.

Most Israeli homes have "safe rooms" in which windows are covered, cracks and vents are sealed, and precautions have been taken to impede any penetration by biological and chemical agents. In the event of such an attack, Israelis will don their protective gear and head for their safe rooms, where water, food, and communications gear such as radios and cell phones are stored.

Terrorists continue to bathe Israeli streets in blood, and Israel—never given to letting such acts go unanswered—continues to respond with powerful and often disproportionate force. Many countries—with a few exceptions, such as the United States—decry the use of what is often called "excessive Israeli force" in retaliation for such attacks. But if you were a tiny nation like Israel, which can be flown over by jet in just a few minutes and is surrounded by a sea of enemies who want to push you into the sea, you might react strongly, too! Many military strategists are convinced that Israel's predictable and powerful responses have spared the nation from potentially more devastating attacks.

TERRORIST REPRISALS

It comes as no surprise that al-Qaeda, whose very purpose is to produce terror and overthrow the hegemony of Western civilization, has again threatened reprisals against America. But it should surprise people to know that, despite the fact that America is living under wartime regulations, it is still broadcasting the positions of its troops—therefore making them living targets for terrorist assaults.

Anyone can go to the Internet and track the movement of battle groups, carriers, troop deployments, and the like. The idea is that family and loved ones can see where their beloved soldiers are at any given time. Reporters with uplinks report via live satellite feeds from our ships and bases.

It causes one to wonder if this is being done intentionally as psychological warfare—if our troops are being set up as bait for terrorist attacks, or if America has simply gone overboard on the dissemination of information.

ON THE BRINK OF WAR

So what does all this have to do with us? Admitting that the world stands on the brink of war would make it easy for us to be overcome with apprehension. And in many ways, our concerns are the same as those of the people around us. Will we survive? Will we face hardship and privation? Will we lose any of those whom we hold near and dear to our hearts?

The truth is, this world is indeed a dangerous place—and it will continue to be so until Jesus comes back to rule and reign on the earth. We face "clear and present danger" every day that we live. But we who are Christians also have the promise of Jesus Christ that "I will come back and take you to be with me" (John 14:3). That will happen at the rapture of the church, when the Lord comes to deliver believers from the Tribulation that is to come. That should allay our fears, quiet our concerns, and build bright anticipation in our hearts.

The world may be on the brink of war, but we who are Christians are already doing battle in a spiritual war—a war against sin and darkness, a battle for the souls of men. In fact, the unsaved world faces a "clear and present danger" that is far greater than that of war and terrorism. It's the danger of dying without Christ, of passing into eternity without making the decision that will save their souls and give them eternal life.

ONLY A MATTER OF TIME

Given the current world situation, nuclear war is inevitable. It is only a matter of time before someone somewhere has nuclear weapons and the capability to deliver them—and is willing to push the button. Initially, it may be a limited explosion in an isolated place. But human nature being what it is, sooner or later the world will face the reality of a nuclear holocaust.

Ed Dobson notes that there are some Bible prophecies that describe destruction that is eerily similar to that caused by a nuclear war. He points to the apostle Peter's prediction that the world will be destroyed by fire in the last days (2 Peter 3:7-12). Dobson points out three major characteristics of these cataclysmic events described by Peter.[16]

1. *Explosion in the heavens:* "The heavens will disappear with a roar" (verse 10). The bomb dropped at Hiroshima in 1945 exploded in the air 500 meters above the city.

2. *Things melting with heat:* "The elements will melt in the heat" (verse 12). In a nuclear explosion, one-third of the energy is given off in heat, creating huge fireballs.

3. *Destruction of the earth:* "The earth and everything in it will be laid bare" (verse 10). In the aftermath of a nuclear explosion, forests, grasslands, and rivers are burned and destroyed.

"The book of Revelation predicts similar events at the end of the world,"

Dobson adds.[17] He notes that Revelation predicts massive global destruction from "hail and fire" and a "huge mountain, all ablaze." These judgments result in:

> A third of the earth burned.
> A third of the trees burned.
> All the green grass burned.
> The sea turned to blood.
> Rivers and waters polluted.
> Darkness and air pollution.

IS THIS ARMAGEDDON?

The term *Armageddon* (Greek, *Harmegedon*) appears only once in the entire Bible—in Revelation 16:16. The location, the hill Megiddo, overlooks the Valley of Jezreel in northern Israel. It was the site of numerous biblical conflicts (see Joshua 12:7,12; Judges 5:19; 2 Kings 23:29). Megiddo itself served as a military stronghold for several generations (see Judges 1:27; 2 Kings 9:27). It is in this great valley in Israel's breadbasket that the New Testament places the final conflict between Christ and the Antichrist. Old Testament prophecies also point to a final conflict between Israel and the nations of the world in the last day (see Joel 3:2-14; Zechariah 14:1-5; Zephaniah 3:8).

Theologically, *Armageddon* is a symbolic term for the final apocalyptic conflict between the forces of Christ and Antichrist. It is not limited to the Valley of Jezreel, but its focus is there. The entire series of battles instigated by the Antichrist will climax at Armageddon, where the kings of the earth converge for the "battle on the great day of God Almighty" (Revelation 16:14). J. Dwight Pentecost notes that this is not an isolated battle but a military campaign that includes several battles and extends throughout the Tribulation period.[18]

Biblical references to the final end-times conflict also refer to events in the Valley of Jehoshaphat (Joel 3:2,12), the Lord's coming from Edom (Isaiah 34:6), and Jerusalem itself being the center of the conflict (see Zechariah 12:2-10; 14:2). While the troops may be deployed from Armageddon, they apparently will spread out to cover the land. The conflict will extend from the plains of Esdraelon on the north, down through Jerusalem, out into the Valley of Jehoshaphat, and southward to Edom.

The Bible describes the nations of the world, under the leadership of the Antichrist, allied against Israel and the people of God in the last days. Differences of opinion exist among some regarding the relationship of the battle of Armageddon to the biblical predictions of the invasion of the king of the north and the king of the south (see Daniel 11:4-45). Revelation 16:12 also refers to the drying up of the Euphrates River as a prelude to this great battle. With this miraculous act, the way will be paved for the kings of the east to join the final battle.

Dr. John Walvoord notes that "the Battle of Armageddon will occur during the final days of the Great Tribulation,"[19] after the pouring out of the bowls of judgment (see Revelation 16). This will be the culmination of the ongoing conflict between the Antichrist and the people of God. Walvoord also notes, "Armies will be fighting in Jerusalem on the very day of the second coming of Christ (Zechariah 14:1-3)."[20] At the point of Christ's return, the battle of Armageddon will be won by Jesus and His triumphant church (the bride of Christ), which will return with Him (Revelation 19:11-14). The Battle of Armageddon will also culminate in the final collapse of political and ecclesiastical Babylon. The kingdom of the Antichrist and its false religious system will be utterly destroyed at the same time (see Revelation 17–18). Again, some disagree on whether *Babylon* here refers to the literal city of Babylon in modern Iraq or whether it is a symbolic term for Rome. In either case, the Scripture makes it clear that Babylon represents the global political and ecclesiastical system of the end times.

At the Battle of Armageddon, Christ is victorious by the power of His spoken word. The Antichrist and the false prophet will be defeated and cast into the lake of fire, and Satan will be bound in the abyss ("bottomless pit," KJV) for 1,000 years during the millennial reign of Christ on earth (Revelation 19:17–20:3). Thus, the last great war will take place in relation to the second coming of Christ.

Prophecy scholars Thomas Ice and Timothy Demy note that the Battle of Armageddon is "a battle that never really takes place" in the sense of achieving its objectives. The war itself leaves the earth devastated, but the final assault on Christ is aborted. They write, "God will intervene and Jesus Christ will return to rescue His chosen people Israel. The Lord and His

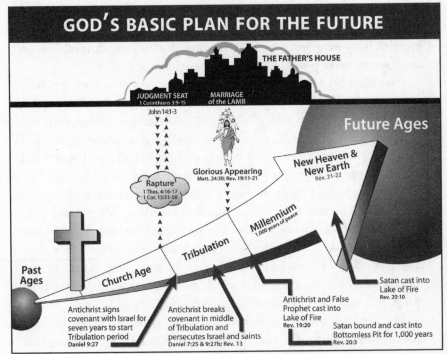

The most accepted understanding of pretribulationist prophecy. God loves mankind and has a wonderful plan for those who accept His son as their Lord and Savior.

angelic army will destroy the armies, capture the Antichrist and the False Prophet, and cast them into the lake of fire."[21]

No rational person wants war. Death and destruction are the consequences of a fallen world. They may be inevitable, but their inevitability is certainly no reason to want to hasten Armageddon. It will come soon enough. In the meantime, we should pray for peace and work for peace so that the gospel of Jesus Christ may be preached in all the world.

THE GOSPEL ACCORDING TO JESUS

Jesus' preaching of the kingdom of God contradicted every prevailing view of religion and politics of His day. He rejected the asceticism and isolationism of the Essenes. He refused to play the games of political accommodation that characterized the Sadducees and Pharisees. He totally confounded the Herodians and refused to give cause to the Zealots (see Matthew 22:15-46). He stood alone with a uniquely new message, emphasizing that the kingdom of God was within the hearts of true believers. Thus, they were free from the suppression of political domination or the corruption of political compromise. They were citizens of heaven as well as earth, and their mission on earth was to make people citizens of the kingdom of God.

Jesus offered the people of His day a whole new way of looking at politics and power. He clearly announced, "My kingdom is not of this world" (John 18:36). Ironically, His own disciples struggled with this issue. At the time of His ascension, they asked, "Lord, are you at this time going to restore the kingdom to Israel?" (Acts 1:6). He reminded them that He had another priority, and that was the preaching of the gospel to the whole world (Acts 1:8).

Jesus stood above them all. Like a divine enigma on the landscape of humanity, He seemed to treat the political as mundane. When asked if He would pay the Roman tax, He asked to see the tribute coin. When it was produced, He asked, "Whose is this image and superscription?" (Matthew 22:20 KJV). When He was told it was Caesar's, He merely responded, "Render therefore unto Caesar the things which are Caesar's; and unto God the things that are God's" (Matthew 22:21 KJV).

Jesus always made it clear that the spiritual supersedes the political and that the political derives its authority from the spiritual. It is no wonder that He who was the embodiment of divine authority confounded His captors, accusers, and even the political governor who sentenced Him to die.

It is the Christian's spiritual success, based upon an adherence to God's Word, that restrains the coming of the Antichrist and the false prophet. Satan's influence in society may seem to be great, but it is, nevertheless, under the restraint of the voice of God through His church. When the church is removed at the rapture, Satan's evil will break completely loose!

We do not know the timetable of God, but we can all smell the ashes of a decadent society that may soon face extinction. It is only a matter of time before the human race faces the prospect of annihilation. But first the deceiver will arise, promising to bring peace to the world.

Spiritual darkness threatens to engulf us. False prophets are everywhere. The world is rushing headlong toward disaster. We who are believers dare not give up until the trumpet sounds and we all go home to glory. We must keep our spiritual balance between our present earthly life and our future hope as we approach the end of the age. And as we do approach the end, we must realize that we live in an increasingly dangerous world.

6

THE ISLAMIC THREAT

"Many false prophets will appear and deceive many people."
—MATTHEW 24:11

THE RELIGION OF ISLAM is now the fastest-growing religion on the planet, claiming some one billion followers. Among them are hundreds of thousands, if not millions, of Islamic extremists whose stated goal is world conquest. They will stop at nothing—they will show no restraint, mercy, nor reason when dealing with those whom they view as the enemies of Islam. Their targets are often innocent bystanders, including women, children, and the elderly.

Islamic terrorists are determined to use every means of attack at their disposal—including suicide bombings, assassinations, military operations, chemical warfare, and even nuclear weapons—to accomplish their stated agenda. Bestselling Canadian author and Middle East expert Grant Jeffrey states, "The strategic goal of Islamic terrorists is nothing less than the annihilation of Judeo-Christian Western civilization."[1] Harvard University professor Samuel Huntington has observed, "Some Westerners...have argued that the West does not have problems with Islam, but only with Islamic extremists." To which he replies: "Fourteen hundred years of history demonstrate otherwise!"[2]

Newspaper columnist Cal Thomas refers to the growing Islamic threat as *Islamofascism* and likens it to the Cold War. During the 50 years of the struggle between Communism and capitalism, it was not always clear who was winning or losing. So it is in the continuing encounter with Islamic terrorism. Thomas clearly observes that the same liberal "who opposed U.S. strategy in standing against communism now stand in opposition to America's position against Islamofascism."[3]

Fellow columnist Paul Greenberg observes, "America's enemies live for re-enactment of this country's 'exit strategy' from Vietnam, which was more exit than strategy."[4] He paints a picture of Vietnamese citizens clinging to the struts of American helicopters as their hopes of freedom disappeared and parallels it to the effect of an American pullout in Iraq.

Whatever the eventual outcome in Iraq, it is painfully obvious to Western observers that Islam is anything but a religion of peace. This is not only true in America; it is now becoming obvious in Europe as well. No one, not even the pope, is exempt from the irrationality of Islamic rage. Despite calling the Holocaust a myth and advocating the elimination of the State of Israel, Iranian president Mahmoud Ahmadinejad recently told the United Nations, "We love everyone in the world—Jews, Christians, Muslims, non-Muslims, non-Jews, non-Christians. Everyone is respected," he insisted while continuing to build a nuclear program that threatens the prospects of peace in the Middle East.[5]

Until September 11, 2001, most Americans and Europeans were ignorant of the extreme hatred that existed within various Islamic factions. Westerners generally viewed the Middle East with a blend of curiosity, suspicion, and downright indifference. They knew that Arabs and Jews didn't get along very well, but they viewed that as a Middle Eastern problem and not a global threat. They were aware that the region controlled most of the world's oil supply but never really understood the economic implications of that control.

Today, one can hardly read a newspaper in the Western world that is not daily emblazoned with some horrific story of death, destruction, and carnage in the Middle East that now threatens the entire world with Islamophobia. People are afraid to confront the dangers of Islamic extremism for fear of reprisal. They realize that we are not dealing with some minor theological argument. It looks more like a religious world war with an enemy who is concealed behind political lines that are not clearly defined, and who is very committed to the annihilation of all things non-Muslim.

MUHAMMAD'S RELIGION

The Islamic religion is based upon Muhammad's claim to receive a divine revelation from God. Assuming the position of a Middle Eastern holy man of noble descent, Muhammad claimed to write his divinely inspired message in the Quran in the Arabic language. However, most of the early sources of information on Muhammad's life were written more than a century after his death.[6] Yet, most Muslim and non-Muslim scholars believe that he was born in Mecca, in western Arabia, around A.D. 570. He was a member of the Quraysh tribe, who were especially devoted to the Ka'ba, where the images of local gods were kept.

Ancient sources portray Muhammad as a seeker after God who wished to be taught, saying, "O God, if I knew how you wished to be worshipped, I would so worship you, but I do not know." Muhammad was living in a remote region frequented by various traders, wanderers, and religious seekers. He is said to have encountered Jewish rabbis, Christian monks, and Arab soothsayers.[7] Unfortunately, the form of Christianity to which he was exposed was Gnosticism, from which he seems to have developed a view of Jesus that regarded Him as a human prophet rather than a divine Savior. Thus, many of the central concepts of Gnostic Christianity can be found within Islam.

Sometime around age 40, Muhammad claimed to have a supernatural revelation from God. Known to later generations as the "Night of Destiny," it changed his perception of himself from a seeker after God to a messenger of God. The prophet's basic message was that God (Allah) would judge the world on the basis of those who would submit to His will, rely on His mercy, and show their gratitude by regular prayer and other religious observances. Thus, the new religion became known as *Islam,* which means "submission."[8]

The practice of the Islamic religion revolves around the five "pillars of Islam" (*arkan-al-Islam*).

1. **Faith** (*Iman*)

   The principle declaration of Islam is, "There is no god but Allah, and Muhammad is His messenger." Known as the *shahadah,* this prayer is central to the life of a devout Muslim who pledges to serve Allah by following the teachings and practices of the prophet

Muhammad, whom they believe to be "the apostle of God, and the seal of the prophets" (Sura 33:40).

2. **Prayer** (*Salah*)

Muslims pray five times each day facing Mecca. The daily prayers are recited at dawn, midday, late afternoon, sunset, and nightfall. Grant Jeffrey explains: "The prayers are preceded by a ceremonial cleansing (ablution) with water or sand if water is not available. The five times of prayer provide a religious cycle or rhythm to the day. The prayers are memorized and recited in Arabic, whether or not the Muslim understands the language."[9]

3. **Fasting** (*Sawm*)

During Ramadan, the ninth month of the Islamic lunar year, Muslims fast from dawn until sundown as an exercise of self-restraint, purification, and devotion to Allah. Muhammad established a lunar calendar of 12 months without additional days to make up the difference with the solar calendar. Thus, Islamic "months" do not occur at the same fixed times every year on the Gregorian calendar, but move a bit from year to year.

4. **Alms** (*Zakah*)

Muslims are encouraged to give alms to the poor and those in need. The general rule of giving is 2.5 percent of what he has in excess of the funds needed to support his family. Certainly any charitable giving is to be commended, but it cannot atone for one's sins.

5. **Pilgrimage** (*Hajj*)

The annual pilgrimage to Mecca occurs in Zul Hijjah, the twelfth month of the Islamic year. Every Muslim is required to make the pilgrimage at least once during his lifetime if he is able to do so, and millions do every year. The pilgrimage, known as the hajj, includes circling the Kaaba (a large, sacred black stone structure) seven times and traveling seven times between the hills of Safa and Marwa. Later, the pilgrims gather on the plain of Arafat in the desert outside Mecca to pray for the forgiveness of their sins. Afterwards is a festival called Id al-Adha, which is celebrated with prayers and gifts. Author Dave Hunt is quick to point out that all the elements of the hajj derive from ancient pagan Arabic practices that preceded Islam and were merely absorbed within it. This includes the often bizarre practice of stoning the three pillars of Satan in the Wadi Mina. In recent years, this symbolic stoning has worked the pilgrims into such a frenzy that hundreds have been trampled to death in the onslaught to attack the devil.

The Quran claims the Kaaba was the "first sanctuary appointed to mankind...where Abraham stood up to pray" (Sura 2:125). In addition, Islamic sources make outrageous claims that have no basis in historical facts. They insist that Abraham put Ishmael, not Isaac, on the altar of sacrifice. They deny both the crucifixion and resurrection of Christ, which are the essential elements of the Christian gospel (see Surh 4:157). They also reject the concept of the deity of Christ, whom they view as a mere human prophet (or messenger). In fact, Islam teaches that Jesus will one day denounce Christianity and affirm allegiance to Islam.[10]

The ceremonial practices of Islam certainly give religions cohesion to the global Muslim community. But the antihistorical basis of the religion often causes Muslims to play loose with the facts when it comes to their responsibilities to the global community. Who can forget, at the beginning of the war in Iraq in 2003, the outright lies of Saddam Hussein's media minister, who insisted there were no American tanks in Baghdad as one rolled past him on the videotaped satellite transmission.

MUHAMMAD'S LEGACY

From the very beginning, Muhammad met with opposition. To many of the local tribesmen, he was viewed as a troublemaker and eventually fled 200 miles north to Yathrib, later known as Medina. From there he attracted a powerful alliance of believers and followers of the new faith. It was also during this time that Muhammad came to believe that God had given him divine permission to fight to protect himself.

Historians claim that much of the change in Muhammad's beliefs were influenced by the Jewish community in Medina, who were originally part of his original alliance with the wider population. It was during this time that he particularly emphasized his descent from Abraham and began to suggest that Ishmael, not Isaac, was placed on the altar of sacrifice and spared by Allah. Eventually the Jews rejected Muhammad's claim to be a prophet of God, and he accused them of perverting the revelation God had given them. Finally, some of the Jewish clans were expelled and others were killed.[11]

From the very beginning of his claim to be God's prophet, Muhammad received objections from both Christian and Jews, whom he then began to view as infidels (unbelievers). The stage was set for his harsh "revelations" against Christians and Jews, which appear frequently throughout the Quran.

In 629 Muhammad appealed to the residents of Mecca to allow his followers to go there on a pilgrimage, and within a year, he had taken over the city and eventually forced the locals to submit to Islam or face the sword. While Muhammad's political power base remained at Medina, he viewed Mecca as the spiritual capital of the Islamic world. In 632, he died in Mecca. Traditional Muslim writings claim that his final message urged Muslims to accept one another as brothers but fight all men until they say, "There is no god but Allah."[12]

CULTURE OF DEATH

It is no wonder that the history of Islam has been bathed in bloodshed in a "culture of death." While there have been Muslims of high intellectual and cultural standing all through history, there have also been millions who have blindly followed the dictates of their religion while threatening to kill all who dare to disagree—especially among their own people.

Immediately after Muhammad's death, conflicts arose over the choice of a successor. In the end, Abu Bakr proclaimed himself the leader (caliph) of the community. His daughter A'isha had been one of Muhammad's wives. By contrast, 'Ali ibn Abi Talib, a cousin of the Prophet who married Muhammad's daughter Fatima, was rejected and eventually assassinated.[13]

The division between Sunni and Shiite Muslims came early in Islamic history. Shiites claim direct descent from the Prophet, whereas Sunnis emphasize the importance of the Quran and the practice (*sanna*) of the prophet. Thomas Abercrombie, writing for the National Geographic's *World of Islam,* explains that the rift began in A.D. 656 after the murder of the third caliph, Othman. Ali, a son-in-law of the Prophet, was duly elected in Medina but quickly moved his capital to Kufa in Iraq. "As descendants of the Prophet, Ali's heirs still command allegiance of the Shias, some ten percent of the Muslim world."[14] By contrast, Sunnis make up nearly 90 percent of the world's Islamic population. Daily telecasts from the Middle East make it painfully clear to even the most casual observer that the two factions are still antagonistic to this day.

Since 9/11 there have been over 7,000 recorded terrorist attacks worldwide, in which over 38,000 people have been killed. Some involve the assassination of one person, such as the Dutch filmmaker Theo Van Gogh, or the Jewish journalist Daniel Pearl. Others involve attacks that have killed hundreds at one time. For example, on March 3, 2004, Islamic militants killed 344 teachers, mothers, and mostly children in a school in Beslan, Russia. A few days later, on March 11, ten coordinated al-Qaeda bomb blasts on commuter trains killed 201 in Madrid, Spain. Hundreds of Christians are being killed regularly in Darfur province in the Sudan. Thousands of people are being killed in Iraq in Sunni versus Shiite religious civil wars. On November 23, 2006, over 200 Shiites were killed by Sunni terrorists. Eighty more Shiites were killed in a similar attack on a mosque on April 7, 2006. And on November 18, 2005, 74 worshippers were killed in a Shia mosque by two Sunni suicide bombers. A detailed list of these atrocities—which is updated daily—can be found online at "Islam: A Religion of Peace?" (www.TheReligionofPeace.com).

THE WARRIOR PROPHET

The Quran states, "Those who believe [Islam] and those who follow the Jewish [scriptures], and the Christians and the Sabians, and any who believe in Allah and the Last Day, and work righteousness, shall have their reward with their Lord" (Sura 2:62; 5:69; 22:17). Robert Spencer points out, "Muslim spokesmen in the West like to quote such verses and to stress the commonality between Islam and Christianity—and sometimes even between Islam and Judaism."[15] He further observes that Western Muslims prefer to paint an irenic picture of Islam's respect for its sister "Abrahamic faiths," assuring Western countries that they can accept Muslim immigrants "without any significant disruptions to their pluralistic societies."[16]

However, quite a different picture emerges from the light of the 9/11 terrorist attacks in America, the July 7, 2005 subway bombings in London, Islamic violence in Spain and France, and the cartoon riots in Denmark. It seems that the overtolerance of Western pluralism is at a loss to identify, explain, and confine Islamic extremism within its own borders, let alone in the Middle East, where it is and has been out of control for centuries.

In reality, Muslim jihadists point to their venerated prophet with pride as an example of one who fought the infidels in the name of God. In *The Truth About Muhammad,* Spencer quotes Ibn Ishaq, an eighth-century Muslim biographer who states that Muhammad participated in 27 battles and fought in nine engagements—at Badr, Uhud, al-Khandaq, Qurayza, al-Mustaliq, Khaybar, Mecca, Hunayn, and al-Ta'if.[17]

Spencer then observes, "Here again Muhammad's example is normative. Jihadists today invoke Badr and Khaybar to exhort Muslims to fight according to the example of the Prophet. It is difficult, if not impossible, to maintain that Islam is a religion of peace when warfare and booty were among the chief preoccupations of the Prophet of Islam."[18]

Despite Western Islamic attempts to whitewash the image of Muslim extremism, the Quran itself is replete with nearly 100 passages calling for the extermination, eradication, or submission of all non-Muslims, especially Christians and Jews. In Dave Hunt's riveting and revealing study *Judgment Day!* are listed numerous passages from the Quran that make the militant goals of Islam all too clear.[19]

> Fight and slay the idolaters wherever you find them…(Surah 9:5).

> Fight against such of those who have been given the Scripture [Bible] as believe not in Allah nor the Last Day…(Surah 9:29).

> Therefore when you meet the unbelievers [in battle] smite at their necks [until] you have thoroughly subdued them (Surah 47:4).

> Truly Allah loves those who fight in His Cause in battle array (Surah 61:4).

> O you who believe: Take not the Jews and Christians for your friends and protectors; they are but friends and protectors of each other (Surah 5:51).

followed Muhammad's example by sending a letter to President George W. Bush calling upon him to convert to Islam before declaring all-out war on him. As far as Ahmadinejad is concerned, the West has already been warned of a coming attack.

he beliefs and prejudices of Islam are deeply entrenched. While picturing a religion of fanatics, terrorists, and warmongers is not fair on the whole, rue of a radical element within the Muslim faith. This radical element es most Westerners to be repulsed by Islamic concepts of justice, revenge, so-called holy wars.

> *The "Islamic Curtain" cuts off the Arab world from outside influences. "Behind that wall of prejudice," Dave Hunt observes, "any religion except Islam is forbidden."*[20]

Muslim political leaders see themselves as protectors of Islam, and those o convert to Christianity are often persecuted, imprisoned, and even ecuted. In many Islamic countries, Muslims who become Christians have en put to death by their own families! Gospel preaching is outlawed and spel literature is banned from public distribution. Freedom of the press, f speech, and of public assembly is forbidden.

The Quran, the sacred book of Islam, advocates the killing of apostates nd unbelievers. Muhammad himself led several battles in which many eople were killed. He claimed that God had called him to spread Islam vith the point of the sword. History tells us that Muhammad's followers swept across the Middle East and North Africa, conquering everyone in their path. They crossed into Europe and took Spain, but they were finally turned back by Charles Martel in the Battle of Tours in France in A.D. 732. Even today it is considered an honorable duty for Muslims to kill Christians and Jews.

Hunt is correct when he writes, "It is impossible to understand the current situation in the Middle East, much less anticipate probable future developments there, except in the context of the religion that grips and motivates the Arab world."[21] This is a world of diverse peoples held together by the bond of a common religion, Islam, and a common language, Arabic. Together, these elements have a viselike grip on the Muslim world.

This is not to say that the Arab people have not made significant con-

And there has arisen between us and you hostilit
until you believe in Allah only (Surah 60:4).

The punishment of those who wage war against
Messenger [is] execution, or crucifixion, or the
hands and feet...or exile from the land: that is th
this world, and a heavy punishment is theirs in
(Surah 5:33).

GLOBAL TERRORISM

The Islamic extremism that fuels global terrorism is
the Quran itself. Notice the following examples:

- March 28, 2003—Palestinian sheikh Muhammad
  Hunud prayed about Americans in Iraq, saying, "Al
  their possessions a booty for Muslims, Allah annihil
  and their weapons, Allah make their children orphans
  women widows."

- November 21, 2003—Muslims in the Nigerian city of
  distributed flyers calling for the use of force to establish
  in their city.

- November 2003—The Web site of the Islamic Affairs Depar
  of the Saudi Arabian embassy in Washington, D.C. cont
  exhortations to Muslims to wage jihad "in order to make
  Word of Allah supreme in this world."

- May 29, 2004—Fawwaz bin Muhammad Al-Nashami, the c
  mander of the jihad group that killed 22 people in an attack
  Khobar, Saudi Arabia, said, "We found Filipino Christians. \
  cut their throats and dedicated them to our brothers the Mu
  hideen in the Philippines...we found Hindu engineers, and w
  cut their throats too, Allah be praised."

- October 2004—The al-Qaeda online journal *Sawt al-Jihad* urges
  jihadists to "sacrifice your souls...in fighting your enemy, as an
  imitation of your Prophet [Muhammad]."

- January 2005—Iranian president Mahmoud Ahmadinejad

tributions to the world in art, literature, architecture, mathematics, and science. The intricate geometric designs of Islamic art are among the most beautiful in the world. The Arab people themselves can be kind, loving, and hospitable. We must be careful not to close the door of the gospel to them by failing to love them for the sake of Christ. But when it comes to religion, there is a strong rejection of Jews and Christians.

We must remember that it is the Muslims who have insisted on destroying Israel at all costs. Israel has never declared such an intention against her Arab neighbors. If there is going to be real and lasting peace in the Middle East, the Arabs must change their stated policy and be willing to coexist with Israel and the West.

John Walvoord observed, "The rapidly increasing tempo of change in modern life has given the entire world a sense of impending crisis."[22] He too raises the difficult questions about how long the world can survive before a madman has nuclear bombs or how long the world economic struggle can be held in check before it ends in a bloodbath.

During the first Gulf War, the world was sitting on the edge of its seat. The entire global community was transfixed. People were ready for any possibility, including chemical or nuclear warfare. Then the war ended as quickly as it had begun. The Western world relaxed, assuming the crisis was over. But in the years that followed further conflicts, crises, and escalations have only intensified those original concerns. Today Iraq stands on the verge of collapse. Iran is making nuclear threats. Muslim extremists among al-Qaeda, Hamas, and Hezbollah are running rampant on campaigns of murder, mayhem, and mass destruction—all in the name of God.

In the postmodern world, the great problem for the Muslim mind is pluralism. It is a struggle for Christians as well. Both Christians and Muslims struggle with the relationship of their faith to a nonbelieving world. We who are Christians believe we must live the lifestyle of Christian discipleship before the unbelieving world as a testimony of God's grace in our lives. We do not believe in forcing others to accept our faith.

Islam, however, is quite different. The attitude of many Muslims is to spread their faith by the sword or kill the infidels who reject it. Tragically, this often leads to a breakdown of civility that results in international "gang war."

Ironically, *jihad* is a word that generically means "struggle," referring to the struggle of the soul against evil. In this regard it is a legitimate concept that Christians, Jews, and Muslims share. But when it is applied to religious war in the name of God, *jihad* becomes an ugly and frightening concept that seems to condone terrorism and mass murder in the name of religion. Here Christians and Jews part company with Muslims. They do not believe in forcing other people to accept their faith, neither at swordpoint nor gunpoint.

Christianity's greatest appeal is found in the moral teachings of its founder, Jesus Christ. He clearly told His disciples to "put away the sword" and spread His message by proclaiming the "good news" of salvation by grace. This is in total contrast to the constant Islamic defiance that now threatens any serious prospects for lasting peace in the Middle East. If the final answer is religious and it comes from the Islamic religion, the result could be catastrophic!

THE ISRAELI FACTOR

"Who has even heard of such a thing?
Who has ever seen such things? Can a country be born in
a day or a nation be brought forth in a moment?"
—ISAIAH 66:8

FOR CENTURIES, CHRISTIANS AND Jews have been anticipating a miracle—the reestablishment of the nation of Israel in its ancestral homeland. The reasons behind this anticipation are the numerous prophecies and promises of God recorded throughout the Bible, which clearly indicate there will indeed be a Jewish homeland in Israel in the last days. The miracle occurred on May 14, 1948, when the United Nations officially recognized the State of Israel.

To understand the significance of this miraculous event, it is necessary to know the history of this land. As a bridge between Asia to the north, Iran to the east, Africa to the south, and the Mediterranean Sea to the west, Israel has long been a battleground for the invading armies of the world.

Nebuchadnezzar of Babylon, Cyrus the Persian, and Alexander the Great all trampled and battled their way across the land which God had originally deeded to the Jews. Eventually the Romans succeeded in conquering everything west of the Euphrates River from Europe to Africa and were in power at the time of Christ. Since then, history has recorded one conflict after another in the Holy Land.

To this very day, the issue of who controls the Promised Land is still the most volatile issue in international politics. As recently as July 2000, then-Israeli prime minister Ehud Barak offered to give East Jerusalem and the entire West Bank to then-PLO chairman Yasser Arafat. For the first time since the capture of Jerusalem by Israeli forces in 1967, the Jewish head of state was proposing the city's redivision under pressure from then American president Bill Clinton. Former Israeli ambassador to the United Nations Dore Gold explains, "Barak was playing a dangerous chess game with...the legacy and history of his own people. His offer to Arafat is inexplicable in light of his advance knowledge, gleaned from his military intelligence chiefs, that Arafat had no intention whatsoever of making peace."[1]

During the Camp David summit, Barak offered Arafat the ultimate Israeli concessions, and still Arafat refused. Some still view Barak's gamble as an attempt to expose the Palestinians' unwillingness to reach any serious and peaceful solutions. In the end, the Camp David summit was a total failure. Gold observes, "On September 29, 2000, barely a month after the Camp David summit ended, Arafat used a visit to the Temple Mount by Ariel Sharon, then head of Barak's parliamentary opposition, as a pretext for launching a long, violent insurrection...called the al-Aksa intifada."[2]

To the Western world, the Palestinians claimed the violence began as a spontaneous reaction to Sharon's visit. In the meantime, however, Arafat's minister of communications, Imad Faluji, told a Lebanese Arabic newspaper, "This Intifada was planned in advance, ever since President Arafat's return from the Camp David negotiations."[3] What is now painfully clear to the entire Western world is that the Arab world does not really want to settle the Israeli-Palestinian issue peacefully. What they really desire is the elimination of the State of Israel altogether. This has been made clear by the recent comments of Iranian president Mahmoud Ahmadinejad, who has said Israel should be "wiped away" and has called the Jewish state a "stain of disgrace."[4]

A TALE OF TWO BROTHERS

The biblical account of the history of both Jews and Arabs is linked to a common ancestor—Abraham. Thus, Judaism and Islam, and even Christianity, are often referred to as the Abrahamic faiths. All three of these religions are founded in one way or another on their connection to Abraham.

Known originally as *Abram* ("father"), Abraham was called by God to leave ancient Ur and set out for the land of Canaan, which God promised to give to him and his descendants after him (Genesis 12:1-3). However, after ten years' residence in Canaan, Abram remained childless and became concerned about a successor. So he proposed adopting his chief steward Eliezer of Damascus, an Aramaean, as his heir (Genesis 15:1-2). Yet God assured Abram that he would have a son of his own as his heir (Genesis 15:4). In response to God's promise, Abram believed and was accounted righteous by God (Genesis 15:6). Abram's faith response was so significant that it is recorded five times in the New Testament as the ultimate example of faith in God (Romans 4:3,9,22; Galatians 3:6; James 2:23).

By the end of the day, God literally cut a covenant with Abram, promising to give the land of Canaan to his descendants (Genesis 15:18). However, when Abram tried to explain this to his wife Sarai, she suggested "they" have the child by a surrogate mother—Hagar, her Egyptian handmaid (Genesis 16:1-3). While this was common practice in the ancient Middle East, it was not what God originally intended. Sarai assumed she was too old to get pregnant and this was a way of helping God keep His promise. *After all,* she may have thought, *what could go wrong?* Hagar eventually became pregnant with Ishmael, the father of the Arabs (Genesis 16:11-16). At this point in the biblical text there follows 13 years of silence between Genesis 16:16 and 17:1. It is as though God were indicating His disapproval with Abram's actions.

While it is very clear that God meant for Abram to have the son of promise by his wife Sarai, we must also observe that none of their actions can be blamed on Ishmael. In fact, God went out of His way twice to spare Ishmael's life (Genesis 16:9-13; 21:9-21). God could have easily solved the Arab-Israeli crisis 4,000 years ago by letting Ishmael and Hagar die in the desert. But He did not. Instead, He allowed Ishmael to live and promised to bless him greatly. Ishmael and the Arab peoples have just as much opportunity to experience God's grace and salvation as any other people.

The God of the Bible offers the gift of eternal life to whoever believes in the atoning sacrifice of His Son, Jesus Christ (John 3:16). From God's perspective, the problem in the Middle East today is religious, not ethnic. Many Arabs are Christian believers and love the Savior deeply. The real conflict is caused by Islamic religious extremists who target all other religions as the "enemies of God."

In the biblical record, God spares Ishmael's life and promises: "I will make him into a great nation" (Genesis 21:18). But then He reaffirms His covenant with Abram, changing his name to *Abraham* ("father of a multitude") and emphasizing that the land of Canaan is promised to his descendants through Isaac, the son of Sarai (now renamed *Sarah*—Genesis 17:1-21). As we read the entire account of the patriarch and his journey of faith, it becomes obvious that God deliberately waited to allow Sarah to conceive a son in her old age, even after menopause, so that the Jewish race would begin with a miraculous conception. Then, 2,000 years later, God would intervene in human history with an even greater miracle—the virginal conception of Jesus Christ, the incarnate Son of God (Matthew 1:18-25).

The Old Testament focuses on God's covenantal promises to Israel, the nation that descended from Abraham through Isaac and Jacob. At the same time, the Hebrew Scriptures include frequent references to God's love and grace toward Gentiles (non-Jews). Ruth, a Moabite, is converted to Jehovah and becomes the great-grandmother of David—Israel's greatest king (Ruth 1–4). Joseph marries an Egyptian, Asenah, who becomes the mother of two of the tribes of Israel—Ephraim and Manasseh (Genesis 41:45-52). While dedicating the Jewish temple, Solomon is promised that prayers could be offered there by "the foreigner who does not belong to your people Israel" (1 Kings 8:41). The prophet Isaiah describes the temple as a "house of prayer for all nations" (Isaiah 56:7), and he predicts God's light and glory will shine on the Gentiles in the future (Isaiah 62:1-2).

The biblical narrative is the story of two mothers (Hagar and Sarah) and two brothers (Ishmael and Isaac). It is the story of a choice made in human history which now affects human destiny. It is a story that reminds all of us that our choices have consequences that often outlive us. For the Jews, it is a story of a promised destiny that is particular to a promised land—the land of Israel.

BIBLICAL HISTORY OF ISRAEL

The Old Testament opens with the stories of the *patriarchs* (Abraham, Isaac, and Jacob) who received and believed the promises of God. Next it moves to the period of the *exodus* from Egypt under Moses' leadership. Then, on to the *conquest* of the Promised Land by Joshua and its *settlement* in the days of the Judges. Finally, the Hebrew Scriptures take us to the era of the *theocratic kingdom*—a literal kingdom of God on earth administered by human rulers under the authority of God. But the failures of those rulers eventually led to the collapse of Judah and the fall of Jerusalem to Nebuchadnezzar and the Babylonians in 586 B.C.[5]

From that point until the end of the Old Testament record, Israel's future was dominated by the Babylonians (ancient Iraq) and the Persians (ancient Iran). During the Persian period, Cyrus the Great decreed that the Jews could return from the Babylonian captivity to rebuild their temple and their future. Thus the Old Testament closes with the Jews benefiting from the Persian benevolence.

Between the Old and New Testaments, both the Greeks and then the Romans dominated the Middle East, including Israel, which was divided into various provinces: Judea, Samaria, and Galilee.[6]

As the New Testament opens, Rome is ruling the world and Christianity is established within its hostile boundaries. In fact, Jesus Himself is executed by a Roman crucifixion ordered by Pontius Pilate. After the resurrection of Christ, the disciples received the Great Commission (Matthew 28:19-20) and were empowered on the Feast of Pentecost to carry out that commission (Acts 2). The rest of the New Testament emphasizes the unique distinction of the church as a separate entity from national Israel. While various Jewish questions remained (dietary laws, eating with Gentiles, social obligations, and religious practices), the New Testament church clearly established an identity of its own.

By the end of the New Testament (the apostolic era), there were more Gentiles than Jews within the burgeoning young church. Peter and Paul were both executed in Rome, while John was later exiled to the island of Patmos, where he received the Revelation (Greek, *Apocalypsis*) as the final book of inspired Scripture. From that point onward, Christianity continued to spread beyond the borders of Israel into Europe, Asia, and Africa. In the meantime, Jewish nationalism reached a fervency that led to a rebellion against the Roman Empire that resulted in the destruction of Jerusalem in A.D. 70.

Destruction of the Temple (A.D. 70). Just as Jesus had predicted four decades earlier (A.D. 30), the Jewish temple was destroyed by the Romans. The Roman general Titus had earlier besieged the city following a Jewish revolt in A.D. 66. The result was a Jewish death toll of somewhere between

500,000 to one million. Interestingly, the Christian Jews in Jerusalem were basically spared from death because they knew of the impending destruction beforehand based on Jesus' prophetic Olivet Discourse as recorded by Luke:

> When you see Jerusalem being surrounded by armies, you will know that its desolation is near. Then let those who are in Judea flee to the mountains, let those in the city get out, and let those in the country not enter the city (Luke 21:20-21).

The Christian Jews had watched as Vespasian and his Roman army surrounded Jerusalem two years earlier in A.D. 68. But before he could lay siege to the city, Vespasian broke off the attack and returned to Rome in order to claim the throne. Vespasian then turned control of the Roman army over to his son Titus, who returned to Jerusalem in A.D. 70 and proceeded to destroy the city and Herod's temple. Heeding Jesus' warning, the Christian Jews had auspiciously believed the prophecy and were thus able to flee the city ahead of time.

The bar Kochba Rebellion (A.D. 135). Following Emperor Hadrian's announcement that he was going to build a pagan temple on the site of the Jerusalem temple ruins and restrict the practice of the Jewish religion, another Jewish rebellion arose in Jerusalem, led by Simon bar Kochba. Over half a million were killed during the fighting and the bar Kochba revolt failed, resulting in the almost total expulsion of Jews from their ancient homeland.

The Roman Period (A.D. 135–640). Under the direction of the Roman government, a new city called Aelia Capitolina was built over the ruins of Jerusalem. Jews were forbidden to set foot inside the new city under penalty of death. A pagan temple was also constructed and the name of the province of Judah was changed to Syria Palestina, from which the name *Palestine* was later derived. In A.D. 325, the Roman emperor Constantine was converted to Christianity and the Roman Empire eventually became Christianized so that Christianity became the dominant religion in Europe, the Middle East, and North Africa during the period known as the Byzantine Empire (A.D. 325–640). While the emperor continued to rule from Constantinople, he lost control of the entire Middle East to the sweeping conquests of the Muslims in the seventh century.[7]

PERIOD OF ISLAMIC DOMINATION

Muslim Period (640–1090). Not long after Muhammad died, his Muslim followers conquered Palestine from the Byzantine Romans and contact with the West was virtually cut off. During this period, the Mosque of Omar (Dome of the Rock) and the al-Aksa Mosque were built on the Temple Mount, where they have now stood for nearly 1,300 years as a symbol of Muslim domination and influence. To this very day, the issue of control of the Temple Mount has prevented the Jews from rebuilding their own temple on this holy site.

Latin or Crusader Period (1099–1291). During this stormy period of time, European Catholic crusaders invaded the Holy Land in an attempt to take it back from the Muslims, who had recently desecrated some ancient Christian sites, including the tomb of the Holy Sepulcher. Both Muslims and Jews were slaughtered as a result of the First Crusade when the overzealous crusaders took Jerusalem and established it as the Latin Kingdom of Jerusalem under the auspices of the Roman Catholic Church. Many today forget that the city was Christianized for over 100 years and other parts of Palestine remained under European control for nearly 200 years.

Saladin and the Mamluks (1187–1517). The Syrian Muslim scholar Ali ibn Tahir al-Sulami revived the idea of calling for jihad ("holy war") to recapture the Holy City from the Crusaders. In response, Saladin rallied 30,000 soldiers in Syria, crossed the Jordan, and overwhelmingly defeated the Crusader force of 20,000 at the Horns of Hittim in Galilee on June 30, 1187. By October 2, Jerusalem surrendered to Saladin after a two-week siege. In the aftermath, the Muslims made a determined effort to re-Islamize Jerusalem. The golden cross of the Crusaders was removed from the al-Aksa Mosque and the Catholic altar was removed from the Dome of the Rock. However, in the years that followed, there were continual conflicts between Muslims and Crusaders. In 1219, Saladius' nephew, al-Mu'azzam, ordered the destruction of Jerusalem's walls and depopulated the city to keep it from the Crusaders. By 1260, the city came under the control of the Mamluks.

Ottoman Turkish Period (1517–1917). The Mamluks were replaced by the Turks in 1517. Jerusalem was rebuilt as a Turkish Muslim city. During this time, the Islamic influence on the culture of Palestine continued to grow. The rebuilding of Jerusalem's walls was completed in 1566 and those walls still stand today, enclosing the Old City. Despite numerous local conflicts, the Turkish period provided general protection from foreign invasions and ultimately opened contact with the Western world during the nineteenth century. However, the fate of Israel changed dramatically during World War I when the Turks allied themselves with Kaiser Wilhelm of Germany. Not only did Germany lose the war, but the Turks lost control of Palestine to the British, who set up a mandate over the region from 1917–1948.

THE MODERN PERIOD
The Zionist Movement

Curiously, it was the Christians of the nineteenth century which stimulated interest in the Jews to return to the Holy Land as well as various movements originating with the Jews themselves.

Increasing attention among Western Christians regarding the second coming of Christ revived thoughts about the Jews returning to their homeland as a sign of the end times.

Prophetic literature and debates on the subject began to materialize, which, in turn, influenced sermons and missionary visions of churches in the West. Not surprisingly, this movement coincided with the revival of the literal interpretation of prophetic Scripture within the church. This, in turn, sparked interest among many displaced and homeless Jews for an Israeli homeland. Simultaneously, Baron Edmund de Rothschild launched a program of agricultural colonies in Palestine that proved to be quite profitable to European Jews.

The Society for Colonizing Palestine was formed in London in 1861. This organization and similar groups throughout Europe eventually helped to popularize the idea of Jewish emigration to Israel. But it didn't happen overnight. Faithful Jewish believers met regularly in their synagogues to read God's promises to Israel as recorded in Deuteronomy and other Old Testament books. They collectively began to pray a prayer that would define their destiny in the decades to come: "Next year in Jerusalem."

Through God's providence, an adverse event that took place in France in 1894 would become an opportunity for the Jews. Captain Alfred Dreyfus, a French Jew and an exceptional army officer, was made the scapegoat for a serious military scandal. He was disgraced and sentenced to Devil's Island as a criminal. It would be several years before his innocence was firmly established. This incident drew worldwide attention in the media and reaffirmed on a global scale that Jews were still the recipients of anti-Semitism and persecution. The Jews concluded that having their own sovereign state and national homeland would be the only means by which they could be kept safe from the kind of discrimination that had followed them for the last 1,900 years.

Austrian journalist Theodor Herzl was disturbed by the Dreyfus affair, which he had written about for his newspaper in 1894. He subsequently convened the First Zionist Congress in Basel, Switzerland, three years later. Jewish leaders from most of the Western countries attended. The Congress quickly adopted a resolution that read, "Zionism strives to create for the Jewish people a home in Palestine secured by public law." Over 75,000 Jews were living in Palestine by the year 1914, which also saw more than 40 agricultural settlements established.[8]

British Rule Begins

In 1917, Arthur Balfour, foreign secretary of Great Britain, issued the following statement, known as the Balfour Declaration, in an attempt to gain support of influential Jews for the war against Germany:[9]

> Dear Lord Rothschild:
>
> I have much pleasure in conveying to you, on behalf of His Majesty's Government, the following declaration of sympathy with Jewish Zionist aspirations, which has been submitted to, and approved by, the Cabinet. His Majesty's Government views with favour the establishment in Palestine of a national home for the Jewish people, and will use their best endeavours to facilitate the achievement of this object, it being clearly understood that nothing shall be done which may prejudice the civil and religious rights of existing non-Jewish communities in Palestine, or the rights and political status enjoyed by Jews in any other country. I should be grateful if you would bring this declaration to the knowledge of the Zionist Federation.
>
> Yours sincerely,
> Arthur James Balfour

The British had grown increasingly impatient in their attempts to mediate the ever-increasing hostilities between the Arabs and Jews who were under their supervision. And it was the United Kingdom's disciplined presence in that tumultuous region that ultimately kept the Arabs from driving the Jews into the sea at a time when they were defenseless and outnumbered.

By 1939, with constant unrest in Palestine, Great Britain began to go back on the Balfour Declaration and instead favor Arab independence and control of the area. Yet Jewish immigration continued, and was accelerated by the intense persecution of the Jewish people under the Nazi regime before and during World War II. By the time Great Britain relinquished control of the region in 1947, some 670,000 Jews inhabited the land, and they were strong enough to defend themselves.

Foundation of the Middle East Crisis

Although the Jewish-Arab conflict can literally be traced all the way back to the time of Abraham, the clash would take on greater significance as the prospect of Israel gaining statehood began to gain momentum.

1939—Emigration of Jews from Europe increases as Hitler builds a network of concentration camps. By the end of World War II, six million Jews will have died at the hands of the Nazis and Russian Communists. Thousands of Jews will flee to Palestine for refuge.

November 2, 1943—Lebanon gains independence from France. Two months later, France relinquishes its mandate powers over Syria, which leads to Syria's establishment as an independent nation. European influence in the Middle East begins to diminish.

March 22, 1945—The Arab League unites Egypt, Syria, Lebanon, Iraq, Saudi Arabia, Yemen, and Transjordan. This is the first move toward unity among the Arabs, who have, as a common bond, an intense opposition to the establishment of a Jewish state.

May 7, 1945—Upon the collapse of Germany at the end of World War II, the Allies liberated the Jewish prisoners from Auschwitz, Dachau, and other concentration camps. Worldwide shock and sympathy along with Jewish wealth from around the world encouraged the relocation of more than a million displaced Jews to Palestine. The process of assimilation began and further inflamed the Arabs.

November 29, 1947—The United Nations voted to partition Palestine into two states, Jewish and Arab. Jerusalem was declared an international city, open to all as the Holy City of Jews, Catholics, Protestants, and Muslims. Although the Jews accepted the plan, the Arabs wanted no part of it. Fearing a civil war, 300,000 Palestinian Arabs fled the country.

May 14, 1948—The United Nations officially recognized the State of Israel. U.S. president Harry Truman determined the deciding vote. The Israeli government established the State of Israel, thus fulfilling the 2,500-year-old prophecy recorded in the Bible in Ezekiel chapter 37. Great Britain ends its mandate in Palestine and removes its troops, leaving behind more than 650,000 Jews to govern themselves. This turn of events was unacceptable to the Arab world. Egypt, Syria, Saudi Arabia, Lebanon, Iraq, and Transjordan united together and immediately declared war on Israel within hours following the declaration of sovereignty. The Arab armies easily outnumbered the Israelis, and although thousands of Jews died in the ensuing combat, Israel miraculously was able to defeat its Arab neighbors. Some 350,000 additional Arabs who refused to recognize the State of Israel fled to neighboring Arab countries such as Lebanon, Syria, Transjordan, Iraq, and Saudi Arabia.

1956—Egypt, under the direction of Colonel Gamel Abdel Nassar, tried to nationalize the Suez Canal following British withdrawal from the area. Israel invaded the Sinai Peninsula and, in eight days, reached the canal, gaining control over the northernmost point of the Gulf of Aqaba. Nassar suffered a military defeat but gained an eventual political victory by retaining control of the Suez Canal.

1964—The Palestinian Liberation Organization (PLO) was founded by Palestinian refugees in order to create an armed force capable of coercing Israel to give up land that could be used for an independent, Arab-controlled Palestine. The move led to inflamed Palestinian nationalism, which resulted in a series of wars and conflicts that continue to this very day.

1967—Six-Day War. The Israeli intelligence agency, Mossad, uncovered

Arab plans to launch an immediate military attack against Israel. Mossad also discovered that Russia was in the process of supplying large shipments of arms to these same Arab countries. Rather than waiting for the Arab assault, Israel launched predawn land and air strikes against Egypt, Jordan, and Syria. Although outnumbered 30 to 1, Israel was able to quickly destroy the Egyptian air force and navy as well as overcome Syria from the air. Israel's tanks reached the Suez Canal and decisively captured Soviet-built missile bases intact.

The war lasted less than a week, hence the name the Six-Day War. After this stunning military victory, Israel controlled the Sinai Peninsula, the West Bank, and the Golan Heights. This more than quadrupled Israel's territory from 8,000 to 34,000 square miles. And for the first time since the Roman era, the city of Jerusalem was under Jewish control. However, within a few days of the victory, Israeli defense minister Moshe Dayan, who met with Muslim leaders at the al-Aksa Mosque, inexplicably returned administrative control of the Temple Mount site over to the Palestinians, declaring Jerusalem to be an international city.

1973—Syria and Egypt attacked Israel while Jews were in their synagogues observing Yom Kippur, the Day of Atonement. This began the three-week long Yom Kippur War. This was the first and final time the Israeli military found itself unready during an attack. Once again, the Arabs, equipped with Russian-supplied armament, attacked Israel in simultaneous operations. Egypt seized large portions of the Sinai, while Syria took the Golan Heights. Israel, however, was able to break through enemy lines and cross the Suez Canal, thereby cutting off the advancing Egyptian army. At the same time, Israel retook the Golan Heights, forged into Syria, and was about to conquer Damascus but was stopped in its tracks by a U.N.-enforced cease fire. Israel won this war, but suffered tremendous casualties.

1978—At a conference hosted by President Jimmy Carter of the United States at Camp David in Maryland, President Sadat of Egypt and Prime Minister Menachem Begin of Israel signed agreements known as the Camp David accords. This event led to the signing of a formal peace treaty between the two countries on March 26, 1979. In keeping with this agreement, Israel officially withdrew its troops from the city of El Arish and returned the Sinai to Egyptian control.

1981—In a daring early-morning raid on Baghdad, 600 miles north of their air base, seven Israeli F-16 fighters—with seven F-15s flying cover—destroyed a French-built nuclear generator. Israel believed that Iraq was planning to utilize the plutonium generator to build atomic weapons for use against Israel. Formally the world was outraged by Israel's actions, but secretly many world leaders were relieved that the hostile and unpredictable Iraq had been set back in its attempts to become a nuclear power.

1981—President Sadat of Egypt is assassinated on October 6 while watching a military parade. The incident is traced to Arab terrorists opposed to Sadat's friendly attitude toward Israel. Hosni Mubarak, Sadat's successor, subsequently opened Egypt's borders to Libya but maintained the official peace treaty with Israel.

1983—A truck bomb blew up a U.S. Marines compound at the Beirut, Lebanon airport, killing 240 Marines who were part of a peacekeeping force. A similar attack at a French compound killed an additional 56 soldiers, shattering confidence in any hopes for a lasting peace in the region.

1984—Eight thousand Jews were secretly rescued from Ethiopia and brought safely to Israel as part of an effort called *Operation Moses*. During the 1980s and 1990s, thousands of Jews were brought to Israel from Iraq, Iran, and the former nations of the Soviet Union.

1987—On December 6, an Israeli was stabbed to death while shopping in Gaza. The next day, four residents of the Jabalya refugee camp in Gaza were killed in a traffic accident. False rumors began spreading among the Palestinians that the four accident victims had been killed by Israelis out of revenge. Mass rioting broke out two days later and spread across the West Bank, Gaza, and Jerusalem in what would become known as the Intifada. The violence, orchestrated by the PLO and directed toward both Israeli soldiers and civilians alike, continued for the next four years. During this time 27 Israelis were killed and more than 3,100 injured. The PLO-dominated Unified Leadership of the Intifada issued leaflets dictating on which days violence was to be escalated and who was to be its target. Methods of violence included the throwing of Molotov cocktails and hand grenades, shootings, stabbings, bombings, and burnings with acid. The PLO also used this period of unrest as an excuse to execute Palestinians whom they believed had "associations" with the Israelis.

1990—On August 2, Saddam Hussein of Iraq invaded Kuwait. Four days later, the U.N. Security Council imposed economic sanctions against Iraq. The next day, the United States began sending troops into the Persian Gulf area. Hussein announced that any military action taken against Iraq will result in a strike on Israel. Iraqi Foreign Minister Tariq Aziz threatened that Iraq would use chemical weapons if Israel strikes back. On December 23, Saddam Hussein announced that Tel Aviv, Israel would be Iraq's first target if Israel were invaded.

1991—The Gulf War began on January 15. Over the next five weeks, 38 SCUD missiles were launched at Israel from Iraq, resulting in one fatality and 172 injuries. On February 28, the Gulf War ended with the expulsion of the Iraqi army from Kuwait by the United States and coalition forces.

1993—Israel secretly signed a peace agreement with the PLO in Oslo, Norway on August 20. Several days later, both groups signed letters formally recognizing each other's right to exist. On September 13, the historic handshake took place between Israel's prime minister Yitzhak Rabin and PLO leader Yasser Arafat. On September 23, the Israeli Knesset ratified the Oslo Agreement by a vote of 61 to 50. One year later, Rabin and Arafat were awarded the Nobel Peace Prize.

1995—Israeli prime minister Yitzhak Rabin was assassinated at a peace rally by a Jewish extremist. Heads of state from all over the world, including Jordan's King Hussein and President Mubarak of Egypt, attended Rabin's funeral in Jerusalem. Yigal Amir was later indicted for the murder. The future of the Israeli-PLO negotiations was now in doubt.

1996—Jerusalem celebrated its 3,000th anniversary as the capital of the Jewish state, dating back to King David's conquest of the city in biblical times. Later that year, newly elected Israeli prime minister Benjamin Netanyahu announced the opening of a new archaeological tunnel alongside the Western Wall in Jerusalem. This triggered a deadly series of Palestinian protests that resulted in 14 Israeli and 56 Palestinian deaths.

1998—The U.S. embassies in Nairobi, Kenya and Dar es Salaam, Tanzania were simultaneously bombed by al-Qaeda terrorists, resulting in 257 dead and more than 4,000 wounded. Islamic terrorist leader Osama bin Laden was later confirmed to be the mastermind behind the massacre. The Israeli Defense Force aided in the rescue efforts in Nairobi. Later that same year at the White House, in the presence of U.S. president Bill Clinton and King Hussein of Jordan, Netanyahu and Arafat signed the Wye River Memorandum to redeploy portions of the West Bank and Gaza Strip.

2000—U.S. president Bill Clinton attempted to negotiate a peace treaty between Israeli Prime Minister Ehud Barak and Palestinian president Yasser Arafat. Barak agreed but Arafat refused, making it painfully obvious that the Palestinians really did not want a peaceful settlement.

September 11, 2001—Islamic terrorists sponsored by al-Qaeda hijacked and crashed jetliners into the World Trade Center in New York and the Pentagon in Washington, D.C. Nearly 3,000 U.S. citizens were killed. Thousands of Palestinians and other Muslims celebrated in the streets while the rest of the world mourned and expressed outrage. The United States retaliated by invading al-Qaeda-dominated Afghanistan and setting up a democratically elected government in the Islamic nation.

2002—Israel erected a security force along the West Bank to help prevent future terrorist infiltrations into Israel. On October 16 of the same year, Israeli prime minister Ariel Sharon met with U.S. president George W. Bush, who proposed a peace plan known as the Road Map, which called for the creation of a permanent Palestinian state.

2005—Mahmoud Abbas was elected the new president of the Palestinian Authority, replacing Yasser Arafat, who had died two months earlier in Paris, France. Early in 2006, Ariel Sharon of Israel suffered a severe stroke and was replaced by Ehud Olmert.

2006—After a series of air and missile attacks between Israel and Hezbollah in Lebanon, Iranian president Mahmoud Ahmadinejad announced that "Israel will one day be wiped out just as the Soviet Union was," drawing applause from participants in a Holocaust-denying rally in Tehran.

We can readily see from this list of significant events that the modern State of Israel is in a very unique and precarious position in history. It is obvious that God is doing something unusual in our times. It has been nearly 2,000 years since the Jewish people have had a nation to call their own. The prophet Isaiah (66:8) asks: "Can a country be born in a day or a nation be brought forth in a moment?" In the case of the modern State of Israel, the answer is a resounding yes!

The significance of Israel's reemergence in her ancient homeland is that this had to occur in order to set the stage for the final fulfillment of biblical prophecies about the future. Israel must be a nation in her own land in order to experience all that God has predicted about her future. Incredible as it sounds, the existence of Israel today is the number-one evidence for the fact that the Bible's prophecies about the future will be fulfilled literally. God said it would happen, and it has come to pass—to His glory and honor.

8

ISRAEL'S FUTURE DESTINY

"I will put my Spirit in you and you will live,
and I will settle you in your own land.
Then you will know that I the LORD
have spoken and I have done it."
—EZEKIEL 37:14

THE LONG AND BLOODY HISTORY of conflict in the Middle East seems to indicate that more of the same can be expected in the future. But this does not mean that a sincere and reasonable peace should not be sought. The Bible clearly tells us to "pray for the peace of Jerusalem" (Psalm 122:6). Most conservative Christians support the right of Israel to exist, but this does not mean that they blindly support all that the secular Israeli government chooses to do. What they do oppose is the unmitigated use of violence against innocent civilians to further political causes in the Middle East.

Unfortunately, violence has become a way of life among Islamic extremists. Bassam Jarrar of Hamas recently wrote an apocalyptic work entitled *The Disappearance of Israel in 2022*. Dore Gold observes, "Clearly, according to Jarrar's worldview, the elimination of Israel is a prerequisite for the emergence of the global Islamic state."[1] Gold also points out that current Islamic apocalyptic scenarios call for the establishment of a new caliphate whose capital is Jerusalem led by the messianic Mahdi.

The Quran itself never mentions the city of Jerusalem. But more recent Muslim apocalyptic literature pictures Jerusalem as the new Islamic capital at the "end of days." Within this context, one can easily see how the issue of Jerusalem is sparking a renewed jihadist effort to reclaim the city from Israel.[2]

The Hebrew prophet Zechariah also foresaw the significance of Jerusalem in the last days. He predicted, "I am going to make Jerusalem a cup that sends all the surrounding people reeling.... On that day, when all the nations of the earth are gathered against her, I wil make Jerusalem an immovable rock" (Zechariah 12:2-3). The prophet associated this warning with the conversion of the Jews when they will "look upon [Christ], the one they have pierced" (Zechariah 12:10). In the space of just a few verses, Zechariah makes several significant predictions about Jerusalem's future:

1. It will be the ultimate issue in the last days (12:2-3).

2. It will be attacked by the nations of the world (12:8).

3. Israel will be converted to Christ, the true Messiah, by the spirit of grace (12:10).

4. There will be great mourning in Jerusalem and the valley of Megiddo—Armageddon (12:11).

5. One-third of the Jews will survive (13:8).

6. The "day of the LORD" will come when the nations gather against Jerusalem (14:1).

7. Christ will return to the Mount of Olives with the raptured saints (14:4-5).

8. Christ will be King over all the earth in His messianic (millennial) reign (14:9).

9. Jerusalem will be secured and safely inhabited (14:11).

10. Jerusalem will finally become the true Holy City, where all the world will worship the King during the messianic reign of Christ (14:16-21).

All the Hebrew prophets predicted the final world conflict of the last days would be centered in Jerusalem and the land of Israel. Each of these prophecies presupposes that the people of Israel will be back in their own land in the last days—and indeed they are there today. While some question whether the modern State of Israel is the final fulfillment of these prophecies, we must observe that Israel's return after nearly 1,900 years of being scattered around the world certainly seems to be prophetically significant.

The prophet Amos predicted, "I will bring back my exiled people Israel; they will rebuild the ruined cities and live in them.... I will plant Israel in their own land, never again to be uprooted from the land I have given them" (Amos 9:14-15). It is clear that Amos foresaw Israel in permanent possession of her land in the last days.

When reading this prophecy, we must remember that Amos predicted this long before the Babylonian captivity (605–535 B.C.) or the Roman destruction of Jerusalem in A.D. 70. In both of these cases, Israel was uprooted and dispersed. But Amos's prediction tells of a future time when Israel would return and be resettled in her own land, never to be removed. We believe this prophecy began to be fulfilled in 1948 when the nation was "born in a day" (see Isaiah 66:8). Israel's presence in the Promised Land today is the single greatest indication that we are living in the days of prophetic fulfillment.

God performed a biological miracle when Abraham and Sarah were beyond the age of child-bearing in order to bring into this world a son named Isaac, who in turn would be the forefather of a special group of people. God intended these people to be the communicators of His Word to the world. As recorded in the Bible, those who obeyed Him, such as the prophets, judges, and certain kings, have been blessings to the world, while those who opposed Him have been a hindrance. Before this world comes to an end, God will once again use the Jews in a very special way as the messengers of His gospel.

Prophetically speaking, God is not finished with Israel. In fact, unlike other nations, Israel has a guaranteed future. The Jews are still "His people" who will again fearlessly share His message of salvation with a lost world— much like the first-century Christian apostles did with their world.

THE FIG TREE PROPHECY

> Now learn this lesson from the fig tree: As soon as its twigs get tender and its leaves come out, you know that summer is near. Even so, when you see all these things, you know that it is near, right at the door. I tell you the truth, this generation will certainly

not pass away until all these things have happened (Matthew
24:32-34).

Many students of prophecy believe that Israel is the "fig tree" mentioned
by Jesus in the above-cited portion of the Olivet Discourse. The nation of
Israel was often referred to symbolically as a fig tree by the Hebrew prophets,
and Jesus was fully aware of their writings. The disciples had asked, "What
will be the sign of your coming and of the end of the age?" (Matthew 24:3).
According to Jesus' response, the budding fig tree was a clue that Israel was
somehow an important key in providing the answer. In fact, Jesus may have
intended that the regathering of Israel into their homeland was the sign that
His second coming would be taking place soon thereafter and that the end
of the age was at hand.

The "season" Christ refers to in Matthew 24:32 is an indeterminate period
of time known only to God. Our seasons here on earth are usually around
three months in length. The budding of the trees lets us know when summer
is coming, but the exact day and time is not known. So it is with the last
days. Israel's regathering in their ancient land indicates the coming of our
Lord will be soon, but exactly when, we do not know. "No one knows about
that day or hour, not even the angels in heaven, nor the Son, but only the
Father" (Matthew 24:36).

Since we can know "the season" or general time frame, and many believe
we are currently in that period, it would certainly be a good idea to live
every day with the anticipation that He could come today or tomorrow.
It's true that we do not know the day, the hour, or even the year of Christ's
return. But if any generation had a logical reason based on biblical prophecy
to assume that the Lord would come in its lifetime, it is ours. We can't be
certain, of course, but we have more reasons to believe Christ could return
in this generation than any other since the time of Christ. This is why
Christians living today should remember that the time for serving Christ
in this present world may be limited.

There are two reasons why Israel's statehood, which was confirmed by
the United Nations on May 14, 1948 is nothing less than a miracle. First,
the fact that there are enough Jews in the world to form a nation after nearly
1,900 years of homelessness is miraculous in and of itself. Second, if one
considers the fact that this nation had a population of "zero" in 1880, and

by 2000 not only had a population of six million but had also become one of the world's strongest military powers—often while waging battles against insurmountable odds—that too is nothing short of miraculous.

> *The fact that the tiny nation of Israel exists today is powerful evidence of the truth that God keeps His promises.*

The Hebrew prophets were so prolific in their prophecies regarding Israel's future destiny that skeptics and atheists would have had a field day discrediting the Bible if indeed the Jews never returned to their homeland. But because of the historical reality of the existence of the State of Israel, these unbelievers have instead lapsed into silence on the subject.

There are scores upon scores of prophecies contained within the pages of the Bible regarding the restoration of the State of Israel, including those found in Ezekiel 5:5, Amos 9:15, Leviticus 26:27-45, and Deuteronomy 28:36-68. One of the greatest of all Hebrew prophets, Isaiah, dedicated many of his prophecies found in Isaiah 40–66 to Israel and its restoration in the last days.

One of Isaiah's lesser-known prophecies is found in Isaiah 19:17-18. It mentions various wars between Egypt and Israel, in which the Egyptians will be in fear of the Jews. This passage of Scripture indicates that these wars would not occur until *after* the Jews had resettled in Palestine. Certainly the Suez Canal war of 1956, the Six-Day War of 1967, and the Yom Kippur War of 1973 all could be said to fulfill this prophecy. In each case, Egypt suffered humiliating defeats at the hands of Israel's military. That is one reason why President Sadat of Egypt sought to negotiate a peace settlement with the Jews. He had come to realize his troops were no match for Israel's.

It was common knowledge among the prophets of the Bible that the Jews would one day return to the Promised Land. The prophet Jeremiah provided details concerning Israel's eventual return to the land when he prophesied:

> Now therefore, thus says the LORD, the God of Israel, concerning this city of which you say, "It shall be delivered into the hand of the king of Babylon by the sword, by the famine, and by the pestilence": Behold, I will gather them out of all countries where I have driven them in My anger, in My fury, and in great wrath; I

will bring them back to this place, and I will cause them to dwell safely (Jeremiah 32:36-37 NKJV).

This is why we have seen, in our lifetime, millions of Jews emigrating from various nations from around the world and settling in the State of Israel. The prophet Ezekiel made it clear that even though Israel would be dispersed among the nations and turn her back and rebel against God, her people would one day return to the land in order to make God's holy name known to all.

> Therefore say to the house of Israel, "Thus says the Lord GOD: 'I do not do this for your sake, O house of Israel, but for My holy name's sake, which you have profaned among the nations wherever you went. And I will sanctify My great name, which has been profaned among the nations, which you have profaned in their midst; and the nations shall know that I am the LORD,' says the Lord GOD, 'when I am hallowed in you before their eyes. For I will take you from among the nations, gather you out of all countries, and bring you into your own land. Then I will sprinkle clean water on you, and you shall be clean; I will cleanse you from all your filthiness and from all your idols. I will give you a new heart and put a new spirit within you; I will take the heart of stone out of your flesh and give you a heart of flesh. I will put My Spirit within you and cause you to walk in My statutes, and you will keep My judgments and do them. Then you shall dwell in the land that I gave to your fathers; you shall be My people, and I will be your God. I will deliver you from all your uncleannesses. I will call for the grain and multiply it, and bring no famine upon you. And I will multiply the fruit of your trees and the increase of your fields, so that you need never again bear the reproach of famine among the nations. Then you will remember your evil ways and your deeds that were not good; and you will loathe yourself in your own sight, for your iniquities and your abominations. Not for your sake do I do this,' says the Lord GOD, 'let it be known to you. Be ashamed and confounded for your own ways, O house of Israel!'" (Ezekiel 36:22-32 NKJV).

A number of other important biblical prophecies point to the rebuilding and subsequent desecration of the Jewish temple. The prophets Daniel and Ezekiel both foretold the destruction of the temple in Jerusalem that would occur during the Great Tribulation in the last days. These prophecies do not refer to the temple built by Solomon, for it was already demolished at the time Daniel and Ezekiel gave their prophecies. Nor do they refer to the second temple built by Herod, because that was destroyed in A.D. 70 without the other aspects of the prophecies being fulfilled. Consequently, these prophecies must refer to a *new* temple yet to be built for the purpose of Jewish worship. This new temple, or the third temple, will be constructed on the original site of the Temple Mount in Jerusalem. Its destiny is to be desecrated and destroyed by the Antichrist—an event that is prophetically referenced by Jesus in Matthew 24:15 and by the apostle Paul in 2 Thessalonians 2:4. Although plans for the rebuilding of the temple have been on hand for decades, the Jews must wait for the right political climate and must have control of the area before they can begin construction. Many prophecy scholars believe these terms will be part of the seven-year agreement between the Jews and the Antichrist mentioned in Daniel 9:27.

THE VALLEY OF DRY BONES PROPHECY

One of the most incredible of biblical prophecies can be found in Ezekiel chapter 37. This chapter precedes the forecast of the Islamic-Israeli war described in chapters 38–39. The following 14 verses are incredibly accurate in their description of the events of Israel's modern-day restoration. Once again, only God could have forecast such events with precision 2,500 years in advance:

> The hand of the LORD came upon me and brought me out in the Spirit of the LORD, and set me down in the midst of the valley; and it was full of bones. Then He caused me to pass by them all around, and behold, there were very many in the open valley; and indeed they were very dry. And He said to me, "Son of man, can these bones live?" So I answered, "O Lord GOD, You know." Again He said to me, "Prophesy to these bones, and say to them, 'O dry bones, hear the word of the LORD! Thus says the Lord GOD to these bones: "Surely I will cause breath to enter into you, and

you shall live. I will put sinews on you and bring flesh upon you, cover you with skin and put breath in you; and you shall live. Then you shall know that I am the LORD." ' "So I prophesied as I was commanded; and as I prophesied, there was a noise, and suddenly a rattling; and the bones came together, bone to bone. Indeed, as I looked, the sinews and the flesh came upon them, and the skin covered them over; but there was no breath in them. Also He said to me, "Prophesy to the breath, prophesy, son of man, and say to the breath, 'Thus says the Lord GOD: "Come from the four winds, O breath, and breathe on these slain, that they may live." ' "So I prophesied as He commanded me, and breath came into them, and they lived, and stood upon their feet, an exceedingly great army. Then He said to me, "Son of man, these bones are the whole house of Israel. They indeed say, 'Our bones are dry, our hope is lost, and we ourselves are cut off!' Therefore prophesy and say to them, 'Thus says the Lord GOD: "Behold, O My people, I will open your graves and cause you to come up from your graves, and bring you into the land of Israel. Then you shall know that I am the LORD, when I have opened your graves, O My people, and brought you up from your graves. I will put My Spirit in you, and you shall live, and I will place you in your own land. Then you shall know that I, the LORD, have spoken it and performed it," says the LORD' " (Ezekiel 37:1-14 NKJV).

Verse 11 clearly states that the bones referred to here represent "the whole house of Israel." For 1,900 years, Israel was indeed "dry bones" whose "hope was lost." All Jews were at the mercy of their host countries, whether it happened to be the United States, England, France, Russia, Poland, Germany, or elsewhere. Humanly speaking, they had essentially no chance of ever becoming their own nation. Nevertheless, the Bible said it would happen, and it did!

After receiving the command from God, Ezekiel obeyed and prophesied to this dry-boned nation scattered around the world. The words of the prophecy referring to Israel included:

- a noise
- a rattling sound

- bones coming together
- tendons and flesh appearing
- skin covering them

But there was no "breath" in them. That would come later. The prophecy as spoken by Ezekiel indicated a gradual coming together of the nation of Israel. The bodies of Jews were scattered all over this figurative graveyard that contained the bones of other civilizations now dead, such as the Hittites, Assyrians, Babylonians, Chaldeans, Medo-Persians, Romans, and so on. But the "dead bones" of Israel would be different; they would gradually leave the graveyard of dead civilizations and once again become a living nation. Indeed, this is what has happened with the resurrection of Israel in the twentieth century.

A noise and rattling sound. The single most influential event that helped to draw the Jews back to Palestine from around the world was the signing of the Balfour Declaration in 1917. Nothing creates a "noise" and "rattling sound" more than a war. But there's actually more to the story of the "noise." By 1916, World War I wasn't going well for England. The United Kingdom was desperate to find a method of manufacturing TNT quickly in order to repel the advancement of the Germans (and nothing makes a "noise" quite like TNT). A brilliant Jew named Chaim Weizmann invented a formula that made rapid production possible, which helped to change the course of the war. In return, the prime minister of England told Dr. Weizmann to name his reward. Rejecting personal recompense, Weizmann requested that Palestine be declared the national homeland for the Jewish people. As a result, the Balfour Declaration was subsequently drafted and signed on November 2, 1917.

Bones coming together. In 1917, there were fewer than 100,000 Jews living in Palestine; but that would quickly change. For the first time, the nation that controlled the land (England) gave official sanction to the scattered Jews to reclaim it. The "bones" were beginning to come together.

Tendons and flesh appearing. By the 1920s the bones were coming together but there was no meat on them. There was little national consciousness among the Jews. The government was British, although a few small Jewish unions called *kibbutzim* were beginning to crop up. However, all this changed when the Arabs began their assaults on the Jewish settlers. The defenseless

Jews marshaled together in strength and unity to resist a common foe. The strength from the "tendons and flesh" was beginning to grow.

Skin covering them. The organizational unity and ability to self-govern became apparent following the establishment of Israel as a sovereign state in 1948 and its recognition by the other living nations of the world. With skin covering the tendons and bones, the body of Israel was now recognizable, but there was still no "breath" within. This prophecy clearly indicates that Israel would be *physically* regathered before she was *spiritually* reborn.

The word *breath* (Hebrew, *ruach*), when used symbolically in Scripture, indicates spiritual life. From the time God breathed into Adam the breath of life to make him a living soul, God has been more interested in man's spiritual life than in his physical. Mankind, for the most part, operates in the opposite manner; and the Jewish emigration to Israel is no exception. Essentially, the regathering of Jews into their homeland beginning in 1917 has been primarily a physically, politically, and economically motivated experience. The majority of Jews who inhabit the Promised Land today have no "breath" in them. That is, they are not committed to God by faith and practice. Many tend to be rather secular and humanistic.

Theodor Herzl was actually an atheist, and the Zionist movement he founded was not a spiritual organization, but instead reflected strong humanistic tendencies. In fact, the Zionists in the Israeli government today frequently find themselves at odds with the orthodox rabbis and other minorities who are likely to deserve and live according to the Old Testament.

But this will one day change. It is significant that Israel is only "a breath away" from completely fulfilling Ezekiel's prophecy in chapter 37, and this fulfillment is forecasted to occur suddenly! Everything the prophets foretold could happen within the very near future. In fact, the greatest prophetic event will take place in a sudden flash and without warning.

9

BATTLE OF GOG AND MAGOG

"After many days you will be called to arms.
In the future years you will invade a land that has
been recovered from war, whose people were gathered from
many nations to the mountains of Israel."

—EZEKIEL 38:8

ONE OF THE MOST IMPORTANT PROPHECIES in the ancient Hebrew text can be found in Ezekiel chapters 38–39. According to noted Bible scholar Mark Hitchcock, this prediction, which was given to the prophet Ezekiel by God, is one of the most dramatic prophecies found in all the Scriptures.[1] It foretells of an invasion of Israel by a multitude of nations and ends with the supernatural annihilation of Israel's enemies through God's direct intervention.

Without question, Ezekiel 38–39 is the most detailed prophecy found in the Bible that outlines a future war. It is also a powerful indicator that we are living in the very period the Bible speaks of just prior to the return of Christ. As you read this text, take note of how many nations mentioned are the very countries which surround Israel today, and who are in fact the sworn enemies of God's *chosen* people.

The fulfillment of the prophecy is clearly stated as happening in the "latter years" (Ezekiel 38:8 NKJV) or "latter days" (38:16 NKJV). In other words, this forthcoming attack on Israel, meticulously detailed by Ezekiel 2,600 years ago, could be right around the corner. There is no clear indication in the text whether this battle will take place *before* the rapture of the church into heaven or *after*. All we know is that it could occur at any time.

Thomas Ice observes,

> The Battle of Gog and Magog in Ezekiel 38 and 39 is one of the most debated items in the area of biblical prophecy.... Almost every aspect of this ancient prophecy has been disputed, including whether it was fulfilled in the past or is still a future prophecy. Who are the peoples involved and how do they relate to modern nations? How should we understand the weapons described? If it is a future event, when does it take place on the prophetic timeline?[2]

Notice the list of nations involved in this invasion: Magog, Persia, Cush, Libya, Gomer, and Togarmah (Ezekiel 38:2-6). Because ancient Persia is modern Iran, the predictions seems to have definite relevance to our times. In fact, prophetic scholars have observed that never before has it seemed more likely that this prophecy is about to be fulfilled. Grant Jeffrey writes, "Today there are abundant signs that the stage is being set for the war of Gog and Magog."[3]

One of the more fascinating aspects of this divinely foretold invasion lies in trying to determine where it fits in with other end-time events. This predicted confrontation has been subjected to countless speculations over the past 26 centuries as to when and how it will occur. The battle described by Ezekiel is clearly different in a number of aspects from the Battle of Armageddon, which is described in the book of Revelation, even though both battles involve the State of Israel. As we will show, the conflict of Ezekiel 38–39 will have a much different conclusion than Armageddon, and will dramatically alter the world as we know it.

The battle described by Ezekiel is known by a number of different names, including the North-Eastern Invasion, the Russian-Islamic Invasion, or the Gog and Magog Invasion. As mentioned, the manner in which this battle concludes will ultimately prove to be unique in the annals of history. God will give indelible evidence of His existence during the closing stages of this prophesied confrontation when He supernaturally rescues Israel at the last minute from certain annihilation in an unmistakable demonstration of His power. At that moment, the world will clearly see that God is who He claims to be. In addition, this incredible event will once again confirm the fact that the Bible is indeed a book of prophecy—or as it is often called, "history written in advance." As with more than 500 Old Testament prophecies that have already been fulfilled, the reliability of the Scriptures will again be credentialed at the conclusion of this earth-shattering event, and the process of taking Bible prophecy literally will again be validated.

THE APOCALYPTIC COALITION

The armies named in the Gog and Magog prophecy are familiar to the biblical text. They can be identified as the grandchildren and great grandchildren of Noah. Magog, Tubal, Meshech, Gomer, Togarmah, Cush, and Put eventually dispersed across Asia and Eastern Europe and gave rise to nations which bore their names. Because the nations identified in Ezekiel's prophecy no longer go by these ancient names, it is necessary to determine their modern-day territorial counterparts in order to discover which countries will ultimately be part of the coalition that will march against Israel. By studying the current complex dynamics of these Middle Eastern countries and their relationships to the Jewish state, one can easily see the stage being set for the fulfillment of this incredible 2,600-year-old prophecy.

Magog, Rosh, Meshech, and Tubal

The descendants of Magog were known as the Scythians, a barbaric and savage race who inhabited central Asia and the southern portions of Russia. In Arabic, the name for the Great Wall of China is in fact *the wall of Al Magog*—which was built in order to keep those who lived in what is now Russia out of China. According to early historians such as Herodotus and Josephus, the Scythians seemed to take pleasure in the act of killing and frequently engaged in the practice of human sacrifice. The homeland of the ancient Scythians is where we today find the former Soviet republics of Kazakhstan, Kyrgyzstan, Uzbekistan, Turkmenistan, and Tajikistan. Incredibly, all five of these now independent nations are under Islamic influence with a combined population in excess of 60 million people. Islam is, of course, the sworn enemy of Israel, so the nations named in this text are pictured as enemy nations.

The fall of the Soviet Union in 1991 set the stage for these former Soviet-controlled republics to begin exercising their own agenda without the fear of repercussions from the Kremlin. In fact, the breakup of the USSR could be classified as the catalyst that may have set the wheels of Ezekiel 38–39 in motion. Most worrisome is the fact that each of these republics now controls the tactical Soviet nuclear weapons that have remained within their borders. And Kazakhstan has retained access to their intercontinental ballistic missile program, thus ranking this particular Muslim nation among the top nuclear powers in the world today.

At the time Ezekiel wrote his prophecy in the sixth century B.C., there were various groups of Rosh people who were known to exist in the areas north of the Black Sea. This, of course, would be consistent with modern-day Russia, and as we shall see, is the only non-Islamic country to partner in this doomed conspiracy. The reference in Ezekiel 38:4 to "hooks in your jaws" along with the statement "I will turn you around...and bring you out" could mean that Russia may somehow find itself coerced or forced to participate in this battle.

Both Meshech and Tubal are mentioned together several times throughout the book of Ezekiel. Although they are sometimes identified as being located in Russia as well, they more likely correspond to areas which today can be found in Turkey, another militant Islamic regime. Bible scholars also identify ancient Gomer as modern Turkey as well.[4]

Persia, Ethiopia (Cush), Libya (Put), Gomer, and Togarmah
Persia

In March 1935, the ancient land of Persia became the nation of Iran. Nearly four-and-a-half decades later, Iran officially changed its name to the Islamic Republic of Iran. Today, with its population of nearly 70 million people, Iran has become a hotbed of militant Islam and blatant anti-Semitic hatred whose fundamentalist leaders and citizens would like to see Israel eliminated as soon as possible. Iranian president Mahmoud Ahmadinejad, while speaking to a group of Islamic students on October 26, 2005, stated that "Israel must be wiped off the map." He then went on to say that "with the force of God [Allah] behind it, we shall soon experience a world without...Zionism."[5] If the Bible's 100-percent accuracy rate regarding prophecy is any indication, President Ahmadinejad will be in for quite a disappointment because when it comes time for the prophesied attempt to wipe Israel off the map, Allah, the god of Islam, will most certainly find himself overpowered by Jehovah, the God of the Bible.

Cush

Cush is a Hebrew word frequently translated in the Bible as "Ethiopia." According to both secular and biblical historians, Cush was originally located due south of Egypt where today we find the country of Sudan. While the ancient term *Cush* may apply specifically to Ethiopia, it more generally applies to the entire region south of Egypt. Although the Sudanese people themselves are divided into different factions, including Muslims and Christians, the government itself is radically Islamic. In fact, the longest war of the twentieth century is still going strong within that country, having entered the twenty-first century with no sign of letting up. Since 1955, the Islamic-controlled government has been engaged in the wholesale slaughter of its own citizens, primarily Christians, through a seemingly unending terrorist campaign that has already cost the country more than two million lives. During the first half of the 1990s, Sudan harbored terrorist leader Osama bin Laden and built numerous Islamic terrorist training facilities within its borders. Not surprisingly, Sudan fully supported Saddam Hussein's regime in Iraq during the Gulf War.

Put, Gomer, and Togarmah

Historians concur that Put was a north African nation located directly west of Egypt. This coincides today with the modern country of Libya, another Islamic nation. Finally, we have Gomer and Togarmah, territories that correspond with the area north of Israel, or modern-day Turkey.

As one can see, the stage is indeed being set for the invasion of Israel as outlined in Ezekiel 38–39. With the exception of Russia (Rosh), all the countries identified in chapter 38 are controlled by openly anti-Semitic Muslim governments who share the goal of annihilating Israel—a goal made more possible than ever with the five former Soviet republics (Magog) already having nuclear weapons and Iran (Persia) desperately trying to develop them. The Bible says the attack against the tiny country of Israel will come from all sides, and this vast network of enemy nations extends from Russia and its associated republics in the north to Iran in the east, Sudan in the south, and Libya in the west. To say that Israel's army will be greatly out-numbered would be the understatement of the century. However, this will only serve to highlight God's divine intervention when Israel's enemies are supernaturally defeated.

WHO IS GOG?

> And you, son of man, prophesy against Gog, and say, "Thus says the Lord GOD: 'Behold, I am against you, O Gog, the prince of Rosh, Meshech, and Tubal; and I will turn you around and lead you on, bringing you up from the far north, and bring you against the mountains of Israel.... You shall fall upon the mountains of Israel, you and all your troops and the peoples who are with you; I will give you to birds of prey of every sort and to the beasts of the field to be devoured. You shall fall on the open field; for I have spoken,' says the Lord GOD" (Ezekiel 39:1-5 NKJV).

Featured among the list of nations referenced in the opening verses of both Ezekiel 38 and 39 is the name Gog. Unlike the other names mentioned, which indicate specific territories, Gog instead refers to an individual and identifies him as coming from "the land of Magog" and "the prince of Rosh, Meshech, and Tubal." Gog is mentioned 11 times in Ezekiel 38 and 39 and denotes the name or title of the leader of the forthcoming invasion. He will become the most important person in this deadly coalition of nations.

The overall tone of Ezekiel's prophecy also indicates that God will supernaturally place the desire for the invasion into Gog's mind, thereby influencing his will in the matter. The only other instance recorded in the Bible of God interacting with a man in such a fashion involves the hardening of Pharaoh's heart in the book of Exodus. This hardening subsequently caused the Egyptian leader to refuse to release the children of Israel from slavery. In that case, God was able to fulfill the promises He made to Israel while at the same time demonstrating to the world His sovereignty and divine power over the situation. The same will hold true regarding the Gog and Magog invasion.

It's ironic that some think this Islamic military alliance will be headed up by someone coming out of Russia, since in the past, Arabs have been at war with the Russians in places such as Chechnya and Afghanistan. However, in this case, a shared virulent anti-Semitic and anti-God obsession might be enough to motivate the formation of the union and override any historic differences between the Arabs and Russians. From their perspective, a coalition of armies will be necessary in any event in order to overpower Israel's superior military capabilities—even though such a coalition is already prophetically doomed to fail. And if anyone should have any lingering doubts about the growth of this military confederation, he should consider the fact that Russia, in recent years, has been providing military training and intelligence to the very countries listed in Ezekiel 38. Not only that, but each of these nations now have massive stockpiles of AK-47s, surface-to-air missiles, and RPG antitank weapons—all supplied by Russian manufacturers. Most of these Islamic-controlled governments routinely use the wealth they derive from the sale of oil to purchase weapons rather than use it to help their own people. This is why the citizens of these nations continue to remain at

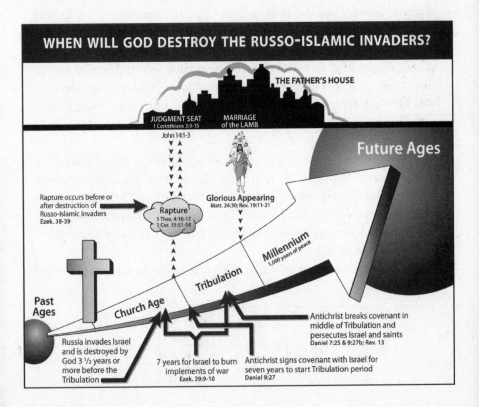

WHEN WILL GOD DESTROY THE RUSSO-ISLAMIC INVADERS?

THE FATHER'S HOUSE

JUDGMENT SEAT
1 Corinthians 3:9-15

MARRIAGE
of the LAMB

John 14:1-3

Future Ages

Rapture occurs before or after destruction of Russo-Islamic Invaders
Ezek. 38-39

Rapture
1 Thes. 4:16-17
1 Cor. 15:51-58

Glorious Appearing
Matt. 24:30; Rev. 19:11-21

Millennium
1,000 years of peace

Tribulation

Church Age

Past Ages

Russia invades Israel and is destroyed by God 3 ½ years or more before the Tribulation

7 years for Israel to burn implements of war
Ezek. 39:9-10

Antichrist signs covenant with Israel for seven years to start Tribulation period
Daniel 9:27

Antichrist breaks covenant in middle of Tribulation and persecutes Israel and saints
Daniel 7:25 & 9:27b; Rev. 13

a third-world status despite the billions that their governments receive in annual oil profits.

Gog is the leader of Magog and is identified as "the prince of Rosh" (Ezekiel 38:2). Some scholars argue that "Rosh," in this verse, is simply the Hebrew term for "head" or "chief." It is, in fact, a common Hebrew word that appears over 600 times in the Hebrew Bible. Others argue that the name *Russia* does not appear in history until the Middle Ages. Some English translations (King James Version and New International Version) translate the word *rosh* as "chief," as in chief prince. However, other English versions (New American Standard Bible and the New English Bible) translate *rosh* as a proper name, indicating a geographical location, rendering it "the prince of Rosh."

Mark Hitchcock provides extensive evidence for interpreting "Rosh" as an identification for Russia.[6] He notes that eminent Hebrew scholars C.F. Keil and Wilhelm Gesenius both held to this view.[7] The Greek translation of the Old Testament, known as the Septuagint, translates "Rosh" as a proper name. Even the International Critical Commentary on Ezekiel identifies Rosh as a place, noting this is "the most natural way of rendering the Hebrew."[8] Hitchcock also points out that the place name Rosh appears at least 20 times in ancient documents, including several Assyrian inscriptions from ancient Iraq. Therefore, he concludes, "Rosh was apparently a well-known place in Ezekiel's day. In the sixth century B.C., when Ezekiel wrote his prophecy, several bands of Rosh people lived in an area north of the Black Sea."[9]

One thing that is very clear in Ezekiel's prophecy is that the invading host will come from the "far north" (38:15). Magog will be the foremost nation in this invasion from the distant north, which will include Meshech and Tubal, the ancient Mushki and Tabal peoples of Assyria; Gomer, the ancient Cimmerians of Turkey; and Beth Togarmah ("house of Togarmah"), a region in northern Turkey.

Hitchcock provides the following chart to identify the invaders in Ezekiel 38–39.[10]

Ancient Name	Modern Name
Rosh	Russia
Magog	Russia
Meshech	Turkey

Tubal	Turkey
Persia	Iran
Cush	Sudan
Put	Libya
Gomer	Turkey
Beth-togarmah	Turkey

It is interesting to note that Iraq (ancient Babylon) is not named anywhere in this prophecy, even though Ezekiel was living in Babylon as a captive Jew at that time. What can we make of this absence? In light of current events in the Middle East, it is possible that Iraq will either 1) break into fragmented, warring pieces; 2) be taken over by Iran; or 3) become an international zone under the auspices of the United Nations?

WHEN WILL IT HAPPEN?

One problem that has puzzled prophecy experts for years about Ezekiel 38–39 is where it fits into the latter-days' timetable. There are a number of conflicting viewpoints as to exactly when this battle will take place. *Preterists* believe that the battle of Ezekiel 38–39 has already occurred. This same group believes that the Tribulation, the reign of the Antichrist, and the battle of Armageddon have already taken place as well! The problem with this viewpoint is that there has never been an invasion of Israel by the nations listed in the first six verses of Ezekiel chapter 38. Nor has any army ever been destroyed by God in the manner described within this passage of Scripture. As pointed out earlier, these events are said to take place in the *latter years* or *last days* and refer to a time when Israel has been restored to the land—making it impossible for the prophesied events to have already occurred if one takes these prophecies literally.

The remaining viewpoints are from the *futurist* perspective. Of these, the one that makes most sense is the *pretribulation* view, which means that the invasion will occur prior to the start of the seven-year Tribulation and possibly before the rapture of the church into heaven. In this scenario, the rapture remains imminent, and the events that are described in Ezekiel 39 do not conflict with the events of the Tribulation.

Should the battle of Ezekiel 38–39 take place before the start of the Tribulation, the seven-month period of cleansing the land of dead bodies and the seven-year period of burning the enemies' weapons would not in any way clash with the Tribulation events that are described in Revelation, Joel, Zechariah, and other prophetic books of the Bible. Both the cleansing of the land and the burning of the weapons (Ezekiel 39:9-16) could even overlap into the seven-year Tribulation if the battle were to take place just prior to the beginning of the Tribulation.

The decimation of Israel's Islamic enemies could open the opportunity for the rebuilding of the Jewish temple on the site of the Temple Mount in Jerusalem. In addition, the manner in which God destroys Israel's enemies may open the hearts of the Jews to the truth of the gospel, which they will be responsible for disseminating to the world during the Tribulation because Christians have been removed by the rapture.

The certainty of Ezekiel's prophecy is emphasized by these words: "It is coming! It will surely take place, declares the Sovereign LORD" (Ezekiel 39:8). Therefore, this is an unconditional prophecy. There is no doubt about its complete and total fulfillment. Ezekiel proclaimed:

> "It will come to pass in the day that I will give Gog a burial place there in Israel, the valley of those who pass by east of the sea; and it will obstruct travelers, because there they will bury Gog and all his multitude. Therefore they will call it the Valley of Hamon Gog. For seven months the house of Israel will be burying them, in order to cleanse the land. Indeed all the people of the land will be burying, and they will gain renown for it on the day that I am glorified," says the Lord GOD. "They will set apart men regularly employed, with the help of a search party, to pass through the land and bury those bodies remaining on the ground, in order to cleanse it. At the end of seven months they will make a search. The search party will pass through the land; and when anyone sees a man's bone, he shall set up a marker by it, till the buriers have buried it in the Valley of Hamon Gog. The name of the city will also be Hamonah. Thus they shall cleanse the land" (Ezekiel 39:11-16 NKJV).

There is some question about the use of the term "safely" in Ezekiel 38:8 (NKJV) to describe the manner in which the Jews are dwelling in Israel at the time of the invasion. As we've seen, Israel has never really been truly safe since the nation was restored to the land. The constant threat of terrorist attacks from its Palestinian and other Islamic neighbors has made life for the Jews precarious at best. However, verse 11 further elaborates on the safety issue by defining the land as "without walls and without gates and bars." This describes present-day Israel quite well. In addition, no one, besides Israel itself, knows for certain the types of weapons it has at its disposal. As the third-strongest military power on earth, it's possible that Israel may even consider itself relatively safe and secure for the time being. The world should not be fooled by Israel's refusal to utilize its full arsenal of weapons when the nation was attacked by Hezbollah in July 2006. That was a political decision that will most likely not be repeated.

The other views for the timing of the invasion described in Ezekiel 38–39 are not without problems. One view places the invasion during the first half of the Tribulation. While this might better explain Israel's feeling of "safety" in the land (due to its peace covenant with the Antichrist), it doesn't account for the seven years of burning the enemies' weapons, which would have to occur during the most horrendous period of the Tribulation, when the majority of earth's inhabitants are fleeing into the wilderness or being wiped out by one plague after another. In addition, the burning process would also have to continue on into the millennial kingdom for a few years in order to complete the full seven-year period of time required to burn the weapons. This possibility is unlikely in view of the nature of the millennial kingdom.

Another viewpoint attempts to equate the battle of Ezekiel 38–39 with the Battle of Armageddon. The justification given for this lies in the similar descriptions that both Ezekiel and Revelation contain regarding the feasting of the birds and beasts on the battle's carnage (see Ezekiel 39:4; Revelation 19:17-20).

While these passages are indeed similar, the other specifics about the two battles are not. Israel is most certainly not at peace during the instigation of the Battle of Armageddon, which takes place at the end of the Tribulation period. In addition, Ezekiel names specific nations that will be involved in the battle of Ezekiel 38–39 and places its location in the mountains of Israel. The Battle of Armageddon, on the other hand, involves *all* the nations of the world, who will gather in the Valley of Megiddo. In addition, the target of the attack by the Russian-Islamic armies, as foretold by Ezekiel, is Israel. In the Battle of Armageddon, it is *all* the armies of the world coming against Christ Himself as He returns to Jerusalem. Finally, there is no mention in

Ezekiel 38–39 of the Antichrist or the Messiah, both of whom play major roles in the Battle of Armageddon and its dramatic conclusion—which again suggests these two battles are not the same (Revelation 16:12-16; Revelation 19:11-16).

Another view attempts to insert Ezekiel's battle into the millennial kingdom, or the 1,000-year period of peace that follows the Tribulation. Some believe that the battle described by Ezekiel may be the same as Satan's final attempted insurrection, which occurs at the end of the millennium as recorded in Revelation 20:7-9. Although the terms "Gog" and "Magog" do appear in the text, this is an entirely different battle altogether, with at least 1,000 years in between the two. This is an ample amount of time for a new population to arise, a portion of whom will become the multitude of rebellious people who will follow Satan—the Gog and Magog of Revelation 20:8. To place Ezekiel's battle here would mean that the seven-month cleanup of

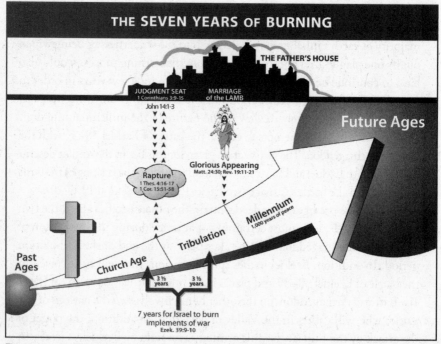

THE SEVEN YEARS OF BURNING

THE FATHER'S HOUSE

JUDGMENT SEAT
1 Corinthians 3:9-15

MARRIAGE
of the LAMB

John 14:1-3

Future Ages

Glorious Appearing
Matt. 24:30; Rev. 19:11-21

Rapture
1 Thes. 4:16-17
1 Cor. 15:51-58

Millennium
1,000 years of peace

Tribulation

Church Age

Past Ages

3 ½ years

3 ½ years

7 years for Israel to burn
implements of war
Ezek. 39:9-10

The seven years of burning these weapons may begin during the Tribulation and continue on into the early "clean up" period of the millennium. However, it is also possible, even probable, that the years of burning may begin before the rapture and continue into the Tribulation. The Jews and saints will be persecuted during the last 3 ½ years of the Tribulation, so they will not be burning the implements of war in Israel during that time. Consequently, the Russo-Islamic invasion of Israel will have to be 3 ½ to 7 or more years before the Antichrist signs the covenant with Israel that starts the Tribulation. So at least the first 3 ½ years of that burning could be during the Church Age. Before our Rapture? No one knows.

the dead bodies and the seven-year weapon-burning period would have to take place in the eternal, heavenly realm—a logical absurdity.

When all aspects of the timing of the battle in Ezekiel 38–39 are taken into consideration, it becomes clear that this event will most likely prepare the world to enter the final phase of earth's history, which includes the seven-year Tribulation followed by the 1,000-year millennial kingdom. Prophecy scholar Grant Jeffrey said it best when he made the statement, "The war of Gog and Magog is the key event that will set the stage for the completion of God's prophetic program."[11] He is, of course, referring to the Russian-Islamic attack against Israel. It is Satan's attempt to thwart God's prophetic plans for the Jewish nation, which will play a key role in the events of the last days.

THE LAST JIHAD

Mark Hitchcock has observed that "when Iran and her allies decide to invade Israel, there will be no stopping them...it will look like the biggest mismatch in history."[12] The invasion force will sweep across the Middle East and cover Israel "like a cloud" (Ezekiel 38:9). The specific details of the prophecy are amazing. The invasion will take place in the "latter days" (38:16 NKJV) at a time when Israel has been regathered from among the nations, is rebuilt, and is dwelling in safety (38:8,12).

Ezekiel 38:13 even names the nations that will object to this invasion. Sheba and Dedan were cities in ancient Arabia, implying that the Saudis will "officially" object to the attack. *Tarshish* is the Hebrew name for Europe, and the "young lions" (NKJV) may refer to European descendants living elsewhere. It is very possible this reference implies that America and Europe also will object but refuse to intervene to protect Israel from this massive horde.

God, however, will be the primary player in the great end-times drama. He Himself will rise up to defend Israel and display His glory to the world. Hitchcock writes, "These nations will arrogantly, boldly swoop down on Israel to take her land, but the only piece of land they will claim in Israel is their burial plots (Ezekiel 39:12). They will set out to bury Israel, but God will bury them."[13]

The prophet Ezekiel predicts the total defeat of the Russian-Islamic allies by both natural and supernatural means. By the end of the battle, only one-sixth of the enemy force will remain, meaning that five-sixths of the force will have been annihilated (Ezekiel 39:2). In describing the battle in detail, the prophet emphasizes several important details:

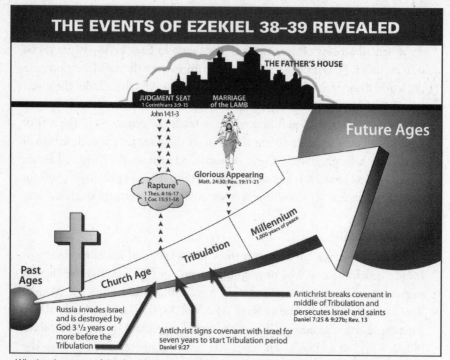

THE EVENTS OF EZEKIEL 38–39 REVEALED

THE FATHER'S HOUSE

JUDGMENT SEAT
1 Corinthians 3:9-15

MARRIAGE
of the LAMB

John 14:1-3

Future Ages

Glorious Appearing
Matt. 24:30; Rev. 19:11-21

Rapture
1 Thes. 4:16-17
1 Cor. 15:51-58

Millennium
1,000 years of peace

Tribulation

Church Age

Past Ages

Russia invades Israel
and is destroyed by
God 3 ½ years or
more before the
Tribulation

Antichrist signs covenant with Israel for
seven years to start Tribulation period
Daniel 9:27

Antichrist breaks covenant in
middle of Tribulation and
persecutes Israel and saints
Daniel 7:25 & 9:27b; Rev. 13

Whether the rapture of the church takes place before the peace treaty is signed, only God knows. It may not, so that the church can serve as "soul harvesters" after God reveals His presence by destroying Russia. Since we will not know beforehand, Christians must watch and be ready for Christ's coming at any time (Matthew 24:42).

1. *Great earthquake* (38:19-20). Ezekiel expresses it like this: "There shall be a great earthquake in the land of Israel." He goes on to explain that the mountains will fall and every wall will collapse. The traumatic effects of this gigantic earthquake will be felt worldwide. At precisely the right moment, God will intervene in human history and the timing and the magnitude of the earthquake will both confuse and destroy the invading force.

2. *Mass confusion* (38:21). In the chaos that follows the earthquake, the troops invading Israel will be thrown into total confusion. This will result in infighting among the various nations: "Every man's sword will be against his brother." The multinational and multilingual invasion forces will begin to kill each other in panic. Such reaction also occurred in the biblical account of Gideon's victory against the Midianites and Amalakites (Judges 7:22).

3. *Disease* (38:22). The prophet describes a horrible "plague" that will decimate the invading host. This lethal plague may accompany the use of biological or chemical weapons. If indeed the multinational invasion forces are thrown into mass confusion, they may well annihilate each other with the very weapons they had planned to use on Israel.

4. *Fire and brimstone* (38:22). These were the very elements God used to destroy Sodom and Gomorrah (Genesis 19:24). Whether this fire will fall from heaven supernaturally or will result from a nuclear blast, only time will tell. As we read the entire prophecy in Ezekiel 38–39, we definitely get the idea that this war escalates out of control and beyond the original intention of the invaders. Their armies will be devastated by this fiery blast.

5. *Fiery destruction* (39:6). Finally, Ezekiel predicts that a consuming conflagration of fire will fall on the nation of Magog itself. The reader is given the impression of either divine destruction or the equivalence of a nuclear blast on the homeland of the enemy perpetrator.

> *No battle in history matches the details of the battle described in Ezekiel's prophecy. Therefore, those who take biblical prophecy seriously believe this battle of Gog and Magog will occur sometime in the future.*

As we compare Ezekiel's prophecy to the events taking shape in the Middle East today, we have great reason to believe that an Iranian-Russian alliance of some type could very easily come together in the near future. The unstable situation in Iraq, the animosity of Iran, and the general tenor of Islamic extremism all point to the possibility of a major war between Israel and Iran and her allies in the near future.

THE END RESULT

When Ezekiel's prophecy comes true, Israel will become the dominant military force in the Middle East. The Islamic jihad will have been decimated by God's own divine intervention and Israel will not only survive, but succeed. It may well be at this time that the Jewish people will rebuilt the temple of the last days.[14]

The temple is the symbol of Israel's national and spiritual life. Its reconstruction in the future will make it Israel's third temple. This temple will be involved in both desecration (in the Tribulation period) and restoration (in the millennium). The temple of the Tribulation period will be built for God but will be desecrated by the Antichrist (2 Thessalonians 2:3-4). The millennial temple will be built by the Messiah and will house the return of the shekinah glory of God (Ezekiel 43:1-7).

Once the dust settles from the battle of Gog and Magog, Israel will become the major player standing on the political field of the Middle East. Her newfound power and status will attract the Western powers, who had abandoned her, to seek her favor again. In time, a powerful world figure will rise in Europe and guarantee Israel's security for the future. But before he rises on the scene, something will happen that will stun the entire world. Millions of people will suddenly disappear without warning. Then, and only then, will this figure be able to rise to power and control the world.

10

GLOBALISM AND THE WORLD ECONOMY

"Globalization is the central reality of our time.
It is coming and you can't stop it!"
—FORMER U.S. PRESIDENT BILL CLINTON[1]

THE TWENTY-FIRST CENTURY WILL GO DOWN IN HISTORY as the century of globalization. It is literally on the lips of nearly every world leader today as the only hope to save mankind from self-destruction. Former secretary general of the United Nations, Kofi Annan, stated, "If one word encapsulates the changes we are living through, it is globalization."[2] Back in the year 2000, the prime ministers of Great Britain, the Netherlands, Sweden, and the chancellor of Germany all banded together to collectively write, "We all embrace the potential of globalization. It is the future of the world as we know it."[3]

In recent years we have witnessed a staggering explosion of computer and related electronic technologies that is driving the countries of this world ever closer to complete interdependence and globalization. This can be seen in the fields of commerce, communications, banking, manufacturing, transportation, space exploration, education, and religion. Even the formerly closed country of China is beginning to spread its global influence.

The Internet is having a major part in changing the way we communicate and do business. It offers easy access to a worldwide network of information and has become the major delivery system of online education, which is revolutionizing our institutions of higher learning. But there is a dark side to all this technology. A recent study by Yahoo revealed that over 50 percent of all Internet traffic involves the accessing of pornography.

A most interesting symbol of globalization appeared on the cover of a recent book. It depicted a man, nearly naked, in what looked like deepest Africa. He was standing in a crudely made canoe with a pole in one hand, pushing himself through some water. In his other hand was a cell phone, held up to his ear. Presumably he was communicating with someone in another part of the world. Despite the planet's circumference of 24,900 miles, anyone can now reach anyone else, anywhere in the world, in less than a second.

The Bible, of course, has much to say about globalization, and none of it is good. God has to go to great lengths early in man's history to prevent globalization from taking place at the Tower of Babel. When the Bible speaks of nations, it's always in the plural sense. Having a multitude of nations is by God's design. A one-world government would inevitably find itself being controlled by a cruel one-world leader. And this is precisely what the Bible predicts is going to happen in the last days. The inhabitants who are left behind on earth following the rapture of the church will enter the seven-year Tribulation period under the command of the Antichrist, who will control a globalized world.

> *The move toward a united world is only one of the many signs that we are entering the last days.*

Globalization could be one of the most important signs of the times, especially in regards to the ecumenical movement. A united world religion will undoubtedly be the number-one enemy of true Christianity as this planet speeds ever so rapidly toward a new world order.

THE BRAVE NEW WORLD?

It was a far different world when Aldous Huxley wrote *Brave New World* in 1932. Yet the insightful Huxley saw ahead through the labyrinth of the future to a time when the World State would rise to power. In many ways, this volume was the most prophetic secular book of the twentieth century. Instead of the Big Brother of George Orwell's *1984,* Huxley foresaw a world gone mad on materialism and pleasure-seeking to deaden its conscience against the value-emptied culture of high technology. His vision of human fertilization "farms" seemed absolutely unthinkable. Artificial insemination and genetic selection sounded like something out of a science fiction horror movie, but somehow Huxley knew the seeds of the future had already been sown in the past.

Huxley pictured people of the future as mindlessly pursuing an existence controlled by machines and soothed by pleasure. The past would become meaningless and the more noble pursuits of life would give way to the all-consuming pursuit of pleasure. One of the most intriguing dialogues in his book takes place between Fanny and Lenina, the one small-talking about the changes in society and the other small-talking about clothes, belts, shoes, and jewelry. The world of the future that Huxley foresaw was one that would readily sacrifice its principles for pleasure. It was a new world, unified politically and economically, whose god was itself—the World State.

Times are changing more rapidly than ever before. So vast and sweeping are these changes that John Naisbitt calls them *megatrends*.[4] These trends of the times are affecting the whole globe simultaneously. No longer can a nation pretend to exist only in its little corner of the world. To the contrary, we are all fast becoming a global village.

Robert Reich of Harvard University recently stated, "We are living through a transformation that will rearrange the politics and economics of the coming century.... Each nation's primary political task will be to cope with the centrifugal forces of the global economy."[5] Reich sees the coming global economy as an inevitable force that will virtually sweep nationalism away. The value of a given society or an individual worker will be its or his ability to contribute to the world economy.

During the nineteenth century, closely knit networks for local economies were transformed into national economies. Today the national economies are being transformed into a global one. Initially, America led the way toward a global economy modeled on American capitalism. Today the New Europe is leading the way to a system that is often viewed as capable of setting the economic standards for the whole world.

Such ideas as "buy American" are becoming obsolete. Reich notes that when an American buys a Pontiac from General Motors, he or she "engages unwittingly in an international transaction." Of $20,000 paid to General

Motors, approximately $5,600 goes to South Korea for routine labor; $3,500 goes to Japan for advanced components; $1,500 to West Germany for styling and design engineering; $800 to Taiwan, Singapore, and Japan for small electronic components; $500 to Britain for advertising and marketing services; and about $100 to Ireland and Barbados for data processing. The balance of $8,000 goes to manufacturers in Detroit, bankers and lawyers in Washington, and General Motors stockholders.[6]

This is a typical example of how globalization already works. In time, the interconnectedness will become even more complex, touching virtually every industry in America. The interrelations of multinational corporations and the international cooperation between corporations within different nations are not a trend of the future; they are already here now.

Gilbert Williamson, president of NCR Corporation, recently said, "We at NCR think of ourselves as a globally competitive company that happens to be headquartered in the United States."[7] Like many American products, American corporations are becoming more and more internationalized. They are fast becoming part of the global web in which much of what they buy and sell comes from other countries.

For example, 40 percent of IBM's world employees are non-Americans. Robert Reich notes that IBM Japan employs 18,000 Japanese workers, and with annual sales of $6 billion, it is one of Japan's leading exporters of computers.[8] The question is whether it is an American or Japanese company—or both!

Whirlpool has an even more complex setup. It recently cut its American work force by 10 percent, shifted production to Mexico, bought Dutch-owned Phillips Appliances, and employs 43,500 people in 45 countries. Is it an American company because it has an American headquarters or because the majority of its stockholders are Americans? Or is it an international company that happens to be headquartered in America?

WHO WILL LEAD THE WAY?

No country is better positioned to lead the way in the economic boom of the twenty-first century than the United States. John Naisbitt and Pat Aburdene write,

In the global economic competition of the information economy, the quality and innovativeness of human resources will spell the difference. In this regard no country in the world is better positioned than the United States.[9]

Naisbitt and Aburdene go on to predict that well-educated, skilled information workers will earn the highest wages in history, further reinforcing an economic boom in the years ahead. They argue that the further the information economy evolves, the better the economy will do in the future as the middle class moves upward in its mobility.

In the meantime, the European Union is trying to catch up to the United States and Japan. Naisbitt and Aburdene note that the changes in Europe are economically driven as a response to the global competition. "Politics is not driving the change," they observe, "but being pulled by it."[10]

The philosophy behind the New Europe is to forge one cohesive market so these players can compete on a global scale. In order for this to become a reality, physical barriers, such as customs posts and border controls, will have to be removed. Technical barriers involving differing standards and regulations will have to be unified. And fiscal barriers, such as taxes, will have to be standardized. When the process is complete, it will mean:

- A Greek lawyer could set up a practice in Barcelona, and a Spanish shoe company could open a shop in Ireland.

- American businesspeople will be able to fly to Europe, pass through customs once, and visit all the other member countries without worrying about border controls.

- A British bank could be a partner in the Paris fashion industry.

All in all, this means there will be more competition at all levels of the single market, bringing a greater choice of goods and services at better prices. For most Europeans this will be a tremendous step forward economically. The high-speed computer network now spreading across Europe will bring the continent together in a manner no military or political action could ever hope to do. Thus, the political unification of Europe will ride on the shoulders of the economy.

IS PROPHECY BEING FULFILLED?

Evangelical Christians view the changes in Europe with some concern.

While economic cooperation could make for more peaceful relations among the European members, it also seems to link together the basic units of the old Roman Empire. Biblical prophecy warns that in the end times, ten nations will emerge out of the old Roman Empire and control Europe politically and economically. Eventually, the Antichrist himself will gain control of that ten-nation conglomerate and attempt to rule the whole world.

Daniel 2:31-35 predicts such a development in the prophecy of the great image, in which the two legs represent the East (Greek) and West (Latin) divisions of the Roman Empire and the ten toes represent the kingdom of the Antichrist. Revelation 13:17 warns of a coming world ruler, "the beast," who will control the world economy: "No one could buy or sell unless he had the mark, which is the name of the beast or the number of his name."

There is nothing morally wrong with computers, televisions, satellites, and cashless financial transactions. But many Christian are concerned about where all this might lead. It appears that we are slowly but surely becoming the victims of our own technological advancements. We are being swept quickly down the corridor of time to an ominous date with destiny. We are moving toward the inevitable globalization of our planet. This requires that national identities and interests yield to a global worldview. In time, America could find herself swept along in the tide with everyone else.

MATERIALISM VS. SPIRITUALITY

The great problem with materialism is that it also elevates an aspect of the creation to the level of idolatry. It is the worship of the almighty dollar that replaces the Almighty God. It is the belief that money and possessions will fill the spiritual void and bring meaning and purpose to one's life. In an age of selfism, issues like the selfish pursuit of money, power, and influence are daily occurrences. Television shows and movies feed the greedy desires of people, leaving little or no room for the pursuit of the spiritual values of life.

Pat Robertson is correct when he says, "The power to create money and to regulate its quantity is the power to control the life of a nation."[11] He goes on to note that when a nation gives the control of its money to an outside source, it has surrendered the control of its future to that outside authority. This is the very issue that cost Margaret Thatcher her job as Britain's prime minister. Linking the British pounds to the European Community's currency unit (euro) would in essence place Britain's economy under the control of the president of the European Community. Today, Britain is helping lead the way into the future for the European Union (EU).

Robertson argues that if the power to create and regulate money is taken away from the president and the Congress of the United States, the American people will also effectively lose democratic control of their own destiny. We in the United States dare not allow ourselves to be drawn into a global money system that is controlled by powers outside the United States, but every pressure will be brought to bear on us to do so.

In the meantime, the spiraling national debt in America is rising out of control. The entire global economy perilously survives from year to year, controlled by large central banking systems. Continued merger of these systems will eventually, in effect, create a one-world economy controlled by a handful of powerful people.

So the idea of a world superstate empowered by a world economy is fast becoming a reality. Whether it takes 10 years or 100 years to be fully in place, we are already on our way toward such a system. Globalists are already promoting the ideas of transnational corporations, universal credit systems, and a world currency controlled by a world bank. In light of this, we have every reason to ask: Can the rise of the Antichrist be right around the corner?

FALSE RELIGION AND THE NEW WORLD ORDER

The greatest conflict of our times will not be fought on a battlefield between nations. It will be fought in heavenly places between the forces of God and Satan. The spiritual conflict of our times is but an extension of the spiritual conflict that has always existed. The deceptions of Satan may appear to change from time to time, but they really remain basically the same: the lust of the eyes, the lust of the flesh, and the pride of life.

Herbert Schlossberg has correctly observed that the personification of these deceptions is idolatry. He writes, "Idolatry in its larger meaning is properly understood as any substitution of what is created for the creator."[12] He goes on to note that Western society, in turning away from Christianity, has turned to materialism and to nature itself ("save the planet") as the two great idols of our time. Yet he adds, "The technological flowering and economic expansion of the twentieth century has been accompanied by an astonishing growth in pessimism, even despair."[13]

The Bible not only predicts the rise of a false messiah (Antichrist) over the world economy, but it also predicts the coming of a false prophet over the world religious system (Revelation 13:11; 19:20). Who he is or when he will arise is a matter of speculation. Medieval Christians viewed Mohammad as the false prophet. Protestant Reformers saw the Catholic pope as the Antichrist. More recent identifications have been suggested as well, including Bill Clinton, Billy Graham, Henry Kissinger, Boris Yeltsin, and Ronald Reagan.

While it may be too soon to guess the identity of the Antichrist, one thing is certain: The cry for religious ecumenism (unity) is growing louder all the time. Some have gone so far as to try to label Hindus, Buddhists, and Muslims as fellow believers. But there is a vast difference between the uniqueness of Jesus Christ and the so-called spirituality of other religions. All other religions teach that we must (by some means) work our way to God. Christianity, by contrast, teaches that God has worked His way to us by sending His Son to die for our sins. All other religions teach, "Try harder." Christianity teaches, "Give up! And trust God to take care of your spiritual destiny."

When Jesus said, "I am the way and the truth and the life. No one comes to the Father except through me" (John 14:6), He was making a narrow and dogmatic statement. He was proclaiming His uniqueness in the plan of divine salvation. This claim and our Lord's great commission to evangelize the entire world stand in opposition to all other religious claims. They set Christianity apart from the other world religions because Christianity is based on *faith in what Christ did,* not faith in what we can do.

We must come to the end of ourselves in order to cast ourselves totally upon God's grace for our salvation. God has made provision for our sins in the sacrifice of His own Son; Jesus' death on the cross was one of substitution. He took our place of punishment and died vicariously for our sins. He also rose from the dead to triumph over sin and death, and He offers everlasting life to all who receive Him by faith.

Ecumenical attempts to ally Christianity with non-Christian religions truly nullify the unique evangelistic appeal of the church. Once we who are Christians drop our beliefs, we have nothing to offer to an unbelieving world. The uniqueness of Christianity *is* Christ! He is the *only* incarnate Son of God, and only He could die for the sins of the world and rise again from the dead. Therefore, we ought to proclaim His uniqueness as the *only* Savior of sinners!

The only real hope of turning our generation away from the mindless pursuit of materialism is to call it back to the spiritual values that give real meaning and purpose to life. That is what Jesus meant when He said, "Seek first his kingdom and his righteousness, and all these things will be given to you as well" (Matthew 6:33).

APOSTASY AND DECEPTION

The Bible warns us that before the Antichrist rises to power, there first will be a "falling away" (Greek, *apostasia*—2 Thessalonians 2:3 NKJV). Most commentators take this to be a warning that in the last days many will depart from the Christian faith. Other such warnings appear throughout the New Testament: "In later times some will abandon the faith" (1 Timothy 4:1). "In the last times there will be scoffers who will follow their own ungodly desires" (Jude 18). "In the last days scoffers will come, scoffing and following their own evil desires. They will say, 'Where is this "coming" he promised?'" (2 Peter 3:3-4).

Such warnings challenge the present generation of believers to hold fast to the truth and beware of the danger of capitulating to unbelief. In the Lord's letters to the seven churches in Revelation 2–3, He often referred to false doctrine as something He hated (Revelation 2:15 KJV). Such hatred is not mere intellectual hatred of a wrongly conceived idea, but a deep-seated hatred of errors that corrupt the truth and pull people away from Him.

These are the warnings of a God whose Word is to be taken seriously. They represent the very nature and character of God. They also express His will and purpose for this world. There is more at stake in the issue of globalism than individualism or nationalism; the ultimate question is, Whose world is this? Is it God's world or man's?

This is the very point where we who are evangelical Christians part company with globalists, New Agers, planetarians, and others who elevate the planet to the place of God. We believe the real, infinite, personal God has a plan for *His* planet. We also believe Christians are to share in that plan.

Even the Old Testament prophets saw beyond the borders of Israel to proclaim God's universal plan for the whole world. "[I will] gather all nations and tongues, and they will come and see my glory" (Isaiah 66:18). "But the

LORD rises upon you and his glory appears over you. Nations will come to your light" (Isaiah 60:2-3). "The wilderness will rejoice and blossom....it will burst into bloom....they will see the glory of the LORD" (Isaiah 35:1-2). "Israel will bud and blossom and fill all the world with fruit" (Isaiah 27:6). "In the last days the mountain of the LORD's temple will be established...and all nations will stream to it" (Isaiah 2:2).

In the New Testament, Christians are clearly commanded to take the gospel to the entire world. Jesus said, "Go and make disciples of all nations, baptizing them in the name of the Father and of the Son and of the Holy Spirit" (Matthew 28:19). He also promised, "You will receive power when the Holy Spirit comes on you; and you will be my witnesses in Jerusalem, and in all Judea and Samaria, and to the ends of the earth" (Acts 1:8).

Our Lord paralleled the *worldwide preaching of the gospel* with the timing of His second coming. He said, "This gospel of the kingdom will be preached in the whole world as a testimony to all nations, and then the end will come" (Matthew 24:14). No date is given to calculate *when* this will be fulfilled, but the promise of Scripture is clear. When the last convert to come to faith in Christ completes the body of Christ, the church age will conclude, and Christ will return to rapture the church to heaven.

Because we do not know when that process will be complete, we must be faithful to preach the gospel to all people everywhere. We can only guess how many nations are left to hear the good news, but the rapid spread of the gospel by radio, television, and satellite must be hurling us toward the end of history faster than ever before.

GOD'S PLAN FOR THE WORLD

The Bible emphasizes the fact that God has a plan for the entire world. His plan includes the people of earth as well as the planet Earth. The whole Earth is pictured as His domain (Isaiah 66:1). It is the place He created (Genesis 1:1) and where He intervenes in the affairs of man (Ephesians 1:9-10; Romans 6:8-21). It is the place to which Christ came (Hebrews 10:5) and where He lived, died, and rose again (Luke 2:11-12; 23:50-53; 24:1-6). It is also the place to which He promised one day to return (John 14:2-3; Acts 1:11).

The Earth is also pictured in Scripture as the place of the last great conflict of mankind. It is God's world, but it is also inhabited by sinful people who pollute, destroy, and defile it. Therefore, the Earth will suffer terrible cataclysmic disasters in the last days. Revelation 8:7–9:21 describes air pollution, water pollution, deforestation, and the annihilation of over half the Earth's population. The prophets described this time as the wrath of the Lord (Isaiah 13:13), the harvest of judgment (see Micah 4:11-12), and the grapes of wrath (see Isaiah 5:1-7). The book of Revelation calls its final phase the Battle of Armageddon (16:16).

The Bible tells us that the coming global holocaust will not yet be the end of the Earth. "If those days had not been cut short," Jesus said, "no one would survive" (Matthew 24:22). Christ's return will come just in time to spare the world. The prophet Zechariah tells us that the survivors of this great battle will go up to Jerusalem year after year to "worship the King, the LORD Almighty" (Zechariah 14:16).

Premillennialists believe that Jesus Christ will reign on the Earth from Jerusalem for 1,000 years (Revelation 20:1-6). We believe this millennial kingdom will be a literal kingdom on the earth because that's what the Bible promises (see Revelation 5:10). The 1,000-year reign of Christ will be marked by unparalleled peace and prosperity on Earth.

Only after the millennium of Christ's rule will the Earth finally be destroyed by fire (2 Peter 3:10-12, Revelation 20:7-9). Or, as the King James Version puts it, the "elements will melt with fervent heat" (2 Peter 3:10). After this, the Bible points to a new heaven and a new Earth as the home of the righteous (see 2 Peter 3:13; Revelation 21–22). The Earth is not our final destiny. We are just pilgrims passing through this vale of tears. Our real destiny is our eternal home in heaven. Yet this does not mean we should be careless with our mandate to care for the Earth. It is still our Father's world, and as the hymn writer put it: "Though the wrong seems oft so strong, God is the Ruler yet."[14]

Man may conceive new world orders or global economies or international systems, but the only world order destined to survive for eternity will be the kingdom of God. The Bible resounds with this great promise: "The kingdom of the world has become the kingdom of our Lord and of his Christ, and he will reign for ever and ever" (Revelation 11:15).

FUTURE POLITICAL SUPERSTATE

"We do not want another committee. We have too many already. What we want is a man of sufficient stature to hold the allegiance of all people, and to lift us out of the economic morass in which we are sinking. Send us such a man and, be he God or the devil, we will receive him."[1]

—PAUL HENRI SPAAK, FORMER PRIME MINISTER OF BELGIUM

THE FUTURE DESIGN OF THE EUROPEAN UNION will lead to economic, monetary, and political unity in the near future. "The vision of a 'United States of Europe' set out in Winston Churchill's famous speech at Zurich in 1946 remains our objective in the process of European unification," announced Helmut Kohl of Germany in *The European,* Europe's first "national" newspaper.[2] Using the reunification of Germany as his model, Chancellor Kohl urged the peoples of Europe to move ahead as quickly as possible.

On February 7, 1992, the 12 nations of the European Community signed a unity treaty paving the way for the fulfillment of the full political union of Europe. The signing of the European Union treaty lays the foundation for a European federation that could one day rival the economic and political influence of the United States.

The modern European Union began when six nations signed the Treaty of Rome in 1957. These six were Belgium, Germany, Luxembourg, France, Italy, and the Netherlands—with a combined population of over 220 million people. In 1973, Denmark, Ireland, and Great Britain joined what was then called the European Economic Community (EEC), bringing 66 million more people into what would become the European Union (EU). In 1981,

Greece joined the EEC. In 1986, Portugal and Spain were added. Less than 30 years after the signing of the Treaty of Rome in 1957, the New Europe was 336 million strong. In 1995, Austria, Finland, and Sweden joined the EU, bringing the total population to 362 million in 15 member nations, with more being added almost yearly.

THE POINT OF NO RETURN

"We have now passed the point of no return," announced Dutch prime minister Ruud Lubbers when the document was signed.[3] Despite earlier restraint, even the British are showing excitement about the New Europe. British foreign secretary Douglas Hurd said, "This is a good treaty for Britain and for Europe." Portugal's prime minister Anibal Silva called the treaty a "wise balance between ambition and prudence, idealism and pragmatism."[4]

The significance of the new treaty is that it sets in motion Europe's desire to increase its international political force in proportion to its growing economic clout. It also sets in motion plans for monetary union, including a central bank and a single European currency. No matter how it shapes up, the future means a New Europe.

Helmut Kohl views this transition with great optimism. He writes, "Love of freedom and respect for the dignity and rights of neighbors is the cornerstone of a future Pan-European order of peace, in which all peoples live together in liberty."[5]

Going even further, Germany's foreign minister Hans-Dietrich Genscher states, "The mentality of the nation-state has been consigned to the past."[6] He adds that Europe "must contribute to a New World Order which focuses on the individual, his dignity and inalienable rights."[7] Genscher also says, "We want to strengthen the United Nations. We want a New World Order in which the human rights covenants of the United Nations will ensure protection for civil rights equality with economic and social rights."[8]

The mind-set of Europe now seems to be cast in cement. Europeans are moving toward economic, political, and military unity, ultimately under the banner of the United Nations. While secularists see this as a renewed hope for international peace and cooperation, many evangelical Christians view it with great concern. The global superstate prophesied in Scripture seems to be just around the corner.

WHERE IS IT ALL HEADED?

Ours may not be exactly the world envisioned by George Orwell or Aldous Huxley, but it is certainly a mix of the two. Somewhere between the Big Brother of Orwell's *1984* and the world gone mad on materialism in a value-emptied culture of high technology in Huxley's *Brave New World* we find the current tension in our world today. Malachi Martin, a former Vatican professor, calls it the great "Millennial Endgame."[9] He predicts a final confrontation between the secularists, socialists, and the church for the new global hegemony which is now upon us. "The competition is about who will establish the first one-world system government that has ever existed in the society of nations," Martin writes.[10]

These are not just the sentiments of a few speculators. Everyone is talking about the possibility of a new world order. Former president George H. W. Bush spoke frequently about this concept. Ever since *Time* magazine (December 11, 1989) flashed the headline "Building a New World Order," the idea has been a hot topic among Christians and secularists alike.[11]

> *With the collapse of the Soviet empire, the unification of Germany, and talk of a United States of Europe, we are certainly on the threshold of a new day of international politics.*

The wheels of change are spinning rapidly across Europe these days. "Europhoria" is the mood of exuberance that has captured the spirit of cooperation within the European Community. The unification in 1992 of the 12 members of the EEC created the largest trading bloc and free-market economy in the world.

Time magazine declared, "Project 1992 has given fresh momentum...to taking Western Europe further down the road to unity."[12] *U.S. News & World Report* predicted a unified Western Europe by 2000.[13] Today, we are there. Europe has the potential, for the first time in some 1,500 years, to become a unified power—the political superstate of the future.

CAN EAST MEET WEST?

The great issue facing the attempt to build a New Europe is whether the Eastern bloc countries can become full participants with the Western bloc. This will not be an easy process. Old hatreds, fears, and jealousies divide

Europe into a patchwork quilt of ethnic rivals and bitter enemies. But let us suppose that the newly united Germany and Russia are able to lead the way in that unification. The end result would be the largest and most powerful nation on earth—a Europe that stretches from the Atlantic to the Pacific!

The world has obviously come to a great crossroads today. On the one hand, peaceful cooperation seems to be the spirit of the times. Everyone is talking democracy, capitalism, peace, and prosperity. For Europe, the future looks brighter than it has since the days of the Roman Empire. On the other hand, the seeds of world destruction may well have been sown to such a degree that there is no retreat from disaster.

The decisions we make today will determine the course of action we take in the years ahead. We who are evangelical Christians need to remind the world of its great spiritual needs. The spiritual emptiness of atheistic communism has left the people of Europe in a vacuum of value-emptied secularism. No matter how hard people try to experiment with freedom, democracy, and free-market enterprise, they cannot build a great society without God. If the democratization of Eastern Europe results in nothing more than empty materialism without God, we have truly failed to set it free from the worst kind of tyranny. Only when the people discover Christian beliefs, values, and principles can they hope to be successful.

Europe is at the crossroads. Which way she goes in the future may well depend on what Christians do today to make Christ and His church known there. Without Him there is no real hope for the future; with Him there could yet be time for spiritual revival on the continent that has so often forgotten God.

TWENTY-FIRST CENTURY EUROPE

Arno Froese, executive director of Midnight Call Ministries, himself a European by background, believes the coming European powerhouse will produce the empire of the Antichrist. He writes, "Not capitalism, or communism, but social-capital democracy is becoming the driving force which will supersede all others."[14] Froese adds, "The phenomenal growth of Europe is based strictly on economy and finance at this point in time."[15]

European economic strategists project the European Central Bank (ECB) will control the new currency.[16] Shortly thereafter the euro will become the dominant world currency. In the meantime, Froese explains that we already have a world currency in the form of credit cards. He notes,

> When you take your credit card and travel to any part of the world, you can instantaneously buy virtually anything in any currency.... We don't have to wait for a one world financial system to appear because it is already working right now at this moment! The world already functions as a global community.[17]

In his controversial but insightful book *How Democracy Will Elect the Antichrist,* Arno Froese correctly emphasizes the relationship of the Antichrist to the New Europe. He writes, "One of the most difficult things to grasp for citizens who have lived under a free system, such as democracy, is the fact that it will usher in the new age of the Antichrist—a temporary time of peace and prosperity."[18]

One of the great ironies of history will be the fact that the most successful human system ever devised will be used by Satan to bring the world dictator to power. While this may sound incredible to some, recall that Adolf Hitler was originally chosen by the German people in a democratic election. Once elected to power, some leaders quickly eliminate further elections and maintain power by force.

Froese astutely observes, "The new European power structure will fulfill the prophetic predictions which tell us that a one world system will be implemented. When established, it will fall into the hands of the Antichrist."[19] What we are now witnessing in Europe are the initial steps leading to the global system of the last days.

WHY EUROPE?

Much has been written about the empire of the Antichrist. Some believe it will be centered in Babylon (Iraq). Others have suggested America as a possibility. But the Bible itself clearly identifies Europe as the location of the final phase of Gentile world power. Americans are quick to ask: "But what about the United States? Where is it in biblical prophecy?" But the better question is, Where is Europe in biblical prophecy?

The United States did not exist when the Bible was written. Therefore, it does not clearly appear in the prophetic Scriptures. One can only make a case for America in prophecy by associating it with Europe. As a nation of predominantly European transplants, the United States could possibly qualify as the "young lions" of Tarshish (Ezekiel 38:13 KJV). The United States also could be included with general references to the revived Roman Empire. Otherwise, prophecy students have to stretch a great deal to find the United States in the biblical text.

By contrast, Israel is the *center* of all biblical prophecy. She is also the "land bridge" between Europe, Asia, and Africa. Therefore, biblical history—as well as biblical prophecy—is focused on Israel and her relationship to those nations that played a role in the Old Testament record.

Note also that Daniel's visions for the nations were given to him in regard to their relationship to Israel. He was taken captive to ancient Babylon by King Nebuchadnezzar in 605 B.C. While still a student in training, Daniel interpreted the king's dream about the great statue with a head of gold, arms of silver, belly of brass, legs of iron, and feet of iron and clay. According to the dream, the statue was obliterated by a great rock that filled the whole Earth (Daniel 2:31-35).

As Daniel stood before the great Nebuchadnezzar to interpret the king's dream, Daniel told the king that God had revealed "what will happen in days to come" (Daniel 2:28). Daniel proceeded to tell Nebuchadnezzar that Babylon was the head of gold and that after Babylon would arise three other kingdoms inferior to his own. Out of the fourth kingdom would come ten toes, "partly strong and partly brittle" (Daniel 2:42). "In the time of those kings," Daniel explained, "the God of heaven will set up a kingdom that will never be destroyed.... It will itself endure forever" (Daniel 2:44). Notice that the supernatural rock, cut out without hands, will strike the ten toes of the statue.

About 50 years later, in 553 B.C., Daniel himself had a vision in which he saw "four great beasts" come up from the sea (Daniel 7:2). These beasts represented the same four great empires Nebuchadnezzar saw in his dream in Daniel 2. What Nebuchadnezzar saw as a beautiful statue, Daniel saw as wild animals about to tear each other apart. He saw a winged lion, which symbolized Babylon. Next came a lopsided bear, stronger on one side than the other. He later identified this second kingdom as Media and Persia (Daniel 8:20). The two arms of the statue and the lopsided appearance of the bear aptly described the dual empire that would eventually be dominated by Persia. Next he saw a four-winged leopard, which he later identified as Greece (Daniel 8:21). Finally, he saw a fourth beast with ten horns (Daniel 7:7). Its teeth were iron, the same metal as the fourth kingdom in the statue, and it subdued "whatever was left."

THE FINAL EMPIRE

Although the fourth beast is never identified by Daniel, it is clearly Rome, the empire that succeeded Greece. The statue's two legs (Daniel 2:33) seem to indicate the division of Rome into Eastern (Greek-speaking Constantinople) and Western (Latin-speaking Rome) empires. The ten horns of this beast parallel the ten toes of the statue (Daniel 2:39-43). They are identified as "ten kings who will come from this kingdom" (Daniel 7:24), after whom will rise "another king," an eleventh king, who will blaspheme God and persecute the saints. Many Bible scholars believe this person is the Antichrist.

Evangelical Christian scholars generally interpret the ten horns of Daniel's fourth beast and the ten toes of the statue as being synonymous. Both grow out of the fourth empire and represent the final phase of it. Premillennialists see a gap of time, the church age, separating the legs and the toes, with the stone falling at the *second* coming of Christ, during the final stage of Gentile history.

In Nebuchadnezzar's vision, the stone fell on the ten toes and obliterated the statue to dust. The wind then blew the dust away, and the stone filled the whole Earth. Premillennialists argue that this has not yet happened. They believe this is a prophetic picture of Christ's return to set up His kingdom on Earth at the beginning of the millennium (His 1,000-year reign).

In the meantime, attempts to identify the ten kings pictured by the toes and horns have proven futile. Daniel's vision of the four beasts clearly dates them at the end of time. The little horn that rises out of the ten horns (Daniel 7:7-8) is said to continue for "a time [one], times [two], and a half a time" (Daniel 7:25), or three-and-one-half times. This is the same time given for the persecution of the "woman" by the beast in the apocalypse (Revelation 12:14; 13:5). This is generally seen to be the three-and-one-half years or 42 months of the Great Tribulation (the last half of the seven-year-Tribulation period).

Daniel's prophecies clearly indicate the dominance of Israel by the Gentiles until the time of the Antichrist. Since Rome (legs) and the revived Rome

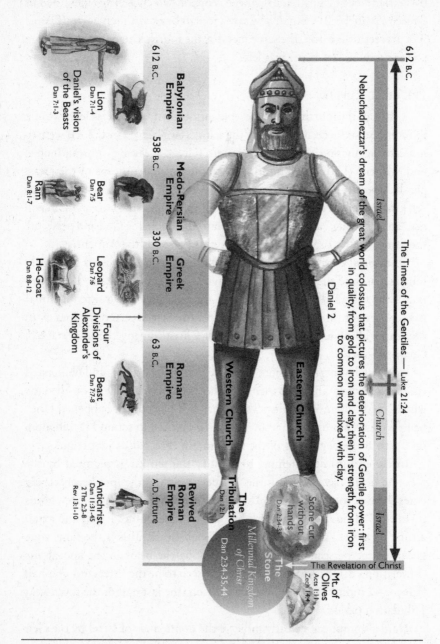

612 B.C.

Nebuchadnezzar's dream of the great world colossus that pictures the deterioration of Gentile power: first in quality, from gold to iron and clay; then in strength, from iron to common iron mixed with clay.

Daniel 2

The Times of the Gentiles — Luke 21:24

Israel

Church

Israel

612 B.C.

Babylonian Empire

Lion
Dan 7:1-4

Daniel's vision of the Beasts
Dan 7:1-3

538 B.C.

Medo-Persian Empire

Bear
Dan 7:5

Ram
Dan 8:1-7

330 B.C.

Greek Empire

Leopard
Dan 7:6

He-Goat
Dan 8:8-12

Four Divisions of Alexander's Kingdom

63 B.C.

Roman Empire

Beast
Dan 7:7-8

Western Church

Eastern Church

A.D. future

Revived Roman Empire

Antichrist
Dan 11:31-45
2 Ths 2:3-8
Rev 13:1-10

The Tribulation
Dan 12:1

Stone cut without hands
Dan 2:34-35

The Stone
Dan 2:34-35, 44

Millennial Kingdom of Christ

The Revelation of Christ

Mt. of Olives
Acts 1:11
Zech 14:4

From Tim LaHaye and Thomas Ice, *Charting the End Times* (Eugene, OR: Harvest House Publishers, 2001), p. 88.

(toes) of the ~~last~~ days are indicated by Daniel's prophecies, Daniel clearly points to ~~Europe/Rome~~ as the final Gentile power. Whether the final form of the ~~fourth~~ kingdom (toes) includes America we can only guess.

WHEN WILL THIS HAPPEN?

Daniel's ~~prophecy~~ of the 70 weeks (Daniel 9) tells us that God put Israel's future on ~~a clock~~. God told Daniel that "seventy 'sevens' ['weeks,' KJV] are decreed ~~for~~ your people [Israel] and your holy city [Jerusalem] to finish transgression, to put an end to sin, to atone for wickedness, to bring in everlasting ~~righteousness~~, to seal up vision and prophecy and to anoint the most holy ~~(Daniel~~ 9:24).

The ~~prophecy goes~~ on to predict that seven "sevens" will pass as Jerusalem ~~is rebuilt, and 62~~ more "sevens" will pass, for a total of 69, until the Anointed ~~One (Messiah)~~ will be cut off. This leaves one "seven" left for the future. ~~Interpreters~~ generally interpret these "sevens" (Hebrew, *shabua*) to refer ~~to seven~~ years; thus 70 sevens would equal 490 years. By ~~this cal~~culation we can determine that the span of time from Arta~~xerxes' decree to~~ Nehemiah to rebuild Jerusalem 445 BC to when the Me~~ssiah is cut~~ off (crucified) is 483 years (69 "sevens"). That would bri~~ng us to~~ the Jewish calendar, which was the year of Christ's cr~~ucifixion.~~

~~...~~ was composed of 360 days or 12 months of 30 ~~...~~ the figures used to calculate that three-and-one-half ~~...~~ 1,260 days (Revelation 12:6-14). By following the ~~...~~ have calculated the beginning date of the Persian ~~...~~ to send Nehemiah to rebuild the city of Jerusalem ~~...~~ Nisan 1 (Jewish calendar) or March 14, 455 B.C. The ~~...~~ Nisan 10 (Jewish calendar), or April 6, A.D. 32. ~~...~~ decree of Artaxerxes and the triumphal entry of ~~...~~ exactly 173,880 days (or 7 x 69 prophetic years of ~~...~~ the days inclusively according to Jewish practice, ~~...~~ first person to work out this computation, and ~~...~~ premillennial scholars since.[21] According to ~~...~~ seven years (483 years) ended on the Sunday of ~~...~~ to Jerusalem. That initiated His final rejection ~~...~~ crucifixion.

DANIEL'S SEVENTIETH WEEK

This leaves one "week" or unit of seven years yet to come. Many pre-millennialists locate this final seven years in the Tribulation period, which will come after the rapture of the church. During these final seven years, God's prophetic clock for Israel will begin to tick again.

Notice that the prophecy of the "seventy sevens" was given Daniel in regard to his people (the Jews) and their holy city (Jerusalem) of the 490 years have to do with *Israel,* not the church. This focuses ention on the fact that Israel plays a prominent role in the Tribulatio d.

In the meantime, Daniel was told that "war will continue u end" (Daniel 9:26). That's what Jesus said in the Olivet Discourse (M 6). Thus, we can conclude that the "times of the Gentiles" will b y wars and by the rise and fall of the four major empires present chapters 2 and 7.

Then Daniel was told of a "ruler" ("prince," KJV) who was and "destroy the city and the sanctuary" (Daniel 9:26). Th make a covenant (peace treaty) with Israel, then break it in t the seventieth "seven" and turn against Jerusalem and cause " and "desolation" (Daniel 9:27), which Jesus also referred to in H message (Matthew 24:15).

THE ABOMINATION OF DESOLATION

After Daniel's time, the Jews returned to Jerusalem and recon temple under Zerubbabel and rebuilt the city walls under Nehe the Old Testament revelation closed. For nearly 400 years there revelation from God—these years are frequently called the silen prophet Malachi, in the final verses of the Old Testament, ha Elijah would come again to turn people's hearts back to God (6). And several prophets had pointed to the coming of this An (Messiah). But as the Old Testament closes, we are left waiti promises to be fulfilled.

During the intertestamental period (the silent years), the severely persecuted by the Selucid ruler Antiochus IV Epipha B.C., he vented his wrath on the Jews, as predicted by Daniel, and the temple (Daniel 11:21-35). (According to historians, this included offering a pig on the holy altar.) Certainly this was an a to the Jews (Daniel 11:31), but notice that it happened *before* the Messiah ever arrived. Soon afterward, the Jews revolted under the leadership of Judas Maccabaeus, whose family fought Antiochus's army from 168 to 165 B.C. Their exploits are recorded in the apocryphal books of 1 and 2 Maccabees. After three years of fighting, the Jews were able to restore worship in Jerusalem, and they cleansed the temple with a great Feast of Dedication (Hanukkah) on December 25, 165 B.C.

Eventually the Romans conquered Jerusalem and installed Herod the Great as a puppet king under their authority. In an attempt to appease the Jews, Herod had the temple remodeled and greatly expanded. The initial work took about ten years, but construction continued from 20 B.C. to A.D. 64. The edifice was a magnificent sight. Jesus' own disciples were so impressed with it that they called Jesus' attention to the building. But our Lord shocked them when He predicted that eventually the temple would be destroyed, and not one stone of it would be left standing (Matthew 24:1-2).

When the Jews revolted against Rome in A.D. 66, the angry Romans decided to retaliate by destroying the temple and burning Jerusalem to the ground. The devastation was carried out in A.D. 70 by Titus, the son of Emperor Vespasian. Jerusalem's occupants were either slaughtered or enslaved. A subsequent revolt in A.D. 135, led by Jesus bar Kochba, a Jewish zealot, also failed. Hadrian, who was Rome's emperor at the time, had the rubble of Jerusalem plowed under, and he erected a Roman city, Aelia Capitolina, from which all Jews were banned. Certainly this was another abomination and desolation.

Over the centuries that followed, either the Romans, the Arabs, or the Crusaders held Jerusalem. The temple was never rebuilt, and the Jews were scattered in the Great Dispersion (*Diaspora*). Yet Daniel's prophecy looks all the way down the corridor of time until the end. He tells us there is one great abomination of desolation still to come.

THE GREAT TRIBULATION

As Jesus looked down this same corridor of time that Daniel saw to the end of the present age—an age that would be launched by the preaching of the gospel message and by the empowerment of His disciples with the Holy Spirit—He warned of a time of great tribulation or great distress that would come upon the whole world (Matthew 24:15-28). The "abomination of desolation" (Matthew 24:15 KJV) refers to when Antiochus Epiphanes profaned Jewish temple worship during the intertestamental period (Daniel 9:27; 11:31; 12:11), foreshadowing an even more serious abomination that would occur in the future. Whereas Antiochus offered an unclean pig on the sacred altar of the temple, the Antichrist will offer himself (2 Thessalonians 2:4).

This future act of desecration by the Antichrist will signal the beginning of the Great Tribulation on earth. Note that Jesus saw this as a future event, so this abomination is not limited to the past actions of Antiochus. Nor was the abomination fulfilled in the Roman destruction of Jerusalem in A.D. 70, since our Lord tied it to the "great tribulation" (KJV) that is "unequaled from the beginning of the world until now—and never to be equaled again" (Matthew 24:21). Our Lord went on to explain that the devastation of the Great Tribulation will be so awful that unless those days were cut short, no one would survive (Matthew 24:22).

Jesus further described this coming day of trouble as a time when the sun and moon are darkened and the heavens will be shaken (Matthew 24:29). His description runs parallel to that found in Revelation 16:1-16, where the final hour of the Tribulation is depicted by atmospheric darkness, air pollution, and ecological disaster. These cataclysmic events will accompany the return of Christ.

THE RAPTURE CHANGES EVERYTHING

"The Lord himself will come down from heaven...
and the dead in Christ will rise first. After that, we who are
still alive and are left will be caught up together with them in
the clouds to meet the Lord in the air."

—1 THESSALONIANS 4:16-17

ONE OF THE MOST EXCITING and compelling prophetic events described in the Bible is the rapture of the church. It will occur instantaneously and without warning. Suddenly, millions of people will be missing—caught up to heaven to meet the Savior in the air. While this prophetic promise is of great comfort and assurance to believers, it will have a shocking impact on those who are left behind.[1]

The rapture will be sudden, but not secret. When Christ calls His living saints to be with Him, millions of people will suddenly vanish from the earth. An unbeliever who happens to be in the company of a believer at that moment will know that his friend has vanished. There will be worldwide recognition of the fact that millions of people have disappeared. Pandemonium, fear, and confusion will impact the entire global community. The ensuing outcry of sorrow, loss, and panic will result in titanic chaos.

Conversations will end in mid-sentence, telephones will suddenly go dead, people will be missing everywhere—all over the world. This will be the most publicized event in all human history. The global media will face the challenge of covering what to many will appear to be a great tragedy.

Families, friends, and co-workers will be separated from each other without warning, for there are no prophetic "signs" that precede the rapture. It is an imminent event that could happen at any moment.

Explanations of what has occurred will probably include a wide range of possibilities—alien abductions, laser-beam weapons, terrorist attacks, divine judgment. Ultimately, the Bible indicates that God Himself will send a "powerful delusion so that they [unbelievers] will believe the lie and so that all will be condemned who have not believed the truth but have delighted in wickedness" (2 Thessalonians 2:11-12). The original text specifically states "the lie," indicating that it is a specific lie that will be told to explain away the rapture.

Now, people will still be converted to Christ after the rapture. Revelation 7:3-14 names 144,000 Jewish converts and "a great multitude that no one could count" (verse 9) of Gentiles who are saved "out of the great tribulation" (verse 14). Those who reject Christ and believe "the lie" will all be lost. Therefore, the Tribulation period will involve seven years of deception and divine judgment. But it will also include a great harvest of souls who will realize that the rapture has come and they have been left behind. Many in Israel will be converted through the ministry of the two witnesses who will proclaim the gospel of salvation in Jerusalem for 42 months, or 3-and-a-half years (see Revelation 11:3-12).

Unfortunately, the vast majority of people will not believe the truth of the gospel. The book of Revelation describes them as resisting God and refusing to repent (6:16; 9:21; 14:20; 16:9). Thus, a final separation will occur between the saved and the lost during the Tribulation period. The saved will be sealed by God Himself but the lost will receive the mark of the beast (Revelation 13:16-18).

THE GLOBAL IMPACT

Christians refer to the rapture as the "blessed hope" (Titus 2:13). But for unbelievers it will be the greatest catastrophe in human history.

Think of what will happen to the world economies, stock markets, the workforces, the militaries, and the police forces. America in particular would suffer great loss because of the high percentage of Christians who live in the

United States. Consider what happened to the city of New Orleans after Hurricane Katrina. The entire city was emptied within a few days, and much of it has yet to recover. Imagine such an impact on every major city in America and the rest of the world.

Can you imagine life on this earth immediately after the rapture? Almost every major profession will have many of its members absent on the first day of work after the rapture. The health-care industry will be without a large percentage of its work force. Many police, fire, rescue, and emergency personnel, as well as teachers, farmers, business people, and more will be gone. All countries in the world that enjoy sizable Christian populations will experience social and cultural collapses of devastating proportions. These countries will never be the same. Second Thessalonians 2:7 mentions that the Holy Spirit is the restraining force of society—through the church, the Holy Spirit holds back the spread and growth of evil. When the church is raptured, the world will be left in the hands of many who could care less about values or their consciences.

The rapture will result in global political, social, and economic chaos. New alliances, political power shifts, and emerging leadership will have to attempt to restore law and order to the planet. This will pave the way for the Antichrist to rise to power, probably in Europe. The rapture would leave America as a second- or even third-rate power and the Western world, making it likely America could turn to Europe for leadership and stability.

And what about the rapture's impact on Europe? It is no secret that Christianity is rapidly eroding in Europe today. Churches and cathedrals are sparsely attended. Religion is viewed as an anachronism from a bygone era. The educational system is dominated by atheism, secularism, humanism, relativism, and mysticism. A tarot card reader, psychic interpreter, or crystal ball gazer receives more intellectual respect in Europe than do most pastors and priests. This is not to deny that there are pockets of revival and evangelism happening in Europe today, but the vast majority of Europeans pay little serious attention to the Christian religion these days.

Surveys that chart religious beliefs, practices, and church attendance in Europe, with the exception of Ireland, reveal very low levels of involvement.[2] Church attendance, for example, is under 20 percent of the population in England, Spain, and Germany and less than ten percent in Norway, Belgium, Sweden, Finland, and Italy. France and Denmark are the lowest at four percent. By contrast, church attendance in America is nearly 60 percent. Polls have stated that as many as 95 percent of Americans believe in God, and 84 percent believe in heaven. Among Europeans, such beliefs are below 50 percent. Statistics on evangelical Christianity show as much as a ten-to-one disparity between Americans and Europeans.

In regard to natural disasters and their impact on the economy, consider the results of Hurricane Katrina on New Orleans and the Gulf Coast. Insurance companies estimated the damage at $25 billion. However, when financial experts considered the loss of revenue while the reconstruction was in progress, the *Financial Times* estimated the total loss at $100 billion.[3]

It would be impossible to estimate the financial impact of the rapture on the global economy. Multiplied trillions of dollars would be lost. Property values would deflate while the general economy would be thrust into an inflationary period. It's no wonder that a superior power would find it necessary to take control of the global network of international commerce and even political, religious, and military control of the entire world in order to bring any semblance of stability out of the ensuing chaos.

WHAT IS THE RAPTURE?

The Bible clearly teaches that there is coming a time when Christ will return for His own. Notice, for example, 1 Thessalonians chapter 4, where the apostle Paul provides us with these details:

> This we say to you by the word of the Lord, that we who are alive and remain until the coming of the Lord will by no means precede those who are asleep. For the Lord Himself will descend from heaven with a shout, with the voice of an archangel, and with the trumpet of God. And the dead in Christ will rise first. Then we who are alive and remain shall be caught up together with them in the clouds to meet the Lord in the air. And thus we shall always be with the Lord. Therefore comfort one another with these words (verses 15-18 NKJV).

From this passage of Scripture we can see that there are five stages to the rapture:

1. The Lord Himself will descend from heaven with a shout and with the sound of a trumpet.

2. The dead in Christ will rise first.

3. Then we who are alive and remain on earth will be caught up together with them in the clouds.

4. We will meet the Lord in the air.

5. And we will always be with Him.

The English word *rapture* comes from the Latin *rapto,* which is a translation of the Greek word *harpazo* in the Greek New Testament. All these terms mean "caught up" or "snatched away." While the word *rapture* does not appear in English translations of the Bible, the concept of the rapture certainly does. It is a sudden and instantaneous event that occurs without warning.

The apostle Paul also unveiled what he referred to as a "mystery" pertaining to the rapture. He explained that there would be some Christians who would not sleep (die), but whose bodies would be instantly transformed:

> Behold, I tell you a mystery: We shall not all sleep, but we shall all be changed—in a moment, in the twinkling of an eye, at the last trumpet. For the trumpet will sound, and the dead will be raised incorruptible, and we shall be changed. For this corruptible must put on incorruption, and this mortal must put on immortality (1 Corinthians 15:51-53 NKJV).

At the moment of the rapture, the bodies of all believers who have died with faith in Christ since the day of Pentecost will suddenly be transformed into new, living, immortal, resurrected bodies. Even those whose bodies have long since decayed or whose ashes have been scattered across the oceans will receive a new body. This new body will be joined together with the person's spirit, which Jesus brings with Him from heaven. Then the bodies of those who are alive on earth and have accepted Christ as their Savior will also be instantly translated into new, immortal bodies.

Notice the similarity between the descriptions of the rapture in 1 Corinthians 15:51-53 and 2 Thessalonians 4:15-18. When Christ comes to take His church (all believers) to heaven in fulfillment of His promise in

John 14:1-3, He will include all New Testament believers, both the living and the dead.

Together, all believers will be instantaneously transported into heaven to meet their loved ones "in the clouds" and then to meet the Lord in the air. Those who have rejected the gift of salvation through Jesus Christ and remain on earth will witness a miraculous event of astonishing proportions—the sudden mass disappearance of millions upon millions of Christians from the face of the earth.

Scripture calls the rapture "the blessed hope" (Titus 2:13) because this event provides comfort not only to those believers who are concerned about the coming tribulations of the last days, but also to those who long to be reunited with their departed loved ones who shared faith in Christ.

The second coming, which encompasses both the rapture and the glorious appearing, is one of the most significant events mentioned in the entire Bible. The New Testament alone has 321 references to this awesome event, making it the second-most prominent doctrine presented in Scripture after the doctrine of salvation. The concept of the second coming is clearly taught in both the Old and New Testaments. It is also affirmed in the doctrinal statement of every major Christian denomination. On average, the New Testament mentions the second coming in one out of every 30 verses, and it is mentioned in every chapter of 1 and 2 Thessalonians, the first books written for the early church. Moreover, all nine New Testament authors mention the second coming, and 23 of the 27 New Testament books reference it. Obviously God intended His church to be motivated to holiness, evangelism, and missionary concern by the study of the second coming of Christ. If Jesus is indeed coming again, we who are Christians need to let the world know it.

THE PHASES OF THE SECOND COMING

When the biblical references pertaining to the second coming are carefully examined, it becomes clear that there are two distinct phases to Christ's return. Let us state that again: There are not two second comings. There are two *phases* to the second coming: 1) the rapture of the church, and 2) the return of Christ with the church. Remember, there were also multiple events related to the first coming of Christ: birth, life, ministry, death, resurrection, and ascension. These were all part of the first coming of Christ. And the reason it's clear the rapture and the return are two separate phases is because there are simply too many conflicting elements in these two phases to merge them into a single event.

In the first phase, Jesus will come suddenly to rapture His church into the air and take all believers to His Father's house in fulfillment of His promise in John 14:1-3. There, they will appear before the judgment seat of Christ (2 Corinthians 5:9-10) and participate in the marriage supper of the Lamb (Revelation 19:1-10).

During this time, those left behind on the Earth will experience the trials of the horrendous seven-year intermission (the Tribulation). Then at the end of the seven years, Christ will come "in His glory" (Matthew 25:31). This time, "all the nations" will see Him (verse 32). The apostle Paul distinguishes between these two phases in Titus 2:13, where he refers to the rapture as "the blessed hope" and the return of Christ to the Earth as the "glorious appearing."

There are some theologians who attempt to dismiss the multiphase aspect of Christ's second coming. They place both the rapture and the glorious appearing at the end of the Tribulation and hold to what is known as the posttribulation view of the rapture. In this scenario, Christians will be required to live through the horrors of the Tribulation. To put it bluntly, this view teaches that Christ (the Bridegroom) will beat up the church (the bride) in order to get her ready for their heavenly marriage!

In order to hold this view, one must ignore numerous passages of Scripture. A careful study of the many biblical references to the second coming clearly shows that the rapture and the glorious appearing are two separate phases of the second coming. Consider the following differences:

The Rapture of the Church	The Glorious Appearing
1. Christ comes *for* believers in the air.	1. Christ comes *with* believers to the Earth.
2. All Christians on Earth are translated into new bodies.	2. There is no translation of bodies.
3. Christians are taken to the Father's house in heaven.	3. Resurrected saints remain on the Earth.

4. There is no judgment upon the Earth.	4. Christ judges the inhabitants of the Earth.
5. The church will be taken to heaven.	5. Christ sets up His kingdom on Earth.
6. It could occur at any time (it is imminent).	6. It cannot occur until the end of the seven-year Tribulation.
7. There are no signs preceding it.	7. There are numerous signs preceding it.
8. It affects only believers.	8. It affects all humanity.
9. It is a time of joy.	9. It is a time of mourning.
10. It occurs before the "day of wrath."	10. It occurs after the "day of wrath."
11. Satan is not bound, but wreaks havoc on the Earth.	11. Satan is bound in the abyss for 1,000 years.
12. Christians are judged at the judgment seat of Christ.	12. Christians have already been judged at the judgment seat of Christ.
13. The marriage supper of the Lamb takes place.	13. The marriage supper of the Lamb has already taken place.
14. Only Christ's own will see Him.	14. All those on Earth will see Him.
15. The seven-year Tribulation follows.	15. The 1,000-year millennium follows.

WHEN WILL THE RAPTURE OCCUR?

While various views exist as to *when* the rapture will occur (before, during, or after the Tribulation), all must acknowledge that there *will* be a rapture. The only real question is, When will it occur? Christ must return at some point to resurrect the "dead in Christ" and rapture the living believers in order to take us all to the Father's house in heaven, as Jesus promised in John 14:1-3.

There are a number of reasons to believe the rapture will occur *before* the Tribulation begins, including these promises of a pretribulational rapture:

1. *The Lord Himself promised to deliver us.* Revelation 3:10 says, "Because you have kept My command to persevere, I also will keep you from the hour of trial which shall come upon the whole world, to test those who dwell on the earth" (NKJV). The Greek word *ek,* which literally means "out of," is translated in this passage as "from." In other words, it is the Lord's intention to keep the church *out of* the Tribulation. Therefore, the rapture must occur before the Tribulation begins.

2. *The church is to be delivered from the wrath to come.* The apostle Paul tells us in 1 Thessalonians 1:10 that we should "wait for His Son from heaven, whom He raised from the dead, even Jesus who delivers us from the wrath to come" (NKJV). The context of this particular passage is the rapture. The church must therefore be removed from the earth before the Tribulation begins in order to be delivered from the wrath to come.

3. *The church is not appointed to wrath.* According to 1 Thessalonians 5:9, "God did not appoint us to wrath, but to obtain salvation through our Lord Jesus Christ" (NKJV). Likewise, as Jesus Himself promises in Revelation 3:10, "I also will keep you from the hour of trial which shall come upon the whole world, to test those who dwell on the earth" (NKJV). Once again, the context of these passages is the rapture. Since the Tribulation is prophesied as a time of God's wrath, and since Christians are not appointed to wrath, it follows that the church must be raptured out of the way before the Tribulation begins.

4. *The church is absent in Revelation chapters 4–18.* Revelation chapters 4–18 detail the events of the Tribulation. The church is mentioned 17 times in the first three chapters of Revelation, but after John (who is a member of the church) is taken up to heaven at the beginning of chapter 4, the church is not mentioned or seen again until chapter 19, when she appears at the marriage supper with Christ in heaven and then returns to earth with Jesus at His glorious appearing. Why is the church missing from those chapters? Because the church doesn't go through the Tribulation. She will be raptured out before it begins.

It is also interesting to note that while the church is mentioned frequently in the first three chapters of Revelation, Israel is mentioned only once in passing (2:14). Then after the church is raptured, Israel is mentioned or referred to 26 times in the next 16 chapters. That is understandable when you recognize that the Tribulation period is for Israel, not the church.

5. *If the church is raptured at the end of the Tribulation, there will be no one left to repopulate the Earth during the millennium.* Just before the millennium begins, all sinners (those who reject Jesus Christ as Savior) who have survived the Tribulation will be cast into hell, according to Matthew 25:46. Should the rapture occur at the end of the Tribulation, as some believe, all Christians would be taken from the earth as well, leaving no one on earth with a natural body to help repopulate the planet during the millennium. The problem here is that we know from numerous Old Testament passages, as well as from Revelation 20:7-10, that there will be a huge population explosion during the millennium. Where do these people come from? The answer is that those who miss the rapture and become believers during the Tribulation (thanks to the preaching of the 144,000 Jews and the two witnesses) and survive to the end will repopulate the earth. While large numbers of believers will be martyred during the Tribulation, there will be some who survive. These people will not be raptured at the end of the Tribulation in some sort of posttribulational rapture, but rather, will enter Christ's millennial kingdom with their natural bodies to help populate that kingdom. In order for this to be possible, the rapture must take place prior to the Tribulation instead of at the end of it.

6. *Only the pretribulational view fulfills Jesus' simple command: "Keep watch" until He comes (Matthew 24:42).* He never told us to watch for the Antichrist, the Tribulation, or the final judgment. He clearly told His disciples to watch for Him to return and to be ready for Him to come for them (Matthew 24:44).

7. *The rapture before the Tribulation also fulfills Jesus' statement to the disciples in the Upper Room, in which He promised to take*

them home to the Father's house in heaven (John 14:1-4). "I am going there to prepare a place for you. And if I go and prepare a place for you, I will come back and take you to be with me that you may also be where I am," Jesus explained. Judas had already left the room en route to betray Jesus. Therefore, he was not a recipient of the rapture promise that Jesus affirmed to the 11 believing disciples.

Among the chief characteristics of the rapture is that it will be sudden and will catch people by surprise. "Of that day and hour no one knows" (Matthew 24:36 NKJV), which is why we should live so as to "be ready, for the Son of Man is coming at an hour when you do not expect" (Matthew 24:44 NKJV). Only a pretribulation rapture preserves that at-any-moment expectation of His coming. Indeed, throughout the ages, the rapture has appeared imminent to Christians of every generation. Nothing could better motivate us to holy living and fervent evangelism than to believe that Jesus could come today. And one day He will! The trumpet will sound, the archangel will shout, and we will all go home to be with Jesus.

THE RAPTURE IS NOT NEW

For God to rapture people to heaven is not new in biblical history. It has already occurred three times.

Enoch: "Enoch walked with God; and he was not, for God took him" (Genesis 5:24 NKJV). The New Testament adds, "By faith Enoch was taken away so that he did not see death, 'and was not found because God had taken him'; for before he was taken he had this testimony, that he pleased God" (Hebrews 11:5 NKJV).

Elijah: "Then it happened, as they continued on and talked, that suddenly a chariot of fire appeared with horses of fire, and separated the two of them; and Elijah went up by a whirlwind into heaven" (2 Kings 2:11 NKJV).

Jesus Christ: After His resurrection, Jesus ascended into heaven:

> Now when He had spoken these things, while they watched, He was taken up, and a cloud received Him out of their sight. And while they looked steadfastly toward heaven as He went up, behold, two men stood by them in white apparel, who also said,

"Men of Galilee, why do you stand gazing up into heaven? *This same Jesus,* who was taken up from you into heaven, will so *come* in like manner as you saw Him go into heaven" (Acts 1:9-11).

All three events describe a natural body of flesh being changed and translated into the presence of God. In our finite body we cannot enter His presence, and thus a sudden translation becomes necessary.

No one saw Enoch's translation. He was walking on the earth one moment, and in the next he was translated. Elijah's rapture was witnessed by his successor Elisha (2 Kings 2:11-14), and Jesus' ascension into heaven was witnessed by many of His disciples (Acts 1:9-14).

The term for the rapture (Greek, *harpazo*) is also used to speak of the experiences of Paul, when he was "caught up" into the third heaven (2 Corinthians 12:2-4) and Philip, when he was "caught away" after witnessing to the Ethiopian eunuch (Acts 8:39).

THE POWER OF THE RAPTURE

Those in Christ who will be snatched up in the rapture do not have to generate their own power. As in all our dealings with God, He provides the impetus. He has not assigned our resurrection to an angel or specifically created being, for "the Lord *Himself* will descend from heaven *with a shout*" (1 Thessalonians 4:16 NKJV). In other words, *He* will do the raising. In John 5:21,28-29 He clearly claimed to possess resurrection power for Himself, using it as proof that He was God in human flesh.

Since so much is at stake here, including our eternal destiny, notice a most comforting truth. Christ has *already* demonstrated His power to raise the dead. Three times He did it during His brief ministry on Earth, the most dramatic of which was Lazarus in John 11:43 when He commanded, "Lazarus, come forth!" (NKJV). To the astonishment of the people of Bethany, a man who had been dead for four days was delivered from his tomb. When that same experienced voice shouts from heaven at the rapture, all those who are in Christ by faith will respond.

The Lord Jesus Himself declared, "I am the resurrection and the life. He who believes in Me, though he may die, he shall live. And whoever lives and believes in Me shall never die" (John 11:25-26 NKJV). For almost 2,000 years, all Christians who died immediately went in spirit to heaven to be with Christ. As Paul said, "To be absent from the body [is] to be present with the Lord" (2 Corinthians 5:8 NKJV). When Christ comes for His church, He will resurrect the bodies of deceased saints, unite them with their soul and spirit in heaven, and translate all living believers to be with them and Him forever. No wonder the early Christians used to greet each other with "Maranatha!" ("The Lord is coming!").

Many who do not believe in the pretribulational rapture falsely assume there will be *no rapture at all*. But if one takes seriously passages such as 1 Thessalonians 4:17, which says "We who are alive and remain will be caught up together with them in the clouds to meet the Lord in the air" (NASB), he or she is forced to conclude that there will be a rapture. The only real debate is over *when* it will occur.

Arguments raised against the rapture on the basis that it is difficult to conceive of what it would be like for millions of people to suddenly disappear are irrelevant. Jokes about bumping your head on the ceiling, or false teeth being left behind, or hundreds of car accidents suddenly occurring are inconsequential in light of the fact that Scripture clearly states that we will be "caught up" (Greek, *harpazo*) into the air.

There *will* be a rapture! The only serious questions are: 1) When will it occur? And 2) what is its relationship to the return of Christ at the time of His second coming? If it can be proved that the body of believers (the church) will be "caught up" into heaven and that this "gathering together" (Greek, *episunagoges,* see 2 Thessalonians 2:1) is a separate event from the return of Christ in judgment, the pretribulationist has more than adequately made his case.

THE NATURE OF HIS COMING

The New Testament clearly teaches that Jesus Christ will "come again" (John 14:3 KJV) and "appear the second time" (Hebrews 9:28 KJV) for His own. He promised this to His disciples in the upper room. "I go to prepare a place for you," the Lord said, "and if I go and prepare a place for you, I will come again, and receive you unto myself; that where I am, there ye may be also" (John 14:2-3 KJV).

This is the Lord's first clear indication that He will return specifically and uniquely for His own. And there is no reference in John 14 to a return in judgment upon the world. The promise of His return is specifically given to comfort the disciples during the time of His absence. Many believe this is the first clear reference in our Lord's teaching to the rapture of the believers.

In Hebrews 9:28, the writer also has believers in view when he states: "So Christ was once offered to bear the sins of many; and unto them that look for him shall he appear the second time without sin unto salvation" (KJV). Again, the promise of our Lord's return for His own is sounded loud and clear.

At least nine terms are used in the New Testament to describe the return of Christ:

1. *Ho erchomenos*—"the coming one," as in Hebrews 10:37: "For yet a little while, and he that shall come will come" (KJV).

2. *Erchomai*—the act of coming. Used often of Christ's return (Matthew 24:30; John 14:3; 2 Thessalonians 1:10; Jude 14; Revelation 1:7; 22:20).

3. *Katabaino*—to "come down" or descend, as in 1 Thessalonians 4:16: "The Lord himself shall descend from heaven with a shout" (KJV).

4. *Heko*—result of one's coming, to have "arrived," as in Revelation 3:3: "I will come like a thief."

5. *Parousia*—denotes arrival and presence (of a ruler) as in 1 Thessalonians 2:19: "What is our hope, or joy, or crown of rejoicing? Are not even ye in the presence of our Lord Jesus Christ at his coming?" (KJV).

6. *Apokalupsis*—meaning to "unveil" or "uncover." Rendered "appearing" (1 Peter 1:7 KJV) or "coming" (1 Corinthians 1:7 KJV), or "revelation" (Revelation 1:1 KJV). Involves the unveiling of His divine glory.

7. *Phaneroo*—to "appear" (John 21:1 KJV), or be "manifested" (1 John 3:5 KJV), as in 1 John 3:2: "It doth not yet appear what we shall be: but we know that when he shall appear, we shall be like him; for we shall see him as he is" (KJV).

8. *Epiphaino*—to "appear" in full light or visibility. Denotes the "brightness" of His coming (2 Thessalonians 2:8 KJV) and the

glory of "that day...unto all them also that love his appearing" (2 Timothy 4:8 KJV).

9. *Horao*—to "see with the eyes," or to "appear" visibly, as in Hebrews 9:28: "unto them that look for him shall he appear the second time" (KJV).

These terms are often used interchangeably to refer to the rapture or the return of Christ. One cannot build a convincing case for the distinction between the two events merely on the basis of the terms themselves.

THE TIME OF HIS COMING

Most evangelical Christians agree as to the *nature* of Christ's coming, but there is substantial disagreement about the *time*. Millard Erickson observes, "The one eschatological doctrine on which orthodox theologians most agree is the second coming of Christ. It is indispensable to eschatology. It is the basis of the Christian's hope, the one event which will mark the beginning of the completion of God's plan." [4]

The New Testament picture of our Lord's return emphasizes at least six distinct aspects of the time of His coming. These may be summarized as follows:

1. *Future.* The entire emphasis of the New Testament points to a future return of Christ. He promised "I will come again" (John 14:3 KJV). The angels promised He would return (Acts 1:11). The apostles taught the certainty of His future return (Philippians 3:20; Titus 2:13; 2 Peter 3:3-8; 1 John 3:2-3).

2. *Imminent.* The return of Jesus Christ is always described as potentially imminent or "at hand" (Revelation 1:3; 22:10 KJV). Every generation of believers is warned to be ready for His coming, as Luke 12:40 states: "Be...ready also: for the Son of man cometh at an hour when ye think not" (KJV). Believers are constantly urged to look for the coming of the Lord (Philippians 3:20; Titus 2:13; Hebrews 9:28; 1 Thessalonians 5:6).

3. *Distant.* From God's perspective, Jesus is coming at any moment. But from the human perspective it has already been nearly 2,000 years since He was on Earth. Jesus hinted at this in the Olivet

Discourse in the illustration of the man who traveled into a "far country" (heaven) and was gone "a long time" (Matthew 25:14,19 KJV). Peter also implies this in his prediction that men will begin to scoff at the second coming after a long period of time has passed (2 Peter 3:3-9).

4. *Undated.* While the rapture is the next major event on the prophetic calendar, it is undated, as is the glorious appearing of Christ. Jesus said: "Of that day and hour knoweth no man, no, not the angels of heaven" (Matthew 24:36 KJV). Later he added, "It is not for you to know the times or the seasons" (Acts 1:7 KJV).

5. *Unexpected.* The mass of humanity will not be looking for Christ when He returns (Matthew 24:50; Luke 21:35). They will be saying "peace and safety" (1 Thessalonians 5:3) when they are suddenly caught unprepared by His return. So unexpected will His return be that "as a snare shall it come on all them that dwell on the face of the whole earth" (Luke 21:35 KJV).

6. *Sudden.* The Bible warns that Jesus will come "as a thief in the night...[and] then sudden destruction" will come upon the unbelieving world (1 Thessalonians 5:2-3 KJV). His return for the bride will occur in a flash: "In a moment, in the twinkling of an eye...for the trumpet shall sound, and the dead [believers] shall be raised incorruptible, and we [living believers] shall be changed" (2 Corinthians 15:52 KJV).

The return of Christ is a series of events fulfilling all end-time prophecies. These include predictions of His coming *for* His church and His coming *with* His church. The concept of the rapture is expressed in the biblical terms "caught up" (Greek, *harpazo*) and "gathered together" (Greek, *episunagoges*).[5] Greek scholars Hogg and Vine observe that *harpazo* is the same verb used of Paul ("whether in the body, or out of the body," 2 Corinthians 12:3 KJV); Philip ("Spirit...caught away Philip," Acts 8:39 KJV); and the man child ("caught up unto God," Revelation 12:5 KJV).[6] This explains that *harpazo* conveys the idea of force suddenly exercised and is best rendered "snatch" (John 10:28-29), where Jesus promises that no one can "snatch" His own out of His hand. He alone does the "snatching" at the time of the rapture!

By contrast, *episunagoges* refers to that which results from the "catching up" (*harpazo*). Once caught up into the clouds, Christians will be "gathered together" with the Lord. In commenting on 2 Thessalonians 2:1, Hogg and Vine observe, "Here it refers to the 'rapture' of the saints into the air to meet and to be forever with the Lord."[7] The basic meaning is to "assemble together." The raptured church is pictured as the great "assembly" (synagogue) in the sky. Milligan observes:

> The world goes back to the saying of the Lord in Mark 13:27 ("gather His elect"), and is found elsewhere in the New Testament only in Hebrews 10:25, where it is applied to the ordinary religious assembling of believers as an anticipation of the great assembling at the Lord's coming.[8]

IT'S A MATTER OF WHEN

Of course there is a rapture! There can be no valid system of biblical eschatology without a rapture. The church will be "caught up" and "gathered together" with her Lord. The only real debate is over the question of when. Any eschatological system that dismisses the rapture has forfeited the essential biblical teaching that Christ will come and snatch away His bride to the great assembly in heaven.

13

THE RISE OF THE BEAST

"Then I saw the beast and the kings of the earth and their armies gathered together to make war."
—Revelation 19:19

BIBLICAL PROPHECIES CLEARLY PREDICT the rise of the Antichrist in the end times. Many people believe those days have already begun. As civilization speeds toward its final destiny, the appearance of a powerful world ruler is inevitable. The ultimate question facing our generation is whether he is already alive and well and moving into power. How can we know who he is? What clues are there to his identity? When will he make his move to control the global economy and world politics?

The Bible predicts that worldwide chaos, instability, and disorder will increase as we approach the end of the age. Jesus predicted there would be "wars and rumors of wars,...[and] famines and earthquakes in various places" (Matthew 24:6-7). Dr. Ed Dobson observes, "The Bible also predicts that this chaos will pave the way for the rise of a new world leader who will be able to negotiate world peace and deliver on the promise of security and harmony. This world leader is a person whom most Bible students call the Antichrist."[1]

Ironically, the term *Antichrist* appears only in 1 John 2:18-22 and 4:3. The apostle John uses it both in the singular ("the antichrist") and in the plural ("many antichrists"). John indicates that his readers have already heard that *the* Antichrist is coming in the future. Then he surprises them by announcing that *many* antichrists have already come. He defines these lesser antichrists as liars who deny that Jesus is the Christ (2:22). In this sense, an antichrist is any false teacher who denies the person and work of Jesus Christ. Such teachers are truly *anti* ("against") Christ.

In 1 John 4:1-3, John warns us to test the spirits to make sure they are from God. Again, he warns that many false prophets (Greek, *psudoprophetes*) are "gone out into the world" (verse 1). These are the people who don't acknowledge that Jesus is from God. In this sense, John announces that the "spirit of the antichrist...is already in the world" (verse 3).

SPIRIT OF THE ANTICHRIST

In the broadest use of the concept of the "spirit of the antichrist," we can say with certainty that it is already at work. It is this anti-Christian spirit that does everything it can to undermine, deny, and reject the truth about Jesus Christ. That spirit has been here since the first century, actively opposing the Word of Christ on earth.

There can be no doubt that the biblical writers believed the "spirit of the antichrist" was alive and well in the first century A.D. Therefore, they were not surprised by opposition, persecution, and even martyrdom. They were convinced that the spiritual war between Christ and Antichrist had already begun.

Grant Jeffrey provides numerous examples of early Christian references to the Antichrist in the *Apocalypse of Peter,* the *Didache,* the *Ascension of Isaiah,* and the *Pseudo-Titus Epistle,* as well as various church fathers such as Irenaeus, Jerome, and Hippolytus.[2] Irenaeus, who studied under Polycarp, who in turn was discipled by the apostle John, said the Antichrist shall come as "an apostate," the very embodiment of "satanic apostasy."[3]

From the very beginning of the Christian era, believers were convinced that a world ruler would eventually come on the scene who was the embodiment of Satan. The book of Revelation (chapters 12–13) presents an "unholy trinity" that aligns Satan (vs. Father), Antichrist (vs. Son), and false prophet (vs. Holy Spirit). Thus, the real power behind the Antichrist is Satan. The "father of lies" is the perpetrator of the human manifestation of the world's greatest liar and the source of the lie that will condemn multitudes under divine judgment (2 Thessalonians 2:11-12).

TITLES OF THE ANTICHRIST

The person we commonly refer to as the Antichrist is actually known by several names and titles throughout the Bible. Each of these provides a glimpse of the many facets of his diabolical character and nature and presents a portrait of the Antichrist in a series of word pictures that leave little to the imagination.

The Beast

"I saw a beast coming out of the sea. He had ten horns and seven heads, with ten crowns on his horns, and on each head a blasphemous name" (Revelation 13:1).

The Man of Destruction

"Don't let anyone deceive you in any way, for that day will not come until the rebellion occurs and the man of lawlessness is revealed, the man doomed to destruction" (2 Thessalonians 2:3).

The Lawless One

"Then the lawless one will be revealed, whom the Lord Jesus will overthrow with the breath of his mouth and destroy by the splendor of his coming" (2 Thessalonians 2:8).

The Abomination

"So when you see standing in the holy place 'the abomination that causes desolation,' spoken of through the prophet Daniel..." (Matthew 24:15).

The Little Horn

"While I was thinking about the horns, there before me was another horn, a little one, which came up among them; and three of the first horns were uprooted before it. This horn had eyes like the eyes of a man and a mouth that spoke boastfully" (Daniel 7:8).

The Insolent King

"In the latter part of their reign, when rebels have become completely wicked, a stern-faced king, a master of intrigue, will arise" (Daniel 8:23).

The Ruler Who Is to Come

"After the sixty-two 'sevens,' the Anointed One will be cut off and will have nothing. The people of the ruler who will come will destroy the city and the sanctuary" (Daniel 9:26).

The Despicable Person

"He will be succeeded by a contemptible person who has not been given the honor of royalty. He will invade the kingdom when its people feel secure, and he will seize it through intrigue" (Daniel 11:21).

The Strong-Willed King

"The king will do as he pleases. He will exalt and magnify himself above every god and will say unheard-of things against the God of gods. He will be successful until the time of wrath is completed, for what has been determined must take place" (Daniel 11:36).

The Worthless Shepherd

"I am going to raise up a shepherd over the land who will not care for the lost, or seek the young, or heal the injured, or feed the healthy, but will eat the meat of the choice sheep, tearing off their hoofs. Woe to the worthless shepherd, who deserts the flock!" (Zechariah 11:16-17).

The Antichrist

"Dear children, this is the last hour; and as you have heard that the antichrist is coming, even now many antichrists have come.... Who is the liar? It is the man who denies that Jesus is the Christ. Such a man is the antichrist" (1 John 2:18,22).

A great deal has been written about the prefix *anti* in connection with the Antichrist. It can mean either "against" (in opposition to) or "instead of" (in place of). That's because this relates to figuring out his identity. If he is the head of a Gentile world government, then he is most likely to be a Gentile himself. If he is a false messiah who is accepted by the Jews, then it would stand to reason that he would be Jewish.

Richard Trench writes, "The distinction, then, is plain...*antichristos* (antichrist) denies that there is a Christ; *pseudochristos* (false Christ) affirms himself to be Christ."[4] The biblical picture is that he is *both*. Initially, he presents himself as the "savior" of Israel by making a covenant to protect her (Daniel 9:27). In this manner, he appears to be her long-awaited Messiah. But in reality, he is against all that the messianic prophecies foretell about the true Messiah.

ANTICHRIST'S NATIONALITY

Whether the Antichrist is a Jew or a Gentile is not clearly answered in the New Testament. Most Bible prophecy scholars believe he will be a Gentile because...

1. He will lead the European union of Gentile nations (Daniel 7:8-24).

2. His covenant with Israel will promise Gentile protection for Israel (Daniel 9:27)

3. His rule is part of the "time of the Gentiles" and their domination over Israel (Luke 21:24).

These passages make it clear that the Antichrist will lead the Western powers, but they do not specifically designate him as a Gentile. It is entirely possible that he could be of Jewish origin or nationality and still be a European or American Jew who leads the final form of the future world government. The fact that Daniel 11:37 says he will not regard the "God of his fathers" (KJV) can also be translated "gods of his fathers" (NIV). This makes his background inconclusive. However, the typical exegesis of Daniel 11:37 has focused on his atheistic beliefs, regardless of whether he is a Jew or Gentile.[5]

Stephen Miller writes, "This verse states that Antichrist will reject whatever religion is practiced by his ancestors."[6] Charles Feinberg, on the other hand, prefers the reading "God of his fathers" (KJV), noting that this is the usual expression in the Old Testament for the "God of Abraham, Isaac, and Jacob." Feinberg adds, "This is the name of God that is used in the prayer book of the Jews to this very day."[7] Either way, the Antichrist is clearly said to be an unbeliever.

The books of Daniel and Revelation associate the Antichrist with a confederation of ten European nations that correspond in some way to the old Roman Empire. Daniel 2:31-45 symbolizes this by the ten *toes* of the great statue in Nebuchadnezzar's dream. Daniel 7:19-28 and Revelation 13:1-9 symbolize this by the ten *horns* on the beast.

In Daniel's prophecies, the Antichrist is always associated with the final phase of the Roman Empire (fourth kingdom). In Revelation 17:9, he is identified with a city that sits on "seven hills" (Rome). While John uses the symbolic term "Mystery Babylon" to describe this city, he clearly indicates that he is talking about Rome.

Arno Froese points out that the entire social-political-legal structure of the Western world is essentially European. He writes,

> The populations of the USA, Canada and South America are made up mainly of European descendants. Our governments are based on Roman principles.... We do well to remember that America, North and South, most of Africa, and Australia are a political reality due to...the greatest power structure ever, Europe.[8]

It is not difficult, given the current international structure and the need for a human leader to guarantee a peaceful coexistence, to imagine a powerful world ruler coming on the scene in the immediate future.

The spirit of Antichrist is at work today, attempting to lure this world into the lap of Satan. Harvard theologian Harvey Cox has warned, "The greatest seducers of history all had one thing in common: they could use the natural needs and instincts of another person for their own selfish ends." He argued that seduction is the most callous form of exploitation because "it tricks the victim into becoming an unwitting accomplice in his own seduction."[9]

ANTICHRIST'S GENIUS AND POWER

The Antichrist will be seemingly the most incredible leader the world has ever known. On the surface he will appear to be the epitome of human genius and power. Arthur W. Pink writes,

> Satan has had full opportunity afforded him to study fallen human nature.... The devil knows full well how to dazzle people by the attraction of power.... He knows how to gratify the craving for knowledge.... He can delight the ear with music and the eye with entrancing beauty.... He knows how to exalt people to dizzy heights of worldly greatness and fame, and how to control that greatness so that it may be employed against God and His people.[10]

Pink provides the following list of the characteristics of the Antichrist:

1. Intellectual genius (Daniel 7:20)
2. Oratorical genius (Daniel 7:20)
3. Political genius (Daniel 11:21)
4. Commercial genius (Daniel 8:25)
5. Military genius (Daniel 8:24)
6. Administrative genius (Revelation 13:1-2)
7. Religious genius (2 Thessalonians 2:4)

Perhaps the most telling of his characteristics is depicted in Daniel 11:21, which tells us that he will come to power and "seize it through intrigue" ("flatteries," KJV). Here is a master of deception, empowered by the "father of lies" (see John 8:44). Some believe he will be Satan incarnate—thus his miraculous recovery in Revelation 13:3.

Grant Jeffrey points out several contrasts between Christ and the Antichrist.[11] These include:

Christ	*Antichrist*
The Truth	The Lie
Holy One	Lawless one
Man of sorrows	Man of sin
Son of God	Son of Satan
Mystery of godliness	Mystery of iniquity
Good Shepherd	Worthless shepherd

Exalted on high	Cast down to hell
Humbled Himself	Exalted himself
Despised	Admired
Cleanses the temple	Defiles the temple
Slain for the people	Slays the people
The Lamb	The beast

A simple survey of the characteristics of the Antichrist confirms the idea that he is both a false Christ (*pseudochristos*) and against Christ (*antichristos*). He masquerades as an angel of light only to plunge the world into spiritual darkness. Like Satan, he is a destroyer, not a builder. Promising peace, he pushes the world into war. In every conceivable way he is just like Satan who indwells and empowers him.

Is Antichrist Alive Today?

The "spirit of the antichrist" is alive and well! It is the Satan-inspired expression of lawlessness and rebellion against God, the things of God, and the people of God. It has been alive since Satan slithered his way around the Garden of Eden. It has been the driving force behind the whole terrible history of the human race—wars, murders, thefts, rapes, and much more. It is the ugly expression of the destructive nature of the great deceiver himself.

The New Testament authors assure us that the "spirit of antichrist" was active in their day over 20 centuries ago. It has remained active throughout the whole of church history, expressing itself in persecutions, heresies, spiritual deceptions, false prophets, and false religions. Satan has battled the church at every turn throughout its long history, waiting for the right moment to indwell the right person—the Antichrist—as his final masterpiece.

Guessing whether certain contemporary figures might be the Antichrist, however, has always proven futile. Those who have attempted to view the future through the eyes of the present have arrived at some incorrect speculations throughout church history: Nero, Charlemagne, Napoleon Bonaparte, various Caesars, popes, czars, and dictators. In the twentieth century alone, several "candidates" have surfaced on the list of possibilities.

Kaiser Wilhelm

The German emperor's title meant "Caesar," and he intended to conquer all of Europe in World War I and reunite what is known as the old Roman Empire.

Benito Mussolini

The Italian strongman from Rome threatened the world after World War I, and prophetic speculators tagged him as the Antichrist long before World War II began.

Adolf Hitler

Hitler has come to represent the ultimate personification of evil. He persecuted and murdered 15 million people (six million of them Jews) and tried to conquer all of Europe, but failed.

Joseph Stalin

This atheistic leader of the former Soviet Union was known for his political intrigues, brutal assassinations, and desire to conquer the world under the banner of communism.

Nikita Khrushchev

Many people still remember this leader of the former Soviet Union pounding his shoe on his desk at the United Nations and his threat to bury us all.

John F. Kennedy

Anti-Catholic fundamentalists were convinced that Kennedy was going to form an alliance with the pope and the Communists and take over the world.

Mikhail Gorbachev

Many believed he was only deceiving the West into reducing its nuclear arsenal. Some even suggested a red mark on his head might be the mark of the beast.

Ronald Wilson Reagan

Yes, even the darling of politically conservative evangelical Christians was targeted as a possible candidate for the Antichrist because he had six letters in each of his three names (666).

Saddam Hussein

Some suggested that he would sign a peace treaty with Israel only to break it and renew his hostilities toward the Promised Land.

Bill Clinton

Some believed that Bill Clinton was the Antichrist and Hillary was the false prophet.

Other candidates for Antichrist have included Henry Kissinger, Margaret Thatcher, and Boris Yeltsin. The problem with these identifications is they are always tentative and viewed through the cultural lens of our own times. The real tragedy is that people guessing dates and selecting possibilities for the Antichrist are claiming to know more than the writers of Scripture. Jesus Himself said, "No one knows about that day of hour, not even the angels in heaven, nor the Son, but only the Father" (Matthew 24:36). Someone will inevitably point out that this says the "day" or "hour," and not the "year." But the obvious point of this passage is that no one knows the time, so don't waste your time trying to guess it. Be ready all the time because Jesus could come at any time!

THE RESTLESS SEARCH

Any apparent delay in Christ's return is not due to God's indecision, but to the fact that He has not let us in on the secret. Nor has He revealed this to Satan, who is a limited, finite being. Satan himself is left guessing when the rapture might occur. This means he must have a man in mind to indwell as the Antichrist in every generation. In other words, any one of a number of people could have been the Antichrist, but only one will be. Satan must keep selecting possible candidates and wait for God's timing.

The apostle Paul comments on this in 2 Thessalonians 2:1-12 when he tells us that the "day will not come" until the "rebellion occurs" and the "man of lawlessness is revealed" (verse 3). Then he tells us that "you know what is holding him back, so that he may be revealed at the proper time" (verse

6). Only after the rapture of the church will the identity of the Antichrist be revealed. In other words, you don't want to know who he is. If you ever do figure out who he is, that means you have been left behind!

Because Satan must prepare a man to serve as his crowning achievement in every generation, it should not surprise us that multiple candidates have appeared on the horizon of human history only to vanish away. Satan must wait on God's timing, which means he is defeated before he ever begins his final assault on God. He can't make his move until God releases the restraining power of the Holy Spirit, who is indwelling the church here on Earth. Therefore, the Spirit is the agent and the church is the means by which God restrains Satan's diabolical plan until the Father calls Christians home to heaven.

Satan's doom is already assured, but the battle is far from being over. He still "prowls around like a roaring lion looking for someone to devour" (1 Peter 5:8). He has fallen from heaven (Isaiah 14:12). He was condemned in Eden (Genesis 3:14). He accuses the believers (Revelation 12:10). Eventually, he will be cast out of heaven permanently and will expend his wrath on the earth (Revelation 12:7-12). Ultimately he will be defeated at Armageddon and cast into the abyss (Revelation 19:11–20:3). And finally he will be thrown into the lake of fire (Revelation 20:10).

In the meantime, Satan waits for his opportunity to destroy the whole world and the ultimate plan of God. He may be a defeated foe, but he has every intention of keeping up the fight to the very end. Even now he is moving about restlessly, searching for the right man to be the Antichrist.

TEN KEYS TO ANTICHRIST'S IDENTITY

The Bible gives us at least ten keys to identifying the Antichrist when he does come to power. They provide enough details to give a general idea of who he will be when Satan inspires him to make his move onto the world scene. These clues also make it clear that only one person in history will fit this description. There have been many prototypes, but there will be only one Antichrist.

1. *He will rise to power in the last days:* "Later in the time of wrath [the time of the end].... a stern-faced king, a master of intrigue, will arise" (Daniel 8:19,23).

2. *He will rule the whole world:* "He was given authority over every tribe, people, language and nation" (Revelation 13:7).

3. *His headquarters will be in Rome:* "The beast, which you saw, once was, now is not, and will come up out of the Abyss.... The seven heads are seven hills on which the woman sits" (Revelation 17:8-9).

4. *He will be intelligent and persuasive:* "The other horn...looked more imposing than the others and...had eyes and a mouth that spoke boastfully" (Daniel 7:20).

5. *He will rule by international consent:* "The ten horns you saw are ten kings.... They have one purpose and will give their power and authority to the beast" (Revelation 17:12-13).

6. *He will rule by deception:* "He will become very strong....and will succeed in whatever he does.... He will cause deceit to prosper, and he will consider himself superior" (Daniel 8:24-25).

7. *He will control the global economy:* "He also forced everyone, small and great, rich and poor, free and slave, to receive a mark on his right hand or on his forehead, so that no one could buy or sell unless he had the mark, which is the name of the beast or the number of his name" (Revelation 13:16-17).

8. *He will make a peace treaty with Israel:* "He will confirm a covenant with many for one 'seven.' In the middle of the 'seven' he will put an end to sacrifice and offering" (Daniel 9:27).

9. *He will break the treaty and invade Israel:* "The people of the ruler who will come will destroy the city and the sanctuary. The end will come like a flood: War will continue until the end, and desolations have been decreed" (Daniel 9:26).

10. *He will claim to be God:* "He will oppose and will exalt himself over everything that is called God or is worshiped, so that he sets himself up in God's temple, proclaiming himself to be God" (2 Thessalonians 2:4).

There are many other details given in the Bible regarding the person we commonly call the Antichrist. But the general picture is that of a European (American?) who rises to power over the Western world. Whether he is Jewish or Gentile is not entirely clear. What is clear, however, is that he will control the last great bastion of Gentile world power. From his base in the West, he will extend his control over the entire world. For all practical purposes, he will administrate the world government and the global economy, and be assisted by the leader of the world religion (Revelation 13:11-18). He may be moving into power at this very moment; only time will reveal his true identity.

When the Antichrist does come to power, he will apparently be promising to ensure world peace through a series of international alliances, treaties, and agreements (see Daniel 8:24; Revelation 17:12-14). Despite his promises of peace, his international policies will inevitably plunge the world into the greatest war of all time.

FALSE PROPHET PREPARES THE WAY

The Antichrist will not rise to power alone. His success will result from a worldwide spiritual deception perpetrated by the false prophet. The false prophet's ability to perform miraculous signs will enable him to convince the public that the Antichrist is the leader for whom they have been looking. The ultimate deception of the end times will involve the worldwide worship of the Antichrist. This will be encouraged by the false prophet (Revelation 19:20; 20:10), who is also known as the second "beast" (Revelation 13:11-17). Like the Antichrist, his identity is not clearly revealed, but several clues are given to help us know who he is.

J. Dwight Pentecost observes that the false prophet serves as the spokesperson for the Antichrist. He states that the spirit of Antichrist "will culminate in the Beasts in their corporate ministries.... The first Beast will be in direct opposition to Christ...and the second Beast will assume the place of leadership in the religious realm which rightly belongs to Christ."[12]

Revelation 13 presents ten identifying features of the false prophet:

1. Rises out of the earth (verse 11)
2. Controls religious affairs (verse 11)
3. Motivated by Satan (verse 11)
4. Promotes the worship of the beast (verse 12)
5. Performs signs and miracles (verse 13)

6. Deceives the whole world (verse 14)

7. Empowers the image of the beast (verse 15)

8. Kills all who refuse to worship (verse 15)

9. Controls all economic commerce (verses 16-17)

10. Controls the mark of the beast (verses 17-18)

Bible scholars are divided on the matter of the identity of the false prophet. Some believe he will be Jewish, while others believe he will be a Gentile. The biblical record itself is inconclusive. However, when we observe the relationship of the false prophet to the great prostitute (Revelation 17), we immediately notice his connection to the city on "seven hills" (see 17:7,9) that rules "over the kings of the earth" (verses 17-18). It seems clear that John is referring to Rome by the terminology that he uses to describe the symbol of "Babylon the Great."

Ironically, little has been written about the false prophet compared to the volumes of material about the Antichrist.[13] Thomas Ice and Timothy Demy comment, "The Antichrist and the False Prophet are two separate individuals who will work toward a common, deceptive goal. Their roles and relationship will be that which was common in the ancient world between a ruler (Antichrist) and the high priest (False Prophet) of the national religion."[14]

The false prophet is depicted in the book of Revelation as one who uses miraculous signs and wonders to deceive the world into worshipping the Antichrist. Ice and Demy remark, "Even though this is yet a future event, the lesson to be learned for our own day is that one must exercise discernment, especially in the area of religion—even when miracles appear to vindicate the messenger."[15]

A century ago, Samuel Andrews argued that the work of the false prophet will be to extend his ecclesiastical administration over the whole earth by establishing the church of the Antichrist as the counterfeit of the true church.[16] Thus, the false prophet does not so much *deny* Christian doctrine as he *corrupts* it. Only in this way can the Antichrist sit in the temple of God and demand to be worshiped as God (see 2 Thessalonians 2:4). Remember, when Satan tempted Christ, he also appealed for worship (Matthew 4:8-10). In fact, Satan offered to surrender the entire world to Christ if He would worship him. Therefore, it should not surprise us that the goal of the

Satan-inspired false prophet will be to get the whole world to bow down to the Antichrist, who is the personification of Satan himself.

Together, Satan (the dragon), Antichrist (the beast of sea), and the false prophet (the beast of earth) comprise an "unholy trinity" that is a counterfeit of the triune God. Satan opposes the Father; the Antichrist will oppose the Son; and the false prophet will oppose the Holy Spirit. This ungodly alliance will comprise Satan's final attempt to overthrow the work of God on earth.

The method of their diabolical attempt is explained in the biblical record. The Antichrist dare not appear until after the "rebellion" (2 Thessalonians 2:3) or "falling away" (KJV) of apostasy. In the meantime, the spirit of Antichrist (lawlessness) is already at work attempting to pervert the gospel and to corrupt the true church. When this process is sufficiently established, the false prophet will arise to prepare for the coming of the Antichrist. To accomplish the final deception, he will have to control the entire world.

14

MARCHING TO ARMAGEDDON

"Then they gathered the kings together to the place that in Hebrew is called Armageddon."

—Revelation 16:16

Armageddon, the last great world war of history, will take place in Israel in conjunction with the second coming of Christ. The battle or campaign of Armageddon is described in Daniel 11:40-45; Joel 3:9-17; Zechariah 14:1-3; and Revelation 16:14-16. It will occur in the final days of the Tribulation, and John tells us that the kings of the world will be gathered together "for the war of the great day of God, the Almighty" in a place known as "Har-Magedon" (Revelation 16:14,16 NASB).[1] The site for the converging of the armies is the plain of Esdraelon, around the hill of Megiddo. The area is located in northern Israel about 20 miles south-southeast of Haifa and 50 miles north of Jerusalem. This area was the scene of many battles in Old Testament times. The book of Judges records it as the location of Barak's conflict with the Canaanites (chapter 4) and Gideon's battle with the Midianites (chapter 7).

WHAT IS ARMAGEDDON?

The term *Armageddon* comes from the Hebrew tongue. *Har* is the word for "mountain" or "hill." *Mageddon* is likely the ruins of the ancient city of

Megiddo, which overlooks the Valley of Esdraelon in northern Israel, where the armies of the world will congregate.

According to the Bible, great armies from the east and the west will gather and assemble on this plain. The Antichrist will defeat armies from the south who would threaten his power, and he will destroy a revived Babylon in the east before finally turning his forces toward Jerusalem to subdue and destroy it. As he and his armies move upon Jerusalem, God will intervene and Jesus Christ will return to rescue His people Israel. The Lord and His angelic army will destroy the Antichrist's armies, capture the Antichrist and the false prophet, and cast them into the lake of fire (Revelation 19:11-21).

When the Lord returns, the power and rule of the Antichrist will come to an end. Charles Dyer states:

> Daniel, Joel, and Zechariah identify Jerusalem as the site where the final battle between Antichrist and Christ will occur. All three predict that God will intervene in history on behalf of His people and will destroy the Antichrist's army at Jerusalem. Zechariah predicts that the battle will end when the Messiah returns to earth and His feet touch down on the Mount of Olives. This battle concludes with the second coming of Jesus to earth.[2]

The campaign of Armageddon—actually at Jerusalem—will be one of the most anticlimactic events in history. Given the huge armies mustered on both sides, we would expect to witness an epic struggle between good and evil. Yet no matter how mighty someone on earth is, that individual is no match for the power of God.

WHAT ARE THE PURPOSES OF ARMAGEDDON?

As with many human events, two purposes are at work at Armageddon: a divine intent and a human rationale. The divine purpose is that the judgment at Armageddon prepares the Earth for the 1,000-year reign of Christ. The satanically inspired human purpose is to once and for all eradicate worldwide Jewry.

The Divine Purpose

The sovereign Lord providentially superintends over all history. Thus, all history is the outworking of the decree of God. Nothing takes place that He did not actively plan. All through history, usually unknown to humanity, the battle rages between God and Satan, good and evil. The war of Armageddon is the culmination of a whole series of events that climax in this final act.

According to God's divine purpose, Armageddon will be the venue by which He will judge His enemies. Both satanic and human opposition will be focused on God's elect nation of Israel, and God will bring them to that location to bring down their foolish schemes of rebellion. The psalmist records God's response of laughter at the puny human plans to overthrow God Himself at Armageddon:

> Why are the nations in an uproar and the peoples devising a vain thing? The kings of the earth take their stand and the rulers take counsel together against the LORD and against His Anointed, saying "Let us tear their fetters apart and cast away their cords from us!" He who sits in the heavens laughs, the Lord scoffs at them. Then He will speak to them in His anger and terrify them in His fury, saying, "But as for Me, I have installed My King upon Zion, My holy mountain" (Psalm 2:1-6 NASB).

The Human Purpose

The demented human perspective leading to the final march to Jerusalem appears to be motivated by these people's effort to solve what they believe to be the source of the world's problems—the Jews. As we follow the buildup to Armageddon in Revelation 11–18, the persecution of Israel begins at the midpoint of the Tribulation, builds, and culminates in the worldwide gathering of armies in Israel.

WHEN WILL ARMAGEDDON OCCUR?

Though today's popular culture often mentions the conflict of Armageddon, it will not take place tomorrow, next month, or next year. It is a military conflict that will occur after the rapture and at the end of the seven-year Tribulation. It will take place at the culmination of the Antichrist's reign and it will end with the second coming of Jesus Christ, who will destroy the Antichrist and his forces.

The conflict is the last major event on the prophetic timeline before the establishment of Christ's millennial kingdom. Armageddon is not an event that any person should desire or anticipate with joy, for it will bring death and destruction to many people. It is, however, a definitely future military conflict that no amount of political negotiation will postpone.

The detailed sequence of events and the terms used in relation to Armageddon show that it is a campaign or series of battles rather than a single battle. Rather than referring to it as the final battle, we should refer to it as a campaign or a war. Armageddon will be a series of conflicts that culminate at the second coming of Jesus Christ. The Greek word *polemos,* translated "war" in Revelation 16:14, usually signifies an extended war or campaign. The events of Armageddon are not a single battle and do not occur in a single day. They are carried out over a wide geographic area to the north and south of Jerusalem and as far east as Babylon. These events will occur over a period of at least several days, and more likely, several weeks.

WHO WILL BE INVOLVED IN ARMAGEDDON?

Scripture indicates that all the nations of the world will gather for war against Israel. This is a fitting climax to the Tribulation, during which the whole world is in rebellion against heaven (except for a remnant of believers). The Bible teaches that this war will involve not only the whole land of Israel but also all the nations of the world (Zechariah 12:3; 14:2; Revelation 16:14).

Scripture mentions the kings (plural) of the East, who take a prominent role in the military buildup in preparation for the war of Armageddon. "The sixth angel poured out his bowl on the great river, the Euphrates; and its water was dried up, so that the way would be prepared for the kings from the east" (Revelation 16:12 NASB). The verse may emphasize the Eastern powers simply because that is where the largest masses of population reside.

When we consider the fact that the whole Tribulation will be a war between God and His opponents—Satan, the fallen angels, and unregenerate mankind—we should not be surprised that it will include a great number of military conflicts throughout. The biblical data lead us to believe that the Tribulation will be a time of great military conflict—so much so that we would not be incorrect to consider the entire Tribulation period as a world war.

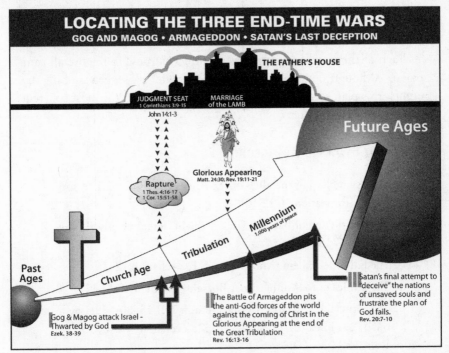

LOCATING THE THREE END-TIME WARS
GOG AND MAGOG • ARMAGEDDON • SATAN'S LAST DECEPTION

THE FATHER'S HOUSE

JUDGMENT SEAT
1 Corinthians 3:9-15

MARRIAGE
of the LAMB

John 14:1-3

Future Ages

Glorious Appearing
Matt. 24:30; Rev. 19:11-21

Rapture
1 Thes. 4:16-17
1 Cor. 15:51-58

Millennium
1,000 years of peace

Tribulation

Church Age

Past
Ages

Gog & Magog attack Israel -
Thwarted by God
Ezek. 38-39

The Battle of Armageddon pits
the anti-God forces of the world
against the coming of Christ in the
Glorious Appearing at the end of
the Great Tribulation
Rev. 16:13-16

Satan's final attempt to
"deceive" the nations
of unsaved souls and
frustrate the plan of
God fails.
Rev. 20:7-10

Many confuse the Russo-Islamic attack on Israel with the Battle of Armageddon, but they are not the same, for several reasons: 1) The Ezekiel 38–39 attack is against Israel alone—not the whole world. 2) Armageddon is the satanically inspired attempt by the nations of the world to meet and destroy Christ when He comes at Megiddo (Revelation 16:13-16). Armageddon is not called Gog and Magog, but is inspired by the same demonic forces.

WHAT ARE THE STAGES OF ARMAGEDDON?

A detailed study of all the biblical passages pertaining to Armageddon reveals a very complex campaign. One of the most thorough studies of the campaign was done by Arnold Fruchtenbaum, who has divided the campaign into eight stages.[3] Although other plans can just as readily be proposed, his evaluation seems to us to be the most logical and comprehensive. Fruchtenbaum writes:

> The two climactic events of the Great Tribulation are the Campaign of Armageddon and the second coming of Jesus Christ. A considerable amount of data is given about this time period in the Scriptures. One of the greatest difficulties in the study of eschatology is placing these events in chronological sequence in order to see what exactly will happen in the Campaign of Armageddon.... The Campaign of Armageddon can be divided

into eight stages, and this in turn will facilitate an understanding of the sequence of events.[4]

Each of these eight stages serves a distinct purpose in the overall campaign. Although no single Bible passage provides a sequence of all the events, this plan seems to put all the pieces together in the most coherent and comprehensive way:

THE EIGHT STAGES OF ARMAGEDDON

1. The assembling of the allies of the Antichrist (Psalm 2:1-6; Joel 3:9-11; Revelation 16:12-16).

2. The destruction of Babylon (Isaiah 13–14; Jeremiah 50–51; Revelation 17–18).

3. The fall of Jerusalem (Micah 4:11–5:1; Zechariah 12–14).

4. The armies of the Antichrist at Bozrah (Jeremiah 49:13-14).

5. The national regeneration of Israel (Psalm 79:1-13; 80:1-19; Isaiah 64:1-12; Hosea 6:1-13; Joel 2:28-32; Zechariah 12:10; 13:7-9; Romans 11:25-27).

6. The second coming of Jesus Christ (Isaiah 34:1-7; 63:1-3; Micah 2:12-13; Habakkuk 3:3).

7. The battle from Bozrah to the Valley of Jehoshaphat (Jeremiah 49:20-22; Joel 3:12-13; Zechariah 14:12-15).

8. The victory ascent upon the Mount of Olives (Joel 3:14-17; Zechariah 14:3-5; Matthew 24:29-31; Revelation 16:17-21; 19:11-21).

Stage 1: The Antichrist's Allies Assemble

The primary biblical reference to this first stage is Revelation 16:12-16, which says the Euphrates River will dry up to prepare the way for the "kings of the east," whose ultimate destiny is Har-Magedon. The assembling of the armies begins at the same time as the divine judgment poured out with the sixth bowl (verse 12). At this time the Euphrates River will be dried up, providing for a faster and easier assembly of the armies of the "kings from the east." In the Bible, "east" refers to the region of Mesopotamia (Assyria and Babylon), and the drying up of the river will allow the forces of the

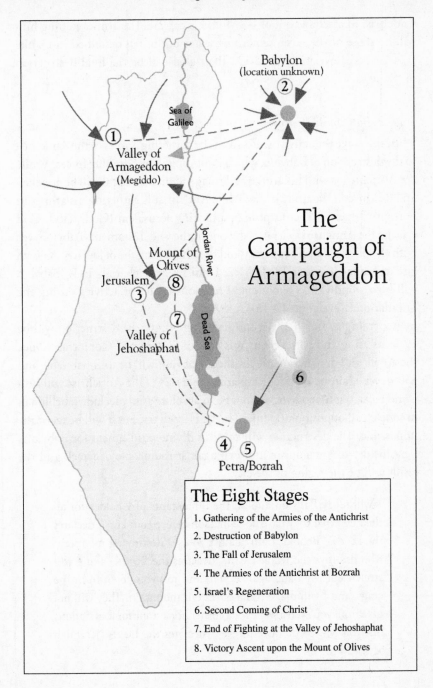

The Campaign of Armageddon

Babylon (location unknown)
②

Sea of Galilee

① Valley of Armageddon (Megiddo)

Jordan River

Mount of Olives ⑧
Jerusalem ③
⑦
Valley of Jehoshaphat

Dead Sea

⑥

④ ⑤
Petra/Bozrah

The Eight Stages

1. Gathering of the Armies of the Antichrist
2. Destruction of Babylon
3. The Fall of Jerusalem
4. The Armies of the Antichrist at Bozrah
5. Israel's Regeneration
6. Second Coming of Christ
7. End of Fighting at the Valley of Jehoshaphat
8. Victory Ascent upon the Mount of Olives

Antichrist to assemble out of Babylon, his capital. The armies joining him
will be those of the seven remaining kings out of ten described in Daniel
7:24-27 and Revelation 17:12-13. Their goal will be the final destruction
of the Jews.

Stage 2: Babylon Is Destroyed

In this stage the activity shifts from the gathering armies of the Antichrist
to the destruction of Babylon, which is his capital, by opposing forces. While
the Antichrist is with his armies at Armageddon, his capital will be attacked
and destroyed. The irony is that while Antichrist is gathering his armies in
northern Israel for the purpose of attacking Jerusalem (God's city), God
attacks the Antichrist's city—Babylon. In the Old Testament, Babylon was
both the place of Israel's captivity and the originating site of idolatry. Known
also as Shinar (Genesis 10:10; 11:2; Daniel 1:2; Zechariah 5:11), Babylon
will be a worldwide economic and religious center of activity during the
Tribulation (Revelation 17–18).

According to Isaiah 13:19 and Jeremiah 50:40, the destruction will be
as devastating and complete as was that of Sodom and Gomorrah. Once
the attack and destruction are finished, Babylon will be uninhabitable and
will never again be rebuilt (Revelation 18:21-24). The Antichrist will be a
world ruler, but his control will not be so absolute as to preclude rebellion or
to squelch all opposition (Daniel 11:41). He will try, but it will be tactically
impossible. The destruction will come as divine punishment for Babylon's
long history of antagonism and evil against the people of Israel, and the
result will be the razing of the city.

> "I will repay Babylon and all the inhabitants of Chaldea for all
> their evil that they have done in Zion before your eyes," declares
> the LORD. "Behold, I am against you, O destroying mountain,
> who destroys the whole earth," declares the LORD, "and I will
> stretch out My hand against you, and roll you down from the
> crags, and I will make you a burnt out mountain. They will not
> take from you even a stone for a corner nor a stone for foundations,
> but you will be desolate forever," declares the LORD (Jeremiah
> 51:21-26 NASB).

Stage 3: Jerusalem Falls

Although the Antichrist's capital will have been destroyed in the second phase of the campaign, his forces will not have been lost. Rather than moving eastward to confront the attackers of his capital, the Antichrist will move south against Jerusalem. We read of this move in Zechariah 12:1-3 and 14:1-2:

> The burden of the word of the LORD concerning Israel.... Behold, I am going to make Jerusalem a cup that causes reeling to all the peoples around; and when the siege is against Jerusalem, it will also be against Judah. It will come about in that day that I will make Jerusalem a heavy stone for all the peoples; all who lift it will be severely injured. And all the nations of the earth will be gathered against it.

The Antichrist's forces will sweep down to Jerusalem, and once again the city will fall into Gentile control. Although Zechariah 12:4-9 and Micah 4:11–5:1 describe a temporary resurgence of Jewish strength and stiff resistance, Jerusalem will fall. The losses on both sides will be enormous, but the Antichrist's forces will prevail, and Jerusalem will fall. With the fall of Jerusalem the campaign's third stage will come to an end.

Stage 4: The Antichrist Moves South Against the Remnant

In the fourth stage, the campaign will shift into the desert and mountains, probably to a location about 80 miles south of Jerusalem to the area of Bozrah and Petra. At the beginning of the second half of the Tribulation, after the Antichrist breaks his treaty with Israel (Daniel 9:27; Matthew 24:15), many of the Jews will flee into the desert for safety. This will fulfill the words and exhortation of Jesus in Matthew 24:16-31. In verse 16, Jesus says of those who see the abomination of desolation, "Then those who are in Judea must flee to the mountains" (NASB). This flight for life is also described in Revelation 12:6,14.

After Jerusalem is captured, the Antichrist will move south in an attempt to destroy those who fled in the previous three-and-a-half years. In Micah 2:12 we read of God's gathering and protection of this remnant: "I will surely assemble all of you, Jacob, I will surely gather the remnant of Israel.

I will put them together like sheep in the fold; like a flock in the midst of its pasture they will be noisy with men."

The area normally associated with this part of the campaign is that of Mount Seir, about 30 miles south of the lower end of the Dead Sea. Two sites are possibilities for the location of the fleeing Jews: Bozrah and Petra (see Isaiah 33:13-16 and Jeremiah 49:13-14). As the forces gather in the rugged wilderness of Mount Seir, the fourth phase will come to an end and the last few days of the campaign will begin.

Stage 5: The Regeneration of the Nation Israel

The Campaign of Armageddon will culminate in the second coming of Christ. But before Christ returns, Israel will confess its national sin (Leviticus 26:40-42; Jeremiah 3:11-18; Hosea 5:15) and plead for the Messiah to return (Isaiah 64:1-12; Zechariah 12:10; Matthew 23:37-39). This will come as the armies of the Antichrist gather to destroy the Jews in the wilderness. According to Hosea 6:1-3, the Jewish leaders will issue a call for the nation to repent. The nation will respond positively and repent for two days.

Fruchtenbaum writes,

> The leaders of Israel will finally recognize the reason why the Tribulation has fallen on them. Whether this will be done by the study of the Scriptures, or by the preaching of the 144,000 or via the Two Witnesses or by the ministry of Elijah, is not clearly stated. Most likely there will be a combination of these things. But the leaders will come to a realization of the nation's sin in some way. Just as the Jewish leaders once led the nation to the rejection of the Messiahship of Jesus, they will then lead the nation to the acceptance of His Messiahship by issuing the call of Hosea 6:1-3, which will begin the last three days before the Second Coming.[5]

The fifth stage will come to completion on the day after Israel's two days of confession and prayer for Messiah's return. In the sixth stage, God, having heard their prayers, will answer them, fulfilling biblical prophecy and the hope of the ages.

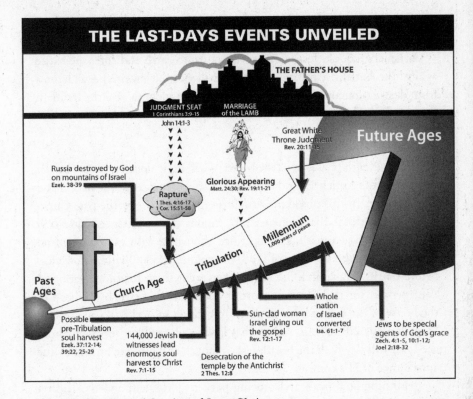

THE LAST-DAYS EVENTS UNVEILED

THE FATHER'S HOUSE

JUDGMENT SEAT
1 Corinthians 3:9-15

John 14:1-3

MARRIAGE
of the LAMB

Great White
Throne Judgment
Rev. 20:11-15

Future Ages

Russia destroyed by God
on mountains of Israel
Ezek. 38-39

Rapture
1 Thes. 4:16-17
1 Cor. 15:51-58

Glorious Appearing
Matt. 24:30; Rev. 19:11-21

Millennium
1,000 years of peace

Tribulation

Church Age

Past
Ages

Possible
pre-Tribulation
soul harvest
Ezek. 37:12-14;
39:22, 25-29

144,000 Jewish
witnesses lead
enormous soul
harvest to Christ
Rev. 7:1-15

Desecration of the
temple by the Antichrist
2 Thes. 12:8

Sun-clad woman
Israel giving out
the gospel
Rev. 12:1-17

Whole
nation
of Israel
converted
Isa. 61:1-7

Jews to be special
agents of God's grace
Zech. 4:1-5, 10:1-12;
Joel 2:18-32

Stage 6: The Second Coming of Jesus Christ

In the sixth stage the prayers of the Jews are answered, and Jesus Christ will return to earth to defeat the armies of the Antichrist at Bozrah and to begin the final portions of the campaign. He will return to earth in the clouds, in the same manner in which He departed (Matthew 24:30; Acts 1:9-11). The fact that Jesus returns first to the mountain wilderness of Bozrah is seen in Isaiah 34:1-7; 63:1-6; Micah 2:12-13; and Habakkuk 3:3. At His second coming, Jesus Christ the Messiah will enter battle against the Antichrist's forces, and He will miraculously defeat them.

According to Jude 14-15 and Revelation 19:11-16, Jesus will return with an angelic army and with the church saints (robed in white at the marriage supper of the Lamb) who had been raptured prior to the Tribulation. Revelation 19:11-16 makes it clear that the second coming will bring destruction to the enemies of Jesus Christ. These verses describe Him as treading the winepress of the wrath of God and ruling with a rod of iron.

At Israel's request, Jesus Christ will return to earth and enter the battle against the Antichrist and his armies. He will save the Jews in the wilderness from destruction and will then continue to Jerusalem to save the remnant there and conclude the campaign (Zechariah 12:7).

Stage 7: The Final Battle

In the seventh phase, Jesus the Messiah will fight alone on Israel's behalf, destroying the Antichrist and those who have come against the nation and persecuted it. In this phase the Antichrist will be slain by the true Christ (Habakkuk 3:13; 2 Thessalonians 2:8). Among the very first casualties will be the Antichrist himself. Having ruled the world with great power and spoken against the true Son of God, the counterfeit son will be powerless before Christ. Habakkuk 3:13 says, "You went forth for the salvation of Your people, for the salvation of Your anointed. You struck the head of the house of the evil to lay him open from thigh to neck" (NASB). Second Thessalonians 2:8 tells us, "Then that lawless one will be revealed whom the Lord will slay with the breath of His mouth and bring to an end by the appearance of His coming" (NASB).

Beginning at Bozrah and moving back to Jerusalem and the Kidron Valley, also known as the Valley of Jehoshaphat, Jesus will engage and destroy the Antichrist's forces (Joel 3:12-13; Zechariah 14:12-15; Revelation 14:19-20). In the Valley of Jehoshaphat, along the eastern walls of Jerusalem, the nations and armies that gathered against the Jews to destroy them will now find themselves being destroyed by Jesus Christ, the Messiah and King of the Jews.

Stage 8: The Ascent upon the Mount of Olives

With the destruction of the Antichrist and his forces complete, the campaign will be over, and Jesus will go and stand upon the Mount of Olives in a symbolic victory ascent. When He does so, a number of cataclysmic events will occur, bringing the Tribulation to an end, as described in Zechariah 14:3-4.

> Then the LORD will go forth and fight against those nations, as when He fights on a day of battle. In that day His feet will stand

on the Mount of Olives, which is in front of Jerusalem on the east; and the Mount of Olives will be split in its middle from east to west by a very large valley, so that half of the mountain will move toward the north and the other half toward the south (NASB).

Revelation 16:17 adds:

Then the seventh angel poured out his bowl upon the air; and a loud voice came out of the temple from the throne, saying, "It is done." And there were flashes of lightning and sounds and peals of thunder; and there was a great earthquake, such as there had not been since man came to be upon the earth, so great an earthquake was it, and so mighty. The great city was split into three parts, and the cities of the nations fell (NASB).

The supernatural calamities that come upon the world at this time correspond to the seventh bowl judgment and include the greatest earthquake the world has ever known. As a result of the earthquake, Jerusalem will split into three parts, and the Mount of Olives will split into two parts, creating a valley and means of escape from the earthquake for the Jewish inhabitants of the city (Zechariah 14:4-5).

WHAT COMES AFTER ARMAGEDDON?

Armageddon will be the last great world war of history, and it will take place in Israel in conjunction with the second coming of Christ.

In a sense, Armageddon is a battle that never really takes place. That is, it does not take place in accordance with its original human intent. Its human purpose will be to gather the armies of the world to execute the Antichrist's "final solution" to the "Jewish problem." This is why Jesus Christ chooses this moment in history for His return to earth—to thwart the Antichrist's attempted annihilation of the Jews and to destroy the armies of the world.

God's purpose in allowing the Tribulation is to bring about the conversion of Israel and multitudes of Gentiles (Revelation 7:4-14). But once the Antichrist attempts to wipe out the Jews, the final wrath of God's judgment will fall at Armageddon. And Jesus Christ will win the victory, vanquish the enemy, and establish His kingdom on earth.

15

HOW SHOULD
WE THEN LIVE?

"So then, dear friends, since you are looking forward to this,
make every effort to be...at peace with him."
—2 PETER 3:14

THE TIMING OF THE LAST DAYS IS IN GOD'S HANDS. From a human stand-point it appears that we are standing on the threshold of the final frontier. The pieces of the puzzle are all in place. As the sands of time slip through the hourglass of eternity, we are all moving closer to an appointment with destiny. The only question is, How much time is left?

The tension between living for today and looking for tomorrow is one of the realities of the Christian life. We often find ourselves caught between the here-and-now and the hereafter. On the one hand, we need to be ready for Jesus to come at any moment. On the other hand, we have God-given responsibilities to fulfill in this world in the meantime.

We are living in a time of great crisis, but it is also a time of great opportunity. We must be prepared for the challenges that lie ahead of us. New technologies will make our lives more convenient, but they will also make us more dependent on those conveniences. Medical advancements will continue to pose enormous challenges in the area of biomedical ethics. The shifting sands of sociopolitical change will also challenge our national and international policies in the days ahead. We will find ourselves living in a very different world from the one into which we were born. All these changes and challenges will confront us in the days ahead.

Preparing for Christ's return is something each one of us must do on our own. You cannot look to others to get your heart ready to meet God. Each person is responsible for his or her eternal destiny. Jesus urges us to do three things in view of His second coming:

1. Keep watching (Matthew 24:42)

2. Be ready (Matthew 24:44)

3. Keep serving (Matthew 24:46)

Erwin Lutzer, the senior pastor of Moody Church in Chicago, has reminded us there are "five unshakable pillars" that enable us to live with eternity in view.[1]

AN EYE TOWARD ETERNITY
1. God still reigns.

Human leaders will come and go. Some will be better, some worse. Some will be what we deserve—a reflection of our own weakness and sinfulness. But behind the scene of human governments, God still reigns over the eternal destiny of mankind. Beyond this temporal world, God rules from the throne in heaven. He guides His children and overrules in the affairs of men and nations to accomplish His will and purposes. The Bible assures us "there is no authority exept that which God has established" (Romans 13:1). Regardless of who our leaders are, we are to offer "prayers, intercession and thanksgiving...for kings and all those in authority" (1 Timothy 2:1-2).

2. The church is still precious.

During this present age, God is still working through His church to evangelize the world. Jesus gave Christians clear direction about what they are to be doing until He returns. He said: "Go and make disciples of all nations, baptizing them in the name of the Father and of the Son and of the Holy Spirit, and teaching them to obey everything I have commanded you.... to the very end of the age" (Matthew 28:19-20). The church may flourish or be persecuted in the days ahead, but she is to be faithful to her mission until Jesus calls her home to glory (1 Thessalonians 4:13-17).

3. Our mission is still clear.

The church stands as the salt and light of God in society. We who are Christians are to "declare the praises of him who called you out of darkness into his wonderful light" (1 Peter 2:9). Lutzer suggests that we can accomplish this by 1) representing Christ to the world by a godly lifestyle; 2) winning people to Christ through intellectual and moral confrontation with a loving persuasiveness; and 3) strengthening our families as a testimony to God's grace. The integrity of sincere and authentic Christian lives and families speaks volumes to a lost world that is desperate for meaning and purpose. We cannot underestimate the spiritual impact that true Christianity has on those who have no answers to the overwhelming problems of life. When we as Christians live out our faith with authenticity and boldness, we capture the attention of the watching world.[2]

4. Our focus is still heaven.

In this day of affluence, it is easy for Christians to forget that heaven is our real destiny. So many believers today are so content and preoccupied with their lifestyles that they forget about heaven. Dave Hunt has observed, "Unfortunately, too many persons—even dedicated Christians—find heaven a topic of only minor interest because they consider it irrelevant to the challenges of this present life."[3]

We must remember, however, that this world is no friend to grace. As time passes, we should expect a continual moral decline in secular society. The Bible reminds us that there will be an "increase of wickedness" and that "terrible times" will come in the last days (Matthew 24:12; 2 Timothy 3:1). In the meantime, whatever success we have in this world must be measured in the light of our eternal destiny. Joseph Stowell reminds us that if we make heaven our primary point of reference it will transform our relationship to everything that is temporary in this world.[4] C.S. Lewis wrote, "Christians who did most for the present world were just those who thought most of the next."[5]

5. Our victory is still certain.

The ultimate Bible prophecies focus on the triumph of Christ and His bride, the church (Revelation 19). They assure us that all believers will share in His victorious reign. Whatever transpires in the meantime must be viewed in light of our eternal destiny. Peter Marshall, former chaplain of the U.S. Senate, said, "It is better to fail at a cause that will ultimately succeed than to succeed in a cause that will ultimately fail."[6] Until the trumpet sounds and the Lord calls us home, we have the Great Commission to fulfill (Matthew 28:19-20) and the world to evangelize. There is no reason to let up now. Because no clear date has been revealed for the end of the present age, we must keep on serving Christ until He comes.

A young African martyr wrote these words in his prison cell before he died:

> I'm part of the fellowship of the unashamed, the die has been cast, I have stepped over the line, the decision has been made—I'm a disciple of Jesus Christ—I won't look back, let up, slow down, back away or be still.
>
> My past is redeemed, my present makes sense, my future is secure—I'm finished and done with low living, sight walking, smooth knees, colorless dreams, tamed visions, worldly talking, cheap giving and dwarfed goals.
>
> My face is set, my gait is fast, my goal is heaven, my road is narrow, my way is rough, my companions are few, my guide is reliable, my mission is clear. I won't give up, shut up, let up until I have stayed up, stored up, prayed up for the cause of Jesus Christ.
>
> I must go till He comes, give till I drop, preach till everyone knows, work till He stops me and when He comes for His own, He will have no trouble recognizing me because my banner will have been clear.[7]

What Should We Be Doing?

Since we who are believers can never be certain when God's purposes for His church will be finalized, we must remain obedient to our Lord's commands regarding His church. This was made clear to the disciples at the time of Christ's ascension to heaven. They had asked if He was going to restore the kingdom to Israel at that time, and Jesus told them, "It is not for you to know the times or dates the Father has set by His own authority" (Acts 1:7). Two facts are clear in this statement: 1) The date has been set;

and 2) we aren't supposed to know it because we have a responsibility to fulfill in the meantime.

In the very next verse, Jesus told the disciples they would be empowered by the Holy Spirit to be His witnesses in Jerusalem, Judea, Samaria, and "to the ends of the earth" (Acts 1:8). Then, to the disciples' amazement, Jesus ascended into heaven, leaving them gazing intently into the sky. Two men in white (probably angels) appeared and asked, "Why do you stand here looking into the sky? This same Jesus, who has been taken from you into heaven, will come back in the same way you have seen him go into heaven" (Acts 1:11).

All too often, today's Christians are just like those early disciples. We spend more time gazing into the sky and speculating about Christ's return than we do serving Him. The angels' point was to remind the disciples that His return is certain. Thus we shouldn't waste time and energy worrying about when or whether Christ will return. Believe that He is coming again on schedule, and be about His business in the meantime.

Jesus left several instructions about what Christians ought to be doing while awaiting His coming:

1. *Witness for Him everywhere you go.* Our Lord told His disciples to be His witnesses everywhere—even to the farthest ends of the earth (Acts 1:8).

2. *"Go into all the world and preach the good news"* (Mark 16:15). This command emphasizes the evangelistic and missionary nature of the church's ministry during the present era. We are to take the gospel to the whole world.

3. *"Repentance and forgiveness of sins will be preached...to all nations,"* our Lord declared in Luke 24:47. Calling men and women to repent and believe the gospel is the twofold nature of the evangelistic enterprise.

4. *"Make disciples of all nations, baptizing them,"* Jesus said in Matthew 28:19. Making converts and discipling them in their walk with God is a major emphasis of the church's mission.

5. *Build the church, in every generation.* Jesus told His disciples that He would build His church with such power that "the gates of hell

shall not prevail against it" (Matthew 16:18 KJV). Jesus pictured the church being on the march until He calls her home.

6. *"Work...until I come back,"* Jesus said in the parable of the talents (Luke 19:13). In this parable, the servants were to "put this money to work" until their master returned. We are to stay busy about the Master's business until He returns.

7. *Remain faithful until He returns.* Our Lord concluded His prophetic message in the Olivet Discourse by reminding His disciples to continue in faithful and wise service even though He might be gone a long time (Matthew 24:45; 25:14-21).

IS THERE ANY HOPE FOR OUR GENERATION?

Throughout history, God often has moved to bless His people in a fresh and powerful way. Genuine revival came as God's people were convicted of their sin, repented, and gained a new zeal and devotion for God in their lives. In revival, the self-centered, halfhearted indifference that so often dominates our lives is swept aside by a new and genuine desire to live for God.

Revival begins to renew our values and redirect our lives. It calls us to a more serious walk with Christ and results in substantial and abiding fruit (see John 15:16; Galatians 5:22-23). The changes that occur, both in individual believers and in the church collectively, speak convincingly to the world about what it really means to belong to Christ. Such revival comes when God's people pray, when God's truth is proclaimed, and when God's Spirit moves in our lives.

Unfortunately, there is little evidence of genuine revival among Christians today. Some have lost hope of it altogether. Others have diluted the gospel message in order to make its appeal more acceptable to today's generation. Bailey Smith has correctly observed,

> The Christ of the Bible has been reduced to a fallible humanitarian. Salvation has been repackaged into a feel-good experience. Forgotten in today's "gospel revisionism" is the message that sent Christ to the cross and the disciples to martyrdom. Today's gospel "lite" is hardly worth living for and certainly not worth dying for.[8]

If we are going to make an impact on our generation for the cause of

Christ, it must be soon. We have no idea how much time is left before Christ returns, and we dare not let the time slip away indiscriminately. If we are going to use wisely whatever time God has given us, we must be about His business with a sense of urgency. On the one hand, we dare not *presume* on God's grace by assuming we have plenty of time left to get the job done. On the other hand, we dare not hinder the grace of God by assuming it is too late for our generation.

Prophecy lovers are especially prone to this second reaction. We are eschatological pessimists. We know all too well that things eventually are going to get worse, not better. We believe that a growing religious apostasy is strangling the spiritual life of our churches. And we have little hope in human efforts to revitalize our dying culture. As a result, we fall into a kind of eschatological "fatalism." If we are not careful, we may end up abandoning our calling and just sitting and waiting for the rapture. But there is no biblical warrant for such fatalism. The Bible never tells us that things will be so bad that we should give up and quit preaching altogether and wait for "the end." Rather, the Bible clearly instructs us to keep preaching, testifying, and witnessing, knowing that Christ will continue to build His church until He comes (Matthew 16:18).

One thing every Christian can do is to help teach and share the gospel both at home and around the world. We should also pray for our country and its leaders. Those who live in democratic societies should be well informed about political candidates who are up for election and support those who stand for religious freedom. Such freedom, of course, allows for the gospel to spread more easily.

In the meantime, we can live with our eyes on the skies—watching for Christ to come—and with our feet on the earth, working for Him until He comes.

> *The balance of expectation (that Jesus could come at any moment) and participation (serving Him faithfully until He comes) is what the Christian life is really all about.*

Living in the light of His coming keeps us focused on what is really important in life. It also keeps our attention on the balance between our present responsibilities and our future expectations.

The hope of the second coming is a powerful incentive for us to live right until Jesus comes. The ultimate encouragement toward right living is the fact that we will face our Lord when He returns. Each of us needs to be ready when that day comes. If we live out faithfully whatever time is left to us, we will surely hear Him say, "Well done, good and faithful servant."

A DATE WITH DESTINY

The world is speeding toward its ultimate date with destiny. Every day that passes moves us closer to the end. The people and the planet have a divine appointment to keep. As the clock of time ticks away, mankind comes closer and closer to earth's final hour.

It is only a matter of time before our planet will experience the most devastating catastrophes imaginable. Global conflagration is clearly predicted in biblical prophecy, and the outcome is certain. How much time is left?

Almost 2,000 years ago, the apostle Peter said, "The end of all things is near. Therefore be clear minded and self-controlled so that you can pray" (1 Peter 4:7). Way back in the New Testament era, Peter and the other apostles sensed that they had moved dramatically closer to the consummation of God's plan for this world. The Old Testament age had come to an end, and they were now part of a new era.

Peter's reference to the end is expressed by a perfect-tense verb in the original Greek text. This means the action involved is a present reality with future consequences. It could just as appropriately be translated, "The end of all things has already begun." For Peter, the end of the age was already a present reality.

The first coming of Christ initiated the end of the age (see Acts 2:14-20; Hebrews 1:2), and His second coming will terminate the end of the age (Matthew 24:30). Therefore, the entire church age is a "last days," or a "last of the last days."

Scripture also speaks of the end as a future event. The apostle Paul predicted, "There will be terrible times in the last days" (2 Timothy 3:1). The opening verse of the apocalypse refers to "things which must shortly come to pass" (Revelation 1:1 KJV) and goes on to warn us that "the time is near" (Revelation 1:3). Scripture also presents Christ's coming as an imminent reality. "Behold, I am coming soon!" Christ promised (Revelation 22:7). He will come suddenly, and He could come at any moment.

That leaves us asking this question: What time is it now? Peter referred to the *present,* saying, "[Christ] was revealed in these last times" (1 Peter 1:20). At the same time, Peter referred to the coming of Christ as a future event, "ready to be revealed in the last time" (1 Peter 1:5). It is clear that he viewed the last times as both a present reality and a future event.

The Bible affirms three basic facts about the coming of Christ at the end of the age.

First, *we are living in the last days.* Every generation of Christians has lived with the hope of the imminent return of Christ. We believe that He could return at any moment. There is no prophetic event that remains to be fulfilled before the way can be opened for Him to return. In fact, certain events, such as the return of Israel to her land, indicate that we are close to the end.

Second, *God's timetable is not our timetable.* Peter himself told us that "in the last days scoffers will come," questioning the promise of His second coming (2 Peter 3:3-4). They will reject the idea of God's intervention in human history and suggest that all things are moving forward at their own pace without any help from God. These skeptics will also fail to anticipate God's coming judgment upon the world (2 Peter 3:8). God's perspective is not limited to human time. But we dare not mistake the patience of God for a change in His plans. He is waiting, giving His people time to repent. The Bible warns: "He who is coming will come and will not delay" (Hebrews 10:37).

Third, *Christ's coming is always growing closer.* The Bible emphatically promises that Christ is coming again (Luke 12:40; Philippians 3:20; Titus 2:13; Hebrews 9:28). Scripture urges us to be watching, waiting, and ready for our Lord to return. Whether He returns next week or 100 years from now, we are to be living as though He were coming today.

LOOKING AHEAD

Anticipation is the key to preparation. If you were expecting an important visitor, you would probably keep looking for him as you await his arrival. Chances are that you would also make proper preparations for his visit. Your anticipation of the visitor's arrival would influence your preparation for his visit. The same is true of our anticipation of the coming of Christ. If we really believe He is coming, we will want to be prepared for Him when He comes.

Jesus illustrated this in His own prophetic teaching with the story of the ten virgins (Matthew 25:1-13). Only those who were prepared for the wedding were invited into the wedding banquet. The others were left out. Jesus used this illustration to remind us to keep watching because we don't know the time of His coming. Dr. John Walvoord comments on this passage, saying, "The important point here…is that preparation should precede the second coming of Christ and that it will be too late when He comes."[9]

If we can take seriously the biblical predictions about the end time, then we must make preparations now for what is coming in the future. We cannot wait until all other options have been exhausted. The time for action is now. If you are not sure about your own relationship with Christ, make sure before it is too late.

There are many things that demand our attention in life. There are many voices calling to us, and many images that flash across our minds. But no matter what our focus in life, one thing is certain: All of us will face death at some point. We cannot avoid it. All of us are vulnerable.

Death is the great equalizer. It makes no difference how rich or poor, famous or infamous, respected or rejected you may have been in this life. When you face death, you are facing an impartial judge. The Bible reminds us that "all have sinned" (Romans 3:23) and the "wages of sin is death" (Romans 6:23). When death comes knocking at your door, all that really matters is that you are ready to face it.

The reason for Jesus' coming was to die for our sins. He came to pay the price for our sins so that we might be forgiven. He is called our Redeemer because He has done what is necessary to redeem us from God's judgment against our sin. The apostle Peter wrote: "You were redeemed…with the precious blood of Christ.… He was chosen before the creation of the world, but was revealed in these last times for your sake" (1 Peter 1:18-20).

What Does the Future Hold?

The Bible predicts the major events of the future. It gives us the big picture of what is coming in the end times. The specific details are not always clear, and we must be cautious about trying to speculate beyond what the Bible itself actually says. Our goal ought to be one of balance. Don't *minimize* or *maximize* the future. Don't make the Bible say *less* than what it says, but also don't try to make it say *more* than what it says.

The question of the interpretation of biblical prophecy always raises the issue of one's eschatological view. Those who prefer a literal interpretation of prophecy foresee Israel back in the Promised Land, the probable rebuilding of the temple, the rise of a literal Antichrist, the making and breaking of a real peace treaty, and the ultimate invasion of Israel, which leads to the Battle of Armageddon.

We do not believe that we can simply "spiritualize" away the basic statements of Bible prophecy. For us, the rapture means being "caught up" into heaven (1 Thessalonians 4:13-17) and the "one thousand years" of Christ's reign means 1,000 years (Revelation 20:4). We do not discount the use of figurative or symbolic language in prophetic passages (e.g., the Lamb, the beast, the dragon). But we believe strongly that prophetic passages pointing to the second coming of Christ refer to specific people and events, as did the prophetic passages pointing to His first coming (e.g., Isaiah 53).

Based on a pretribulational viewpoint, we believe that Jesus Christ will return to rapture the church prior to the tribulation period. In commenting on this spectacular event, the apostle Paul wrote: "For the Lord himself will come down from heaven, with a loud command, with the voice of the archangel and with the trumpet call of God, and the dead in Christ will rise first. After that, we who are still alive and are left will be caught up [Greek *harpazo*, "snatched away"] with them in the clouds to meet the Lord in the air. And so we will be with the Lord forever" (1 Thessalonians 4:16-17).

The general picture of the future in biblical prophecy centers around 15 key predictions:

1. Spread of the gospel message and the growth of the church

Jesus established the church and promised to continue to build it until He returns (Matthew 16:18). He also predicted that the gospel "will be preached in the whole world as a testimony to all nations" (Matthew 24:14). The growth of the church and world evangelism will continue until the body of Christ is complete. There is no specific prediction of how long the Church Age will last. It will continue until the Lord returns to call the church home.

2. Increase of wickedness and the spread of evil

The Bible also predicts that the "increase of evil" will continue until the end of the age (Matthew 24:12). Paul predicted that "there will be terrible times in the last days" and then defined those days as a time of unparalleled greed, avarice, and selfishness (2 Timothy 3:1-5). Today, these prophecies are being fulfilled at a startling pace.

3. Rise of false prophets and apostate religion

Jesus Himself warned about the coming of "false Christs" and "false prophets" (Matthew 24:4,24). Peter predicted: "there will be false teachers" (2 Peter 2:1). Paul called them "false apostles, deceitful workmen, masquerading as apostles of Christ" (2 Corinthians 11:13). The Bible seems to indicate that false prophets and apostate religion will become worse as we get closer to the end (Jude 17-18).

4. Return of Israel to the Promised Land

"I will bring you from the nations...where you have been scattered," wrote the prophet (Ezekiel 20:34). "I will bring your children...from the ends of the earth," promised Isaiah (43:5-6). In 1948, these ancient prophecies were fulfilled when Israel became a nation again after nearly 1,900 years in exile. Ezekiel predicted a two-stage return: 1) physical regathering; and 2) spiritual rebirth (Ezekiel 37:1-14).

5. Conflict in the Middle East

The general picture of the future is one of turmoil between the Jews and the Arabs in the Middle East. Jesus warned that there would continually be "wars and rumors of wars" in the future (Matthew 24:6-7). The prophet Joel predicts the nations invading Israel in the last days—"multitudes, multitudes in the valley of decision: for the day of the Lord is near in the valley of decision" (Joel 3:2-14 KJV). Ezekiel (38:1-6) predicts a massive invasion of Israel in the "latter days" by a coalition of nations—Magog, Persia, Libya, Ethiopia, Gomer, and Togarmah. Collectively, the prophets foresee Israel back in the land but under constant threat of attack.

6. The rapture of the church

At some undated time in the future, Jesus will return to rapture the church (believers) to heaven. When He was preparing to return to heaven, Jesus promised, "I will come back and take you to be with me" (John 14:3).

Paul predicted that those who had died in Christ "will rise first," then the living believers "will be caught up" into the clouds and united with those who have been resurrected (1 Thessalonians 4:13-17). The rapture will happen "in a flash, in the twinkling of an eye, at the last trumpet" (1 Corinthians 15:51). The rapture precedes the tribulation period and fulfills the Lord's promise: "I will keep you from the hour of trial that is going to come upon the whole world" (Revelation 3:10).

7. Marriage of Christ and the church in heaven

After the rapture and prior to the return of Christ to the earth, the "wedding of the Lamb" will take place in heaven (Revelation 19:7-9). The marriage is followed by the "wedding supper" (the reception) and appears to last for seven years during the tribulation period. Christ is pictured as the husband or bridegroom, and the church is pictured as the bride of Christ (see Ephesians 5:25-27; 2 Corinthians 11:2). Following the pattern of traditional Jewish weddings in biblical times, Jesus pictured the promised engagement, followed by the departure of the groom to prepare a place for the bride, followed by the groom's sudden return at "midnight" to call the bride away (Matthew 26:1-6).

8. Rise of the Antichrist and the false prophet

Paul predicts the rise of the "lawless one" after the restrainer (indwelling Spirit in the church) has been removed (2 Thessalonians 2:3-8). "Then the lawless one will be revealed," Paul writes. This seems to indicate that the identity of the Antichrist will remain a mystery until after the rapture. John calls him "the beast" in Revelation 13:1-10, and "the antichrist" in 1 John 2:22. John also pictures this last great political leader being assisted by the "false prophet"—a false religious leader (Revelation 13:11-18). Together, they deceive the whole world during the tribulation period.

9. Development of a global system

The book of Revelation clearly predicts the world of the future will combine a global economy (Revelation 13:16-17) with a world government (13:8; 17:1-18) and a world religion (13:8-12). The global economy is already a reality! The world government is already in the process of forming under the banner of democracy. At the present time, the United States is the major player in the attempt to ensure global peace and security. While there is no real consensus of world religion today, such could easily happen after the rapture. In the meantime, the sentiment of apostate Christendom continues to favor a religion of universal tolerance.

10. The tribulation period

Despite efforts at world peace, the rule of the Antichrist will be marked by wars of mass destruction, environmental disasters, and divine judgments (Revelation 6:1-16; 9:16-18). Daniel (12:1) calls this period a "time of distress." Zephaniah (1:14) calls it the "great day of the LORD." Jeremiah (30:7) calls it "a time of trouble for Jacob." John calls it the "wrath of the Lamb" (Revelation 16:16). Most pretribulationalists view the tribulation period as being simultaneous with the seven years of Daniel's seventieth week (Daniel 9:24-27). We believe the Antichrist will make a peace treaty with Israel during this period only to break the treaty at the midpoint of the tribulation period (Daniel 9:27).

11. The Battle of Armageddon

The prophetic picture indicates a series of wars of mass destruction are coming in the future (Revelation 6–18). These will result in nearly half the population of the world being destroyed (Revelation 8:7; 9:16-18). Eventually, these wars will culminate in a final battle at "the place...called Armageddon" (Revelation 16:16). The mountains will be "soaked with blood" (Isaiah 34:3). "All the nations that fought against Jerusalem" will be destroyed (Zechariah 14:12-13). In the end, Christ Himself will return and conquer the beast and the false prophet, casting them into the lake of fire (Revelation 19:11-20). Satan will be bound in the abyss for a thousand years (Revelation 20:1-2). The greatest battle in the history of the world will be won when Jesus conquers the enemies of God by the power of His spoken word (Revelation 19:15,21).

12. Triumphal return of Christ

Jesus predicted that one day "the sign of the Son of Man will appear in the sky.... They will see the Son of Man coming on the clouds of the sky, with power and great glory" (Matthew 24:30). Zechariah (14:3-4) predicted that "his feet will stand on the Mount of Olives" and it will "split in two" when He returns. Isaiah (63:1-4) pictures Christ marching in triumph in blood-splattered garments on the "day of vengeance." Revelation 19:11-16 describes Him coming on a white horse with the church, robed in white, at His side. He "judges" with eyes of "blazing fire" and "makes war" with the "sharp sword" of His spoken word. He treads the "winepress...of the wrath of God" when He comes to rule as "King of kings and Lord of lords."

13. Millennial kingdom

The Old Testament prophets picture the coming Messianic Age as a time of peace and prosperity for Israel when "they will beat their swords into plowshares" and "nation will not take up sword against nation" (Isaiah 2:2-4). They also foresaw the Messiah reigning "on David's throne and over his kingdom" (Isaiah 9:6-7). The New Testament pictures this as a time when Christ rules on earth with His bride, the church, for 1,000 years (Revelation 20:1-6). During this time we will "reign on earth" as kings and priests with Christ (Revelation 5:10). Those who have survived the Tribulation will live on into the millennial kingdom as life continues on earth for 1,000 years.

14. Great white throne judgment

After the 1,000-year reign, Satan will be loosed from the abyss and attempt one last time to overthrow the kingdom of God (Revelation 20:7-10). This time he will be permanently defeated and cast into the lake of fire. The millennial kingdom will be transferred into the eternal kingdom of God (1 Corinthians 15:24), and the great white throne judgment settles the eternal condemnation of all the lost of all time whose names are "not found written in the book of life" (Revelation 20:11-15). At that time, even "death and hell" will be thrown into the lake of fire that is the "second death."

15. Eternity

The Bible pictures the eternal state as one of perpetual bliss where paradise is regained. The "tree of life" is restored (Revelation 22:2) and the redeemed of all time live together in the "new heavens" and "new earth" with the "new Jerusalem" as their central dwelling place (Revelation 21:1-23). Tears are wiped away and there will be "no more death or mourning or crying or pain" (Revelation 21:41). Isaiah (65:19) predicted, "the sound of weeping and crying will be heard no more." God the Father and Christ the Lamb are pictured as the light and the temple of the eternal city (Revelation 21:22-23). The twelve gates of the city are named for the twelve tribes of Israel and the twelve foundations for the twelve apostles, emphasizing the eternal unity of the redeemed people of God (Revelation 21:11-14).

Jesus said: "I am the resurrection and the life. He who believes in me will live, even though he dies" (John 11:25). This is the great promise of Christ. He calls us to faith in Him and then promises to reward us with eternal life (John 3:16; 4:36; 5:24). The Bible pictures eternity as a place of great activity where we serve Christ forever. In the meantime, we are "pilgrims" passing through the temporary domain of Earth on our way to our ultimate home. Joseph Stowell writes: "To claim the pilgrim's identity means that we always know we're not home yet. For us, the best is yet to come."[10]

Until the trumpet sounds, or death comes to usher us into eternity, we are to keep our eyes on the Savior (Hebrews 12:2). He is the focus of Bible prophecy. The prophets predicted His first coming with incredible accuracy, and they have done the same for His second coming. Jesus said, "When these things begin to take place, stand up and lift up your heads, because your redemption is drawing near" (Luke 21:28).

Whatever else is coming in the future, we can rest assured that Jesus is coming again!

WHAT ABOUT YOU?

"I write these things to you who believe in the name of the Son of God, so that you may know that you have eternal life."
—1 John 5:13

No matter who we are or what we do, there is one thing that is the same for all of us. We are certain to die at some point. We cannot avoid it. All of us are vulnerable to that final reality.

As we said earlier, death is the great equalizer. We cannot escape it. "All have sinned" (Romans 3:23), and the "wages of sin is death" (Romans 6:23). Are you ready to face death when it comes knocking?

"How can I be ready?" Tom asked us recently. "I know that I am running out of time." He had been resisting God for quite a while.

"You must respond by faith to God's promise to save you," we replied. "Christ died for your sins and rose from the dead to give you eternal life. Trusting Him for your salvation means believing that when He died, He died for *you* and that when He rose, He rose for *you*. The basic invitation of Scripture says, 'Everyone who calls on the name of the Lord will be saved'" (Romans 10:13).

"Have you ever asked Him to save you and believed that He really would?" we asked.

"No," Tom replied, lowering his head.

"Would you like to ask Him to forgive your sins, save your soul, and take you to heaven?" we asked further.

"Yes, I would!" he said emphatically.

As we bowed our heads and prayed, Tom called upon the Lord Jesus Christ by faith to save him.

When we finished praying together, Tom looked at us and said, "Now I'm ready because I believe the Lord will keep His promise to me."

You can have that same kind of assurance in your life. You may have been drawn to an interest in prophecies of the end times so that you could think through the question of your own destiny. Perhaps you've heard people talk about Armageddon, the coming of Christ, and the end of the age, and you've realized that you are not ready to meet Jesus when He comes. Perhaps you have recognized that the end could come at any moment and you are not prepared to step into eternity.

There is no better time to settle the question of your eternal destiny than right now. John the Baptist called Jesus "the Lamb of God, who takes away the sin of the world" (John 1:29). Won't you let Him take away your sin? Bow your heart, soul, mind, and head before Him and ask Him to save you right now.

When Billy Graham was asked on a popular television show to summarize what his life and ministry were all about, he simply quoted John 3:16: "For God so loved the world that he gave his one and only Son, that whoever believes in him shall not perish but have eternal life."

The clock of human history is ticking away. It neither speeds up nor slows down. It just keeps on ticking continually and relentlessly, moving us closer and closer to the end of the age. How close we are to the end will be revealed only by time itself. Don't gamble with your eternal destiny. Time may very well be running out. Jesus is coming. The question is, Is He coming for you?

25 AMAZING PROPHECIES OF THE END TIMES

THE PROPHECIES IN THIS appendix are listed in 25 categories and taken directly from Scripture. These are for personal study and easy cross-reference. The Bible is the only source of the "sure word of prophecy" (2 Peter 2:19 KJV). And God's Word is the only true prophecy of future events. More important than human opinion is what God says about the future. Search these scriptures for yourself and see what the Holy Spirit has revealed about the end times.

1. *Spread of the Gospel Message and Growth of the Church*

"I will build my church, and the gates of Hades will not overcome it" (Matthew 16:18).

"This gospel of the kingdom will be preached in the whole world as a testimony to all nations, and then the end will come" (Matthew 24:14).

"The kingdom of heaven is like a mustard seed, which a man took and planted in his field. Though it is the smallest of all your seeds, yet when it grows, it is the largest of garden plants and becomes a tree" (Matthew 13:31-32).

2. *Increase of Wickedness and the Spread of Evil*

"Because of the increase of wickedness, the love of most will grow cold" (Matthew 24:12).

"But mark this: There will be terrible times in the last days. People will be lovers of themselves, lovers of money, boastful, proud, abusive, disobedient to their parents, ungrateful, unholy, without love, unforgiving, slanderous, without self-control, brutal, not lovers of the good, treacherous, rash, conceited, lovers of pleasure rather than lovers of God—having a form of godliness but denying its power" (2 Timothy 3:1-5).

"You must understand that in the last days scoffers will come, scoffing and following their own evil desires. They will say, 'Where is this "coming" he promised?'" (2 Peter 3:3-4).

"Remember what the apostles of our Lord Jesus Christ foretold. They said to you, 'In the last times there will be scoffers who will follow their own ungodly desires'" (Jude 17-18).

3. *Rise of False Prophets and Apostate Religion*

"The Spirit clearly says that in later times some will abandon the faith and follow deceiving spirits and things taught by demons" (1 Timothy 4:1).

"Jesus answered: 'Watch out that no one deceives you. For many will come in my name, claiming, "I am the Christ," and will deceive many.... For false Christs and false prophets will appear and perform great signs and miracles to deceive even the elect—if that were possible'" (Matthew 24:4,24).

"There were also false prophets among the people, just as there will be false teachers among you. They will secretly introduce destructive heresies.... In their greed these teachers will exploit you with stories they have made up" (2 Peter 2:1-3).

"For such men are false apostles, deceitful workmen, masquerading as apostles of Christ. And no wonder, for Satan himself masquerades as an angel of light" (2 Corinthians 11:13-14).

4. *Continuation of "the Times of the Gentiles"*

"Jerusalem will be trampled on by the Gentiles until the times of the Gentiles are fulfilled" (Luke 21:24).

"I do not want you to be ignorant of this mystery, brothers...Israel has experienced a hardening in part until the full number of the Gentiles has come in" (Romans 11:25).

"I ask then: Did God reject his people? By no means!...at the present time there is a remnant chosen by grace" (Romans 11:1,5).

"How long will it be before these astonishing things are fulfilled?... It will be for a time, times and half a time. When the power of the holy people has been finally broken, all these things will be completed" (Daniel 12:6-7).

5. *Return of Israel to the Land*

"I will bring you from the nations and gather you from the countries where you have been scattered" (Ezekiel 20:34).

"Therefore prophesy and say to them: 'This is what the Sovereign LORD says: O my people, I am going to open your graves and bring you up from them; I will bring you back to the land of Israel....and I will settle you in your own land'" (Ezekiel 37:12,14).

"This is what the Sovereign LORD says: 'I will take the Israelites out of the nations where they have gone. I will gather them from all around and bring them back into their own land'" (Ezekiel 37:21).

"I will bring your children from the east and gather you from the west. I will say to the north, 'Give them up!' and to the south, 'Do not hold them back.' Bring my sons from afar and my daughters from the ends of the earth" (Isaiah 43:5-6).

"I will bring back my exiled people Israel; they will rebuild the ruined cities and live in them" (Amos 9:14).

6. *Conflict in the Middle East*

"When you see Jerusalem being surrounded by armies, you will know that its desolations is near.... For this is the time of punishment in fulfillment of all that has been written" (Luke 21:20,22).

"The word of the LORD came to me: 'Son of man, set your face against God, of the land of Magog, the chief prince of Meshech and Tubal.... Persia, Cush and Put will be with them...also Gomer will all its troops, and Beth Togarmah from the far north with all its troops—the many nations with you'" (Ezekiel 38:1-2,5-6).

"I will gather all nations and bring them down to the Valley of Jehoshaphat.... Proclaim this among the nations: Prepare for war!... Multitudes, multitudes in the valley of decision! For the day of the LORD is near in the valley of decision" (Joel 3:2,9,14).

"You will hear of wars and rumors of wars, but see to it that you are not alarmed. Such things must happen, but the end is still to come. Nation will rise against nation, and kingdom against kingdom" (Matthew 24:6-7).

7. *The Rapture of the Church*

"If I go and prepare a place for you, I will come back and take you to be with me that you also may be where I am" (John 14:3).

"I will also keep you from the hour of trial that is going to come upon the whole world" (Revelation 3:10).

"Concerning the coming of our Lord Jesus Christ and our being gathered to him, we ask you, brothers, not to become easily unsettled or alarmed" (2 Thessalonians 2:1-2).

"The dead in Christ will rise first. After that, we who are still alive and are left will be caught up together with them in the clouds to meet the Lord in the air" (1 Thessalonians 4:16-17).

"Listen, I tell you a mystery: We will not all sleep, but we will all be changed—in a flash, in the twinkling of an eye, at the last trumpet. For the trumpet will sound, the dead will be raised imperishable, and we will be changed" (1 Corinthians 15:51-52).

"They came to life and reigned with Christ a thousand years.... This is the first resurrection" (Revelation 20:4-5).

8. *Marriage of Christ and the Church in Heaven*

"Let us rejoice and be glad and give him glory! For the wedding of the Lamb has come, and his bride has made herself ready" (Revelation 19:7).

"I am jealous for you with a godly jealousy. I promised you to one husband, to Christ, so that I might present you as a pure virgin to him" (2 Corinthians 11:2).

"Husbands, love your wives, just as Christ loved the church and gave himself up for her to make her holy…and to present her to himself as a radiant church, without stain or wrinkle or any other blemish, but holy and blameless" (Ephesians 5:25-27).

"At midnight the cry rang out: 'Here's the bridegroom! Come out to meet him!'" (Matthew 25:6).

9. *Rise of the Antichrist and the False Prophet*

"Don't let anyone deceive you in any way, for that day will not come until the rebellion occurs and the man of lawlessness is revealed, the man doomed to destruction. He will oppose and will exalt himself over everything that is called God or is worshiped, so that he sets himself up in God's temple, proclaiming himself to be God.... And then the lawless one will be revealed, whom the Lord Jesus will overthrow with the breath of his mouth and destroy by the splendor of his coming" (2 Thessalonians 2:3-4,8).

"Who is the liar? It is the man who denies that Jesus is the Christ. Such a man is the antichrist—he denies the Father and the Son" (1 John 2:22).

"I saw a beast coming out of the sea. He had ten horns and seven heads.... resembled a leopard…a bear…a lion. The dragon gave the beast his power and his throne and great authority.... The whole world was astonished and followed the beast....and they also worshiped the beast and asked,

'Who is like the beast? Who can make war against him?'" (Revelation 13:1-4).

"I saw another beast, coming out of the earth. He had two horns like a lamb, but he spoke like a dragon. He...made the earth and its inhabitants worship the first beast....he deceived the inhabitants of the earth. He ordered them to set up an image in honor of the beast.... He also forced everyone, small and great, rich and poor, free and slave, to receive a mark on his right hand or on his forehead, so that no one could buy or sell unless he had the mark, which is the name of the beast or the number of his name.... 666" (Revelation 13:11-12,14-18).

10. *Development of a Global Economy*

"He also forced everyone, small and great, rich and poor, free and slave, to receive a mark on his right hand or on his forehead, so that no one could buy or sell unless he had the mark, which is the name of the beast or the number of his name" (Revelation 13:16-17).

"The merchants of the earth grew rich from [Babylon's] excessive luxuries.... The merchants of the earth will weep and mourn over her because no one buys their cargoes any more—cargoes of gold, silver, precious stones and pearls; fine linen, purple, silk and scarlet cloth; every sort of citron wood, and articles of every kind made of ivory, costly wood, bronze, iron and marble.... Your merchants were the world's great men. By your magic spell all the nations were led astray" (Revelation 18:3,11-12,23).

11. *Formation of a World Government*

"It will be different from all the other kingdoms and will devour the whole earth, trampling it down and crushing it" (Daniel 7:23).

"All inhabitants of the earth will worship the beast—all whose names have not been written in the book of life belonging to the Lamb that was slain from the creation of the world" (Revelation 13:8).

"He exercised all the authority of the first beast on his behalf, and made the earth and its inhabitants worship the first beast, whose fatal wound had been healed" (Revelation 13:12).

the night. While people are saying, 'Peace and safety,' destruction will come on them suddenly, as labor pains on a pregnant woman, and they will not escape" (1 Thessalonians 5:1-3).

"They called to the mountains and the rocks. 'Fall on us and hide us from the face of him who sits on the throne and from the wrath of the Lamb! For the great day of their wrath has come and who can stand?' " (Revelation 6:16-17).

16. *Conversion of Israel*

"I will make known my holy name among my people Israel.... It is coming! It will surely take place, declares the Sovereign LORD. This is the day I have spoken of" (Ezekiel 39:7-8).

"I will pour out on the house of David and the inhabitants of Jerusalem a spirit of grace and supplication. They will look on me, the one they have pierced, and they will mourn for him as one mourns for an only child, and grieve bitterly for him as one grieves for a firstborn son" (Zechariah 12:10).

"On that day a fountain will be opened to the house of David and the inhabitants of Jerusalem, to cleanse them from sin and impurity.... If someone asks him, 'What are these wounds on your body?' he will answer, 'The wounds I was given at the house of my friends' " (Zechariah 13:1,6).

"Israel has experienced a hardening in part until the full number of Gentiles has come in. And so all Israel will be saved, as it is written: 'The deliverer will come from Zion; he will turn godlessness away from Jacob. And this is my covenant with them when I take away their sins' " (Romans 11:25-27).

"I heard the number of those who were sealed: 144,000 from all the tribes of Israel" (Revelation 7:4).

17. *Battle of Armageddon*

"They gathered the kings together to the place that in Hebrew is called Armageddon" (Revelation 16:16).

"See, the LORD is going to lay waste the earth and devastate it…. Therefore earth's inhabitants are burned up, and very few are left" (Isaiah 24:1,6).

"The LORD is angry with all nations; his wrath is upon all their armies. He will totally destroy them….the mountains will be soaked with their blood" (Isaiah 34:2-3).

"The LORD will strike all the nations that fought against Jerusalem. Their flesh will rot while they are still standing on their feet, their eyes will rot in their sockets, and their tongues will rot in their mouths. On that day men will be stricken by the LORD with great panic" (Zechariah 14:12-13).

"The beast was captured, and with him the false prophet…. The two of them were thrown alive into the fiery lake of burning sulfur" (Revelation 19:20).

18. *Fall of Babylon*

"Fallen! Fallen is Babylon the Great! She has become a home for demons and a haunt for every evil spirit…. Give her as much torture and grief as the glory and luxury she gave herself…. Therefore in one day her plagues will overtake her: death, mourning and famine. She will be consumed by fire, for mighty is the LORD God who judges her. When the Kings of the earth…see the smoke of her burning, they will weep and mourn over her…. Woe! Woe, O great city, O Babylon, city of power! In one hour your doom has come!" (Revelation 18:2,7-10).

"With such violence the great city of Babylon will be thrown down, never to be found again" (Revelation 18:21).

19. *Judgment Seat of Christ*

"We will all stand before God's judgment seat…. So then, each of us will give an account of himself to God" (Romans 14:10,12).

"We must all appear before the judgment seat of Christ, that each one may receive what is due him for the things done while in the body, whether good or bad" (2 Corinthians 5:10).

"His work will be shown for what it is.... It will be revealed with fire, and the fire will test the quality of each man's work.... If it is burned up, he will suffer loss; he himself will be saved, but only as one escaping through the flames" (1 Corinthians 3:13-15).

"I have fought the good fight, I have finished the race, I have kept the faith. Now there is in store for me the crown of righteousness, which the Lord, the righteous Judge, will award to me on that day—and not only to me, but also to all who have longed for his appearing" (2 Timothy 4:7-8).

20. *Triumphal Return of Christ and His Church*

"There will be signs in the sun, moon and stars....heavenly bodies will be shaken. At that time they will see the Son of Man coming in a cloud with power and great glory. When these things begin to take place, stand up and lift up your heads, because your redemption is drawing near" (Luke 21:25-28).

"At that time the sign of the Son of Man will appear in the sky, and all the nations of the earth will mourn. They will see the Son of Man coming on the clouds of the sky, with power and great glory" (Matthew 24:30).

"The LORD will go out and fight against those nations.... On that day his feet will stand on the Mount of Olives, east of Jerusalem, and the Mount of Olives will be split in two from east to west" (Zechariah 14:3-4).

"Who is this coming from Edom, from Bozrah, with his garments stained crimson? Who is this, robed in splendor, striding forward in the greatness of his strength?... I trampled them in my anger and trod them down in my wrath; their blood splattered my garments, And I stained all my clothing. For the day of vengeance was in my heart, and the year of my redemption has come" (Isaiah 63:1,3-4).

"Multitudes, multitudes in the valley of decision! For the day of the LORD is near in the valley of decision. The sun and moon will be darkened, and the stars no longer shine. The LORD will roar from Zion and thunder from Jerusalem the earth and the sky will tremble. But the LORD will be a refuge for his people, A stronghold for the people of Israel" (Joel 3:14-16).

"I saw heaven standing open and there before me was a white horse, whose rider is called Faithful and True. With justice he judges and makes war. His eyes are like blazing fire, and on his head are many crowns. He has a name written on him that no one knows but he himself. He is dressed in a robe dipped in blood, and his name is the Word of God. The armies of heaven were following him, riding on white horses and dressed in fine linen, white and clean. Out of his mouth comes a sharp sword with which to strike down the nations. He will rule them with an iron scepter. He treads the winepress of the fury of the wrath of God Almighty. On his robe and on his thigh he has this name written: King of kings and Lord of lords" (Revelation 19:11-16).

21. *Judgment of the Nations*

"In those days and at that time, when I restore the fortunes of Judah and Jerusalem, I will gather all nations and bring them down to the Valley of Jehoshaphat. There I will enter into judgment against them concerning my inheritance, my people Israel" (Joel 3:1-2).

"When the Son of Man comes in his glory, and all the angels with him, he will sit on his throne in heavenly glory. All the nations will be gathered before him, and he will separate the people one from another as a shepherd separates the sheep from the goats. He will put the sheep on his right and the goats on his left. Then the King will say to those on his right, 'Come, you who are blessed by my Father; take your inheritance, the kingdom prepared for you since the creation of the world....' Then he will say to those on his left, 'Depart from me, you who are cursed, into the eternal fire prepared for the devil and his angels'" (Matthew 25:31-34,41).

22. *Millennial Kingdom*

"The beast was captured, and with him the false prophet.... The two of them were thrown alive into the fiery lake of burning sulfur.... And I saw an angel coming down out of heaven, having the key to the Abyss and holding in his hand a great chain. He seized the dragon, that ancient serpent, who is the devil, or Satan, and bound him for a thousand years.... into the Abyss" (Revelation 19:20;20:1-3).

"You have made them to be a kingdom and priests to serve our God, and they will reign on the earth" (Revelation 5:10).

"They came to life and reigned with Christ a thousand years.... This is the first resurrection.... The second death has no power over them, but they will be priests of God and of Christ and will reign with him for a thousand years" (Revelation 20:4-6).

"In the last days the mountain of the LORD's temple will be established as chief among the mountains; it will be raised above the hills, and all nations will stream to it. Many peoples will come and say, 'Come, let us go up to the mountain of the LORD, to the house of the God of Jacob.'... The law will go out from Zion, the word of the LORD from Jerusalem.... They will beat their swords into plowshares and their spears into pruning hooks. Nation will not take up sword against nation, nor will they train for war anymore" (Isaiah 2:2-4).

"For to us a child is born, to us a son is given, and the government will be on his shoulders. And he will be called Wonderful Counselor, Mighty God, Everlasting Father, Prince of Peace. Of the increase of his government and peace there will be no end. He will reign on David's throne and over his kingdom, establishing and upholding it with justice and righteousness from that time on and forever" (Isaiah 9:6-7).

23. *Great White Throne Judgment*

"When the thousand years are over, Satan will be released from his prison and will go out to deceive the nations...to gather them for battle.... But fire came down from heaven and devoured them. And the devil, who deceived them, was thrown into the lake of burning sulfur, where the beast and the false prophet had been thrown. They will be tormented day and night for ever and ever.

Then I saw a great white throne and him who was seated on it. Earth and sky fled from his presence, and there was no place for them. And I saw the dead, great and small, standing before the throne, and books were opened. Another book was opened, which is the book of life.... death and Hades gave up the dead that were in them, and each person was judges according to what he had done. Then death and Hades were thrown into the lake of fire. The lake of fire is the second death. If anyone's name was not found written in the book of life, he was thrown into the lake of fire" (Revelation 20:7-15).

24. *New Heavens and New Earth*

"Behold, I will create new heavens and a new earth. The former things will not be remembered, nor will they come to mind.... I will rejoice over Jerusalem and take delight in my people; the sound of weeping and of crying will be heard in it no more.... This is what the LORD says: 'Heaven is my throne, and the earth is my footstool. Where is the house you will build for me? Where will my resting place be? Has not my hand made all these things, And so they came into being?'" (Isaiah 65:17,19; 66:1-2).

"I saw a new heaven and a new earth, for the first heaven and the first earth had passed away, and there was no longer any sea. I saw the Holy City, the new Jerusalem, coming down out of heaven from God, prepared as a bride.... One of the seven angels...said to me, 'Come, I will show you the bridge, the wife of the Lamb....and he...showed me the Holy City, Jerusalem, coming down out of heaven from God. It shone with the glory of God.'... I did not see a temple in the city, because the Lord God Almighty and the Lamb are its temple. The city does not need the sun or the moon to shine on it, for the glory of God gives it light, and the Lamb is its lamp" (Revelation 21:1-2,9-11,22-23).

25. *Eternal State*

"Multitudes who sleep in the dust of the earth will awake: some to everlasting life, others to shame and everlasting contempt. Those who are wise will shine like the brightness of the heavens, and those who lead many to righteousness, like the stars for ever and ever" (Daniel 12:2-3).

"Your dead will live; their bodies will rise. You who dwell in the dust, wake up and shout for joy" (Isaiah 26:19).

"Jesus said to her, 'I am the resurrection and the life. He who believes in me will live, even though he dies; and whoever lives and believes in me will never die'" (John 11:25-26).

"Then the end will come, when he hands over the kingdom to God the Father after he has destroyed all dominion, authority, and power. For he must reign until he has put all his enemies under his feet. The last enemy to be destroyed is death.... When the perishable has been clothed with the imperishable, and the mortal with immortality, then the saying that is written will come true: 'Death has been swallowed up in victory'" (1 Corinthians 15:24-26,54).

"I heard a loud voice from the throne saying, 'Now the dwelling of God is with men, and he will live with them. They will be his people, and God himself will be with them and be their God. He will wipe every tear from their eyes. There will be no more death or mourning or crying or pain, for the old order of things has passed away'" (Revelation 21:3-4).

"The angel showed me the river of the water of life, as clear as crystal, flowing from the throne of God and of the Lamb.... On each side of the river stood the tree of life.... The throne of God and of the Lamb will be in the city, and his servants will serve him. They will see his face, and his name will be on their foreheads.... And they will reign for ever and ever" (Revelation 22:1-5).

"Whoever believes in the Son has eternal life, but whoever rejects the Son will not see life, for God's wrath remains on him" (John 3:36).

"Everyone who calls on the name of the Lord will be saved" (Romans 10:13).

Endnotes

CHAPTER 1—AT THE BRINK OF DISASTER

1. Seymour M. Hersh, *The Samson Option* (New York: Random House, 1991), p. 177.

2. Rush Limbaugh in Harry Valentine, "It's a Religious War!" *Christian Worldwide Network,* August 19, 2006.

3. Weston Kosova and David Gerlach, "Terror in Our Time," *Newsweek,* August 28, 2006, pp. 54-55.

4. Adapted from the Center for Defense Information's article "What If the Terrorists Go Nuclear?" October 1, 2002. Accessed at http://www.cdi.org/terrorism/nuclear-pr.cfm.

5. "Pascal's New Wager: The Dirty Bomb Threat Heightens," *Center for Defense Information,* February 4, 2003.

6. Eben Kaplan, "America's 'Gravest Danger,'" *Council on Foreign Relations,* March 31, 2006.

7. See http://orise.orau.gov/reacts/.

8. "Testimony of Dr. Henry Kelly, President Federation of American Scientists before the Senate Committee on Foreign Relations," March 6, 2002.

9. "Nuclear Power Plant Security: Voices from Inside the Fences," *Project for Government Oversight,* September 12, 2002.

10. Such as the 2005 CRS Report to Congress at http://www.vnf.com/security/rs21131.pdf.

11. "Security Effectiveness: Independent Studies and Drills," *Nuclear Energy Institute,* 2002.

12. John Mintz, "U.S. Called Unprepared for Nuclear Terrorism," *Washington Post,* May 3, 2005.

13. From the Nuclear Weapons Archive at http://nuclearweaponarchive.org/Nwfaq/Nfaq4.html.

14. "Terrorists' Nuclear Capabilities," *Council on Foreign Relations,* January 2006.

15. "Mubarak Says Egypt Will Develop Nuclear Energy," *People's Daily Online,* September 22, 2006.

16. Cited in "Arab Nations Seeking Nukes?" *Israel Today,* December 2006, p. 9.

17. Graham Allison, *Nuclear Terrorism: The Ultimate Preventable Catastrophe* (New York: Owl Books, 2004), pp. 161-62.

18. "Israel: Iran Must Not Acquire Nuclear Weapons," *CNN,* January 17, 2006.

19. Alireza Jafarzadeh, *The Iran Threat* (New York: Palgrave Macmillan, 2007), p. 201.

20. Benjamin Netanyahu, *Fighting Terrorism* (New York: Farrar, Straus & Giroux, 1995), p. 96.

21. Duncan Long, *The Bio-Terrorism Manual* (Plantation, FL: Life and Health Research Group, 2003).

22. "A Lexicon of Terror: Post 9-11," *St. Petersburg Times,* September 8, 2002.

23. "Lab Tests Could Link Saddam's Missing WMDs to Jordan Plot," Newsmax.com, April 20, 2004.

24. Grant R. Jeffrey, *The Next World War* (Colorado Springs, CO: WaterBrook, 2006), p. 82.

25. "Securing U.S. Water Supplies," *Center for Defense Intelligence,* July 19, 2002.

26. See http://www.epa.gov/nhsrc/.

27. Justin Bloom, "Terrorists Have Oil Industry in Cross Hairs," *Washington Post,* September 27, 2004.

28. Roger Howard, "Oil Price Warfare," *The National Interest,* September/October 2006, p. 85.

29. Shibley Telhami, "The Persian Gulf: Understanding the American Oil Strategy," *The Brookings Review,* Spring 2002, Vol. 20 No. 2, pp. 32-35.

30. From the Energy Information Administration at http://www.eia.doe.gov/emeu/cabs/topworldtables1_2.html.

31. Cited in John Ankerberg and Dillon Burroughs, *Middle East Meltdown* (Eugene, OR: Harvest House Publishers, 2007), p. 67.

32. Eben Kaplan, "America's Gravest Danger," *Council on Foreign Relations,* March 31, 2006.

33. Joseph Garah, "Iran Plans to Knock Out U.S. with 1 Nuclear Bomb," *World Net Daily,* April 25, 2005 (emphasis added).

34. "Nuclear Weapon EMP Effects," *Special Weapons Primer,* Federation of American Scientists Web site, October 21, 1998. Accessed at http://www.fas.org/nuke/intro/nuke/emp.htm.

35. M. CaJohn, "Electromagnetic Pulse—from Chaos to a Manageable Solution," GlobalSecurity.org.

36. "Flying Robot Attack Unstoppable," PhysOrg.com, May 7, 2006.

37. Ibid.

38. David Hambling, "Terrorists' Unmanned Air Force," *Defense Tech.com,* May 1, 2006.

39. "Flying Robot Attack Unstoppable," PhysOrg.com, May 7, 2006.

40. "Remote Controlled Spy Planes," *CBS News,* November 6, 2002.

41. Randy Hall, "Al Qaeda Uses Web as 'Virtual Sanctuary,' Experts Say," CNSNews.com, May 12, 2006.

42. *The 9/11 Commission Report: Authorized Edition* (New York & London: W.W. Norton, 2004), pp. 157, 164, 495.

43. Gabriel Weimann, "Terror on the Internet: The New Arena, The New Challenges," seminar held at the United States Institute of Peace, Washington, D.C., April 10, 2006. Note that in the year since Professor Weimann completed his book, the number of terrorist Web sites increased from approximately 4,300 in May 2005 to 4,800 in May 2006.

44. Bruce Hoffman, "The Use of the Internet by Islamic Extremists," CT-262-1, May 2006. Testimony presented to the House Permanent Select Committee on Intelligence, on May 4, 2006.

45. Dana Priest, "Iraq New Terror Breeding Ground," *Washington Post,* January 14, 2005.

46. Jack Kelly, "Terror Groups Hide Behind Web Encryption," *USA Today,* February 7, 2001, p. 1.

47. Grant R. Jeffrey, *The Next World War* (Colorado Springs, CO: WaterBrook, 2006), pp. 88-89.

48. See http://earth.google.com/.

49. Thomas Harding, "Terrorists Use Google Maps to Target UK Troops," *UK Telegraph,* January 13, 2007.

50. "Protecting the Top Five Most Protective Targets, 2006," *The Strategy Page.*

51. Mark Hitchcock, *Iran: The Coming Crisis* (Sisters, OR: Multnomah Publishing, 2006), p. 103.

52. Matthew 16:2-3.

CHAPTER 2—IT'S LATER THAN YOU THINK

1. Mark Hitchcock, *Iran: The Coming Crisis* (Sisters, OR: Multnomah, 2006), p. 29.

2. Ibid., p. 15.

3. "Experts Warn of Future WMD Attack," *CBS News,* June 22, 2005.

4. Jason Lewis, "Outcry As Border Guards Seize British 'Dirty Bomb' Lorry Heading for Iran," *Daily Mail,* July 22, 2006.

5. "5 Minutes to Midnight," *The Bulletin Online,* 2007.

6. James Kanter and Andrew Revkin, "World Scientists Near Consensus on Warming," *New York Times,* January 30, 2007.

7. Richard Lindzen, "Earth in the Balance: Don't Believe the Hype," *Wall Street Journal,* July 2, 2006. Cf. also *Drudge Report,* February 12, 2007.

8. "5 Minutes to Midnight," *The Bulletin Online,* 2007. Accessed at http://www.thebulletin. org/minutes-to-midnight/.

9. Matthew 24:1-8.

10. See it at www.thewall.org.

11. Matthew 24:5.

12. "How Many Protestant Denominations Are There?" April 12, 2005. Accessed at http://www .bringyou.to/apologetics/al20.htm.

13. According to http://www.adherents.com/.

14. Tim LaHaye and Jerry Jenkins, *Are We Living in the End Times?* (Carol Stream, IL: Tyndale, 1999), p. 38.

15. "Gingrich Says World War III Has Begun," NewsMax.com, July 16, 2006 (emphasis added).

16. See also 2 Chronicles 15:1-7; Isaiah 19:1-2.

17. LaHaye and Jenkins, *Are We Living in the End Times?,* p. 39.

18. Matthew White, "Source List and Detailed Death Tolls for the Twentieth Century Hemoclysm." Accessed at http://users.erols.com/mwhite28/warstat1.htm.

19. Stephen Devereux, "Famine in the Twentieth Century," working paper of the Institute of Developmental Studies, 2006. Accessed at http://www.ids.ac.uk/ids/bookshop/wp/wp105.pdf.

20. See http://www.worldvision.org for more information.

21. "Africa's Famine: Country by Country," *BBC,* November 11, 2002.

22. Bernd Sebastian Kamps and Gustavo Reyes-Terán, "Influenza 2006," *Influenza Report,* 2006.

23. Bruce Kennedy, "Beating Back the Bugs," *CNN,* 1999. Accessed at http://www.cnn.com/SPECIALS/1999/century/episodes/05/currents/.

24. "HIV/AIDS," from the Global Health Council Web site. Accessed at http://globalhealth.org/view_top.php3?id=227. Based on 2005 statistics.

25. For instance, see the emphasis on this issue from Rick and Kay Warren at http://www.purposedriven.com/en-US/HIVAIDSCommunity/HIV_homepage.htm, including video footage of them speaking to over 22,000 college students on the issue at Urbana 2006.

26. "Most Recent Natural Disasters Were Not the Century's Worst, USGS Says," December 30, 1999.

27. Jennifer Rosenberg, "Top 10 Deadliest Earthquakes of the 20th Century," from 20th Century History at About.com. Accessed at http://history1900s.about.com/od/horribledisasters/a/deadlyquakes.htm.

28. "Tsunami Deaths Soar Past 212,000," *CNN,* January 19, 2005.

29. James Brandon, "The Caliphate: One Nation, Under Allah, with 1.5 Billion Muslims," *Christian Science Monitor,* May 10, 2006.

30. Roee Nahmias, "Salah: Caliph Will Sit in Jerusalem," Ynetnews.com (Israel), September 15, 2006. Accessed at http://www.ynetnews.com/articles/0,7340,L-3304384,00.html.

31. "U.S. General: Anbar Insurgents Mostly Iraqis," *CNN,* January 29, 2007.

32. Dick Cheney, "Vice President's Remarks and Q&A at a BC'04 Roundtable in Lake Elmo, Minnesota," Web site of The White House.

33. Elisabeth Bumiller, "White House Letter: Watchword of the Day: Beware the Caliphate," *International Herald Tribune,* December 11, 2005.

34. Abdullah Al-Araby, *The Islamization of America* (Los Angeles, CA: The Pen vs. The Sword, 2003), p. 19.

35. Charles Krauthammer, "In Iran, Arming for Armageddon," *Washington Post,* December 16, 2005, p. A35 (emphasis added).

36. Kenneth R. Timmerman, "Iranian President Sees End of World Order," NewsMax.com, January 24, 2006.

37. James M. Murk, *Islam Rising: Book One* (Springfield, MO: 21st Century Press, 2006), p. 241.

38. John von Heyking, "Iran's President and the Politics of the Twelfth Imam," *Ashbrook Center for Public Affairs,* November 2005.

39. Ibid.

40. Translation from The Middle East Media Research Institute at http://memri.org/bin/articles .cgi?Page=archives&Area=sd&ID=SP143607#_edn1.

41. Joel Rosenberg, "Ahmadinejad Coming to U.S. to Challenge Bush for Global Supremacy," September 6, 2006.

42. Ibid.

43. The Sahih [hadith collection] of Abu Dawud as cited in James M. Murk, *Islam Rising: Book One,* pp. 240-41.

44. Yaakov Lappin, "Bernard Lewis: Iran in Apocalyptic Mood," Ynetnews.com (Israel), January 29, 2007.

45. Ibid.

46. John Walvoord, quoted in Tim LaHaye and Jerry Jenkins, *Are We Living in the Last Days?* (Carol Stream, IL: Tyndale, 1999), p. 364.

CHAPTER 3—SETTING THE STAGE FOR THE LAST DAYS

1. "Don't Get Left in the Dust," *Newsweek,* September 27, 1993, pp. 20-29. Cf. also "History in a Handshake," *Time,* September 27, 1993.

2. John Ankerberg and Dillon Burroughs, *Middle East Meltdown* (Eugene, OR: Harvest House, 2007).

3. This position is advocated by John Walvoord in *Armageddon, Oil and the Middle East Crisis* (Grand Rapids: Zondervan, 1990), pp. 129-35.

4. Ibid., p. 131.

5. See John Lamb. "Power to the People," in *1992 Now,* published by IBM Europe, March 1989, pp. 8-9; and "Reshaping Europe: 1992 and Beyond," *Business Week,* December 12, 1988, pp. 48-51.

6. See Dave Hunt, *Global Peace and the Rise of the Antichrist* (Eugene, OR: Harvest House, 1990); David Reagan, *The Master Plan* (Eugene, OR: Harvest House, 1993). This position was argued earlier by Tim LaHaye, *The Coming Peace in the Middle East* (Grand Rapids: Zondervan, 1984).

7. Nicholas de Lange, *Atlas of the Jewish World* (New York: Facts on File, 1984), pp. 38-41. He cites large Jewish populations in Baghdad, Cairo, Ghazna, and Samarkand during the Middle Ages.

8. Abba Eban, *My People: The Story of the Jews* (New York: Random House, 1968), p. 51.

9. John Phillips, *Only God Can Prophesy!* (Wheaton, IL: Harold Shaw, 1975), p. 61.

10. John Walvoord, *Armageddon, Oil and the Middle East Crisis,* pp. 49-51.

11. Ibid., p. 129.

12. Charles Colson, *Against the Night* (Ann Arbor, MI: Servant Publications, 1989), p. 19.

13. Henrik Bering-Jensen, "Germany Resurgent," *Insight on the News,* March 23, 1992, p. 7.

14. Ibid., p. 8.

CHAPTER 4—EXPANDING THE AXIS OF EVIL

1. Cited in Randall Price, *Unholy War: America, Israel and Radical Islam* (Eugene, OR: Harvest House, 2001), p. 17.

2. George W. Bush, 2002 State of the Union address, January 29, 2002 (emphasis added).

3. Mark Hitchcock, *Iran: The Coming Crisis* (Sisters, OR: Multnomah Publishing, 2006), p. 103.

4. As cited in Frederick Kempe, "Aligning the Planets in Iran," *Wall Street Journal Online,* November 24, 2004 (emphasis added).

5. Michael Duffy, "What Would War Look Like?" *Time,* September 17, 2006.

6. "Iran: We'd Hit Back at Attacker," *CNN,* February 8, 2007.

7. Sean Yoong, "Ahmadinejad: Destroy Israel, End Crisis," *ABC News,* August 3, 2006.

8. William M. Arkin, "Secret Plan Outlines the Unthinkable," *Los Angeles Times,* March 9, 2002.

9. Zuckerman, "Moscow's Mad Gamble," January 30, 2006, p. 1.

10. Kenneth M. Pollack, *The Persian Puzzle: The Conflict Between Iran and America* (New York: Random House, 2005), p. 345.

11. "Bush Vows Firm Response to Iranian Military Actions," *CNN,* January 30, 2007.

12. Zuckerman, "Moscow's Mad Gamble," p. 1.

13. Hitchcock, *Iran: The Coming Crisis,* p. 103.

14. "Iran's Leader Calls for TV Debate with Bush," *CNN News,* August 29, 2006.

15. "Report: Iran Set to Unveil Herbal AIDS Cure," *Fox News,* February 6, 2007.

16. Ann Leslie, "Why This Man Should Give Us All Nightmares," *Daily Mail,* August 23, 2006.

17. Sebastian Usher, "Iran's Leaders Harness Media Power," *BBC,* March 14, 2006.

18. "North Korea," *Council on Foreign Relations,* December 2005.

19. Ibid.

20. Alireza Jafarzadeh, *The Iran Threat* (New York: Palgrave Macmillan, 2007), p. 204.

21. George W. Bush, "Address to a Joint Session of Congress and the American People," September 20, 2001.

22. Joel Rosenberg, "Mideast War Spinning Out of Control," July 14, 2006.

23. "Moscow Wants to Build 40 to 50 Nuclear Reactors Abroad," *AFX News,* September 7, 2006.

24. Ibid.

25. John Thorne, "Putin in Morocco for Middle East Talks," AP News, September 7, 2006.

26. Joel Rosenberg, *Epicenter* (Carol Stream, IL: Tyndale, 2006), p. 113.

27. Ibid.

28. "Putin to Remain Leader After Leaving Kremlin," Breitbart.com News, December 23, 2006.

29. Jon E. Dougherty, "Iran, China Forming Major Alliance," NewsMax.com, November 18, 2004.

30. Gary H. Kah, "War with Iraq: The Aftermath," http://www.johnankerberg.org/Articles/editors-choice/EC0403W4.htm.

31. Roger Howard, "Oil Price Warfare," *The National Interest,* September/October 2006, p. 85.

32. "Special Report with Brit Hume," *Fox News,* August 25, 2006.

33. "Growing Anti-Semitism in Venezuela," *Israel Today,* December 2006, p. 8.

34. "Venezuela Threatens to Sell F-16 Fleet to Iran," *Fox News,* May 16, 2006.

35. David Horowitz, "Al-Qaeda," from the Discover the Network Web site. Accessed at http://www.discoverthenetwork.org/groupProfile.asp?grpid=6211.

36. "Hezbollah," *Council of Foreign Relations,* July 17, 2006.

37. Ibid. Note the corresponding links at this source for additional resources.

38. "Lebanon: The Israel-Hamas-Hezbollah Conflict," *CRS Report for Congress,* August 14, 2006.

39. Adapted from "Hamas," *Council on Foreign Relations,* January 2006.

40. "Hamas Issues Daily Terror Report," *Israel Today,* December 2006, p. 10.

41. "Bin Laden Adheres to Austere Form of Islam," *New York Times,* October 7, 2001.

42. Stephen Swartz, "Wahhabism & Islam in the U.S.," *National Review,* June 30, 2003.

43. "Al-Mahdi Army/Active Religious Seminary/Al-Sadr's Group," GlobalSecurity.org.

44. David Horowitz, "Islamic Jihad," from the Discover the Network database. Accessed at http://discoverthenetwork.org/groupProfile.asp?grpid=6957.

45. Rusty Wright, "Why Radical Muslims Hates You," *Probe,* 2004.

46. *Al-Riswāla,* September 13, 2001; cited in Bernard Lewis, *The Crisis of Islam: Holy War and Unholy Terror* (New York: The Modern Library, 2003), pp. 156-57.

47. Helen Gibson, "Islam's Other Hot Spots: Britain: No Pause in the Recruiting," *Time,* September 15, 2003.

48. Bernard Lewis, *What Went Wrong? The Clash Between Islam and Modernity in the Middle East* (New York: Perennial/HarperCollins Publishers, 2002), p. xxvii.

49. Chuck Colson, "The Clash of Civilizations," *Breakpoint,* August 16, 2006.

50. John L. Esposito, *Unholy War: Terror in the Name of Islam* (New York: Oxford University Press, 2003), p. 135.

51. Matthew 22:21, NLT.

52. Lewis, *What Went Wrong?* p. 79.

53. Cited in Jonathan D. Halevi, "Al-Qaeda's Intellectual Legacy: New Radical Islamic Thinking Justifying the Genocide of Infidels," *Jerusalem Viewpoints,* December 1, 2003.

54. John Hagee, *Jerusalem Countdown,* rev. ed. (Lake Mary, FL: FrontLine, 2007), p. 35.

55. As cited in "Target Iran—Air Strikes—2006 Developments," GlobalSecurity.org.

56. Cited in Halevi, "Al-Qaeda's Intellectual Legacy." *Jerusalem Viewpoints,* December 1, 2003.

CHAPTER 5—THE NUCLEAR NIGHTMARE

1. William Langewiesche, "How to Get a Nuclear Bomb," *Atlantic,* December 2006, p. 83.

2. Adolf Berle, *Power* (New York: Harcourt, Brace & World, 1967), p. 17.

3. Ibid., pp. 37-38.

4. Ibid., p. 37.

5. John Kotter, *Power in Management* (New York: American Management Association, 1979), pp. 13-23.

6. Charles Colson, *Against the Night* (Ann Arbor, MI: Servant Publications, 1989), p. 55.

7. Aleksandr Solzhenitsyn, *A World Split Apart* (New York: Harper & Row, 1978), p. 61.

8. Stephen Budiansky, "The Nuclear Epidemic," *U.S. News & World Report,* March 16, 1992, p. 40.

9. Ibid., pp. 40-44.

10. Carla Anne Robbins, "The X Factor in the Proliferation Game," *U.S. News & World Report* March 16, 1992, p. 45.

11. Ed Dobson, *The End* (Grand Rapids: Zondervan, 1997), pp. 14ff.

12. Ibid., p. 15.

13. Alvin and Heidi Toffler, *War and Anti-War* (Boston: Little, Brown & Co., 1993), p. 3.

14. Ibid., p. 14.

15. Ibid., pp. 247-50.

16. Dobson, *The End,* p. 17.

17. Ibid.

18. J. Dwight Pentecost, *Things to Come* (Grand Rapids: Zondervan, 1965), p. 340.

19. John Walvoord, *Major Bible Prophecies* (New York: Harper Collins, 1991), p. 420.

20. Ibid., p. 422.

21. Thomas Ice and Timothy Demy, *Fast Facts on Bible Prophecy* (Eugene, OR: Harvest House, 1997), p. 24.

CHAPTER 6—THE ISLAMIC THREAT

1. Grant Jeffrey, *The Next World War* (Colorado Springs: WaterBrook Press, 2006), p. 2.

2. Samuel Huntington, *Clash of Civilizations* (New York: Simon & Schuster, 1998), p. 10.

3. Cal Thomas, "The Exit Interview," Tribune Media Services, December 17, 2006.

4. Paul Greenberg, "One Sure Guide in Iraq: Follow Honor," *The News and Advance*, December 17, 2006, D6.

5. "Iran's Leader Uses U.N. as Image Booster," Associated Press, September 22, 2006.

6. For an excellent overview of Islamic history, see Albert Hourani, *A History of the Arab Peoples* (Cambridge, MA: Harvard University Press, 1991), p. 15.

7. A. Guillame, *The Life of Muhammad* (London: University Press, 1955), p. 118.

8. See discussion in Winfried Corduan, *Neighboring Faiths* (Downers Grove, IL: InterVarsity Press, 1998), p. 78.

9. Jeffrey, p. 51.

10. For an excellent examination of Islamic beliefs, see Ergun and Emir Caner, *Unveiling Islam* (Grand Rapids: Kregel, 2002).

11. Hourani, *A History of the Arab Peoples,* pp. 17-18.

12. Ibid., p. 19.

13. Ibid., p. 25.

14. Thomas Abercrombie, "The Sword and the Sermon," in D. Belt, ed., *The World of Islam* (Washington, D.C.: National Geographic Society, 2001).

15. Robert Spencer, *The Truth About Muhammad* (Washington, D.C.: Regnery Publishing, 2006), p. 177. Cf. also Serge Trifkovic, *The Sword of the Prophet* (Boston: Regina Orthodox Press, 2002).

16. Ibid.

17. Ibid., pp. 175-76.

18. Ibid., p. 176.

19. Dave Hunt, *Judgment Day!* (Bend, OR: Berean Call, 2005), pp. 151-52.

20. Dave Hunt, *Judgment Day!* see Robert Spencer, pp. 186-90, for details.

21. Dave Hunt, *Global Peace and the Rise of the Antichrist* (Eugene, OR: Harvest House, 1990), p. 220.

22. John Walvoord, statement made in a message given at the Pre-Trib Conference in Dallas, Texas, December 1995.

CHAPTER 7—THE ISRAELI FACTOR

1. Dore Gold, *The Fight for Jerusalem* (Washington, D.C.: Regnery Publishing, 2007), p. 3.

2. Ibid., p. 5.

3. *Al-Safir,* March 3, 2001, trans. MEMRI. Quoted by Gold, *The Fight for Jerusalem,* p. 329.

4. *Time,* September 26, 2006, p. 32.

5. On the biblical history of Israel, see Alec Motyer, *The Story of the Old Testament* (Grand Rapids, MI: Baker, 2001); Walter Kaiser, *A History of Israel* (Nashville: Broadman & Holman, 1998); Eugene Merrill, *Kingdom of Priests* (Grand Rapids, MI: Baker, 1987); K.A. Kitchen, *On the Reliability of the Old Testament* (Grand Rapids, MI: Eerdmans, 2003).

6. On Jewish history during the Second temple period, see Josephus, *Jewish Antiquities,* Book IX-XI (Cambridge, MA: Harvard University Press, 1956); Elias Bickerman, *From Ezra to the Host of the Maccabees* (New York: Schocken Books, 1966); D.S. Russell, *Between the Testaments* (London: SCM Press, 1960).

7. On the history of Jerusalem during the Byzantine, Muslim, and Crusader eras, see Karen Armstrong, *Jerusalem: One City, Three Faiths* (New York: Ballantine Books, 1997).

8. On the history of the conflict over Jerusalem for biblical and modern times, see Gold, *The Fight for Jerusalem.*

9. Thomas Ice, "History of Zionism," *Pre-Trib Perspective,* March 2005.

CHAPTER 8—ISRAEL'S FUTURE DESTINY

1. Dore Gold, *The Fight for Jerusalem* (Washington, D.C.: Regnery Publishing, 2007), p. 238.

2. Ibid., p. 239.

3. See Randall Price, "Ezekiel," in Tim LaHaye and Ed Hindson, eds., *Popular Bible Prophecy Commentary* (Eugene, OR: Harvest House, 2007), p. 300ff.

CHAPTER 9—BATTLE OF GOG AND MAGOG

1. Mark Hitchcock, *Iran: The Coming Crisis* (Sisters, OR: Multnomah, 2006), p. 10.

2. Thomas Ice, "Ezekiel 38 and 39, Part 1," in *Pre-Trib Perspectives,* January 2007, p. 6.

3. Grant Jeffrey, *The Next World War* (Colorado Springs: WaterBrook, 2006), p. 10.

4. For a detailed discussion of these names, see Hitchcock, *Iran: The Coming Crisis,* pp. 156-67 and Tim LaHaye and Ed Hindson, eds., *Popular Bible Prophecy Commentary* (Eugene, OR: Harvest House, 2007).

5. Quoted in *Time,* September 25, 2006, p. 32.

6. Hitchcock, *Iran: The Coming Crisis,* pp. 180-84.

7. Ibid., p. 210. Note his reference to Gesenius's original Latin version of his lexicon.

8. G.A. Cooke, *A Critical and Exegetical Commentary on the Book of Ezekiel* (Edinburgh: T. & T. Clark, 1936), pp. 408-09.

9. Hitchcock, *Iran: The Coming Crisis,* p. 182.

10. Ibid., p. 187.

11. Grant Jeffrey, op. cit., p. 13.

12. Hitchcock, *Iran: The Coming Crisis,* p. 170.

13. Ibid., p. 172.

14. See Randall Price, *The Battle for the Last Days Temple* (Eugene, OR: Harvest House, 2004).

CHAPTER 10—GLOBALISM AND THE WORLD ECONOMY

1. Bill Clinton, State of the Union address, January 27, 2000.

2. Quoted by Gary Frazier, *Signs of the Times* (Arlington, TX: Discovery Press, 2002), p. 46.

3. "The New Left Takes on the World," *Washington Post,* September 6, 2000, p. A19.

4. John Naisbitt and Pat Aburdene, *Megatrends 2000* (New York: William Morrow, 1990).

5. Robert Reich, *The Work of Nations* (New York: Alfred Knopf, 1992), p. 3.

6. Ibid., p. 113.

7. Quoted by Reich, Ibid., p. 119.

8. Ibid., p. 120.

9. Naisbitt and Aburdene, *Megatrends 2000,* p. 39.

10. Ibid., p. 54.

11. Pat Robertson, *The New World Order* (Dallas: Word, 1991), p. 118. This is probably the finest chapter in Robertson's book. See also Dinesh D'Souza, *The Enemy at Home* (New York: Doubleday, 2007).

12. Herbert Schlossberg, *Idols for Destruction* (Nashville: Thomas Nelson, 1983), p. 6.

13. Ibid., p. 1.

14. Maltbie D. Babcock, *This Is My Father's World,* written in 1901.

CHAPTER 11—FUTURE POLITICAL SUPERSTATE

1. Quoted by Gary Frazier, *Signs of Christ's Coming* (Arlington, TX: Discovery Press, 2002), p. 13.

2. Helmut Kohl, "This Unity Is Just the Beginning," *The European,* October 11-17, 1991, special report, p. 1.

3. As cited in *The European,* February 10, 1992.

4. Commonly reported in the press, *USA TODAY,* February 1992, p. 1.

5. Kohl, "This Unity," p. 1.

6. "Charging Ahead," *Time,* September 18, 1989, p. 45.

7. Ibid.

8. Ibid.

9. Malachi Martin, *The Keys of This Blood* (New York: Simon & Schuster, 1990).

10. Ibid., p. 15.

11. See Pat Robertson, *The New World Order* (Dallas: Word, 1991); and Ed Hindson, *End Times, the Middle East and the New World Order* (Chicago: Victor Books, 1991).

12. "Charging Ahead," *Time,* September 18, 1989, pp. 40-45.

13. *U.S. News & World Report,* October 15,1990, p. 64.

14. Arno Froese, *How Democracy Will Elect the Antichrist* (Columbia, SC: The Olive Press, 1997), p. 165.

15. Ibid., p. 172.

16. *The European,* July 6, 1995, p. 17.

17. Froese, *How Democracy,* p. 173.

18. Ibid., p. 200.

19. Ibid., p. 210.

20. See J. Dwight Pentecost, *Things to Come* (Grand Rapids: Zondervan, 1964), pp. 239-50; Alva McClain, *Daniel's Prophecy of the Seventy Weeks* (Grand Rapids: Zondervan, 1940).

21. Robert Anderson, *The Coming Prince* (London: Hodder & Stoughton, 1909).

CHAPTER 12—THE RAPTURE CHANGES EVERYTHING

1. See Tim LaHaye, *The Rapture* (Eugene, OR: Harvest House, 2002); Tim LaHaye and Richard Mayhue, "Rapture," in Tim LaHaye and Ed Hindson, eds., *Popular Encyclopedia of Bible Prophecy* (Eugene, OR: Harvest House, 2004), pp. 309-16.

2. This theme is developed and supported with statistical tables in Richard Neuhaus, ed., *Unsecular America* (Grand Rapids, MI: Eerdmans, 1986). It is also expressed in Tim LaHaye and Bob Phillips, *The Europa Conspiracy* (New York: Bantam Books, 2005).

3. See Tim McMahon, "Are Hurricanes Inflationary or Deflationary?" at www.inflationdata.com.

4. Millard Erickson, *Christian Theology* (Grand Rapids: Baker Books, 1985), p. 1186.

5. William Mounce, *Mounce's Complete Expository Dictionary of Old & New Testament Words* (Grand Rapids: MI: Zondervan, 2006), p. 666.

6. C.F. Hogg and W.E. Vine, *The Epistles to the Thessalonians* (London: Exeter Press, 1959), pp. 144.

7. Ibid., p. 242.

8. George Milligan, *St. Paul's Epistle to the Thessalonians* (Old Tappan, NJ: Revell, 1958), p, 96.

CHAPTER 13—THE RISE OF THE BEAST

1. Ed Dobson, *The End* (Grand Rapids: Zondervan, 1997), pp. 97-98. This fascinating and insightful study of end-time prophecies discusses the rise and fall of the Antichrist in detail on pp. 97-110.

2. Grant Jeffrey, *Prince of Darkness* (Toronto: Frontier Research Publications, 1994), pp. 48-55.

3. Quoted by Jeffrey, Ibid., p. 53. See also Ed Hindson, *Antichrist Rising* (Springfield, MO: 21st Century Press, 2003).

4. Richard Trench, *Synonyms of the New Testament* (Grand Rapids: Eerdmans, n.d.), p. 107.

5. See Charles Feinberg, *Daniel* (Chappaqua, NY: Christian Herald Books, 1981); Robert Culver, *Daniel and the Latter Days* (Chicago: Moody Press, 1954); Stephen Miller, *Daniel: New American Commentary*, vol. 18 (Nashville: Broadman & Holman, 1994); John Walvoord, *Daniel: Key to Prophetic Revelation* (Chicago: Moody Press, 1971); John Whitcomb, *Daniel* (Chicago: Moody Press, 1985).

6. Miller, *Daniel: New American Commentary*, p. 307.

7. Feinberg, *Daniel*, pp. 174-75.

8. Arno Froese, *How Democracy Will Elect the Antichrist* (Columbia, SC: The Olive Press, 1997), pp. 113, 138-39.

9. Harvey Cox, *The Seduction of the Spirit* (New York: Simon & Schuster, 1973), p. 16. See also Ed Dobson and Ed Hindson, *The Seduction of Power* (Old Tappan, NJ: Revell, 1988).

10. Arthur W. Pink, *The Antichrist* (Minneapolis: Klock & Klock, 1979), p. 77.

11. Jeffrey, *Prince of Darkness*, pp. 29-30; see also Pink, *The Antichrist*, pp. 83-88.

12. J. Dwight Pentecost, *Things to Come* (Grand Rapids: Zondervan, 1965), p. 339.

13. See Mal Couch, ed., *Dictionary of Premillennial Theology* (Grand Rapids: Kregel, 1996), p. 117.

14. Thomas Ice and Timothy Demy, *Fast Facts on Bible Prophecy* (Eugene, OR: Harvest House, 1997), p. 77.

15. Ibid., pp. 78-79.

16. Samuel Andrews, *Christianity and Anti-Christianity* (Chicago: Moody Bible Institute, 1898), p. 320.

Chapter 14—Marching to Armageddon

1. Adapted from Thomas Ice, "Armageddon," in Tim LaHaye and Ed Hindson, eds., *Popular Encyclopedia of Bible Prophecy* (Eugene, OR: Harvest House, 2004), pp. 36-42.

2. Charles Dyer, *World News and Bible Prophecy* (Wheaton, IL: Tyndale House, 1991), pp. 237-38.

3. Arnold Fruchtenbaum, *Footsteps of the Messiah: A Study of the Sequence of Prophetic Events* (Tustin, CA: Ariel Press, 2003).

4. Ibid., p. 314.

5. Ibid., p. 337.

Chapter 15—How Should We Then Live?

1. Erwin Lutzer, *Where Do We Go from Here?* (Chicago: Moody Press, 1993), pp. 25-48.

2. Bill Hybels, *Becoming a Contagious Christian* (Grand Rapids, MI: Zondervan, 1994), pp. 43, 59.

3. Dave Hunt, *Whatever Happened to Heaven?* (Eugene, OR: Harvest House, 1988), p. 7.

4. Joseph Stowell, "Set Your Mind on Heaven," in *10 Reasons Why Jesus Is Coming Soon* (Sisters, OR: Multnomah Books, 1998), p. 235ff.

5. C.S. Lewis, *Mere Christianity* (New York: Macmillan, 1943), p. 118.

6. Quoted by Lutzer, p. 46.

7. Quoted by Lutzer, p. 47.

8. Bailey Smith, *Taking Back the Gospel* (Eugene, OR: Harvest House, 1999), p. 8.

9. John Walvoord, *Matthew: Thy Kingdom Come* (Chicago: Moody Press, 1974), p. 197.

10. Stowell, "Set Your Mind on Heaven," p. 252.